THE

WASHINGTON

LOBBY

CONGRESSIONAL QUARTERLY

1735 K STREET, N. W., WASHINGTON, D. C.

Congressional Quarterly Inc.

Congressional Quarterly Inc., an editorial research service and publishing company, serves clients in the fields of news, education, business and government. It combines specific coverage of Congress, government and politics by Congressional Quarterly with the more general subject range of an affiliated service, Editorial Research Reports.

Congressional Quarterly was founded in 1945 by Nelson and Henrietta Poynter. Its basic periodical publication was and still is the CQ *Weekly Report*, which is mailed to clients every Friday. The *Weekly Report* is cross-referenced quarterly in a cumulative *Index*.

The CQ *Almanac*, a compendium of legislation for one session of Congress, is published every spring. *Congress and the Nation* is published every four years as a record of government for one presidential term.

Congressional Quarterly also publishes paperback books on public affairs. These include the twice-yearly *Guide to Current American Government* and such recent titles as *Civil Rights Progress Report 1970* and *Nixon. the Second Year of His Presidency.*

CQ Direct Research is a consulting service which performs contract research and maintains a reference library and query desk for the convenience of clients.

Editorial Research Reports covers subjects beyond the specialized scope of Congressional Quarterly. It publishes reference material on foreign affairs, business, education, cultural affairs, national security, science and other topics of news interest. Service to clients includes a 300-word report five times a week and a 6,000-word report four times a month. Editorial Research Reports also publishes paperback books in its fields of coverage. Founded in 1923, the service was merged with Congressional Quarterly in 1956.

The Washington Lobby was organized by Associate Editor Robert A. Barnes, who wrote major portions of the book.

Other contributors: Thomas J. Arrandale, Barbara Coleman, Robert E. Cuthriell, Peter A. Harkness, David M. Maxfield, June Spira, Stanley N. Wellborn and Elder Witt.

Book Service Editor: Robert A. Diamond.

Library of Congress Catalog No. 78-168708
Standard Book No. 0-87187-020-7

Copyright 1971 by Congressional Quarterly Inc.
1735 K Street, N.W., Washington, D.C. 20006

TABLE OF CONTENTS

Congress shall make no law...abridging the freedom of speech, or of the press; or the right of the people peaceably to assemble, and to petition the Government for a redress of grievances.

—U.S. Constitution, First Amendment

INTRODUCTION

The Washington Lobby: A Continuing

Struggle to Influence Government Policy

The efforts of organized interests to influence government policy are an inseparable part of the American political process. They are based largely on the guarantees of free speech and the people's right "to petition the Government for a redress of grievances" in the First Amendment to the U.S. Constitution.

A factor in government from early days, interest groups have multiplied at the national level as power moved toward the Federal Government. Specialized interests seek out the power that can determine their fortunes.

Private interests have expanded their activities in the nation's capital since the 1930s, with particular impetus since World War II. Mass communications provide new weapons for an old technique: the molding of public opinion which can turn pressure on public officials. It is a rare moment when Government and public do not hear some of the many voices of the Washington lobby.

Modern Group Pressures

As the 1970s opened, the governmental arenas in Washington were the setting for a broad variety of interest group operations aimed at influencing Congress or the Executive Branch. For example:

• A coalition of aerospace companies and labor unions pushing for government-financed development of a supersonic transport plane capable of carrying 300 passengers at 1,800 miles an hour—and battled in Congress by another coalition led by groups interested in environmental problems and in competing national priorities.

• Temporary coalitions of groups which combined their pressure on policymakers in repeated campaigns to force an end to U.S. military involvement in the Vietnam War.

• Bipartisan coalitions of labor, civil rights and other groups successfully opposing confirmation by the Democratic-controlled Senate of two successive Supreme Court appointments by the Republican President.

• A quietly successful effort by lobbyists for drug interests to block legislation to place two high-selling tranquilizers, Librium and Valium, under mandatory Government controls.

• A bitter battle between U.S. manufacturing and labor interests who urged restrictions on certain foreign imports and a combination of free trade exponents, foreign interests and American-based multinational corporations who opposed import curbs.

• A coalition of shipping companies, unions and shipbuilders successfully culminating years of attempts to enact a Federal subsidy program to rebuild the aging U.S. merchant fleet—efforts which were frustrated earlier largely by disunity in the industry and lack of support in the Executive Branch.

• The American Petroleum Institute successfully pressing Congress and the Executive Branch for continued protective quotas on oil imports—and countered by factions which opposed import restraints.

• The AFL-CIO speaking on a continuing basis, though with varying indications of unanimity, as the organized voice of 14 million labor union members, whose lobbyists listed an interest in "all bills affecting the welfare of the country generally"—and joined or opposed on specific issues by groups as different in general outlook as the business-oriented Chamber of Commerce.

• Ideological pressure groups such as Americans for Democratic Action on the left and Americans for Constitutional Action on the right, working in opposing directions to influence the general trend of U.S. Government policy.

These were a few of many organized interests attempting separately or in combinations to influence government policy. In these cases as in many others, group tacticians on opposing sides generally sought as a matter of course to present their objectives as in the public interest. The resulting decisions were not always simple for Congress or for the general public.

Growth of Pressure Groups

Depending on where decision-making power in specific fields resided, there have always been various specialized interests represented on the local, state and national governmental scenes. The railroad and lumber interests were among those which conducted organized efforts to influence government in the nineteenth century.

Earlier, President Washington warned Congress against what he called "the insidious wiles of foreign influence" as "one of the most baneful foes of republican government."

In 1908 in a pioneer study of pressure group activity Arthur Bentley wrote in *The Process of Government: A Study of Social Pressures:*

"There is no political process that is not a balancing of quantity against quantity. There is not a law that is passed that is not the expression of force and force in tension. There is not a court decision or an executive act that is not the result of the same process....All phenomena of government are phenomena of groups pressing one another, and pushing out new groups and group representatives (the organs or agencies of government) to mediate the adjustments."

Many instances of powerful influence by groups or individuals at the state level have come to light through the years. One of the most publicized was that of Arthur H. Samish, representative for the California State Brewers' Institute. *Colliers'* magazine described him in 1949 as the "secret boss" of the California legislature and quoted Earl Warren, then Governor, as saying: "On matters that affect his clients, Artie unquestionably has more power than the governor."

As Chief Justice, Warren a few years later wrote the landmark Supreme Court opinion which narrowed the scope of the Federal Regulation of Lobbying Act of 1946 while upholding its constitutionality. *(Court opinion p. 118)*

At the national level, few if any other individuals outside of public office have attained the heights of influence reached by Wayne B. Wheeler, legislative counsel for the Anti-Saloon League. The key organization in the drive that produced national prohibition, the league stands as a prototype for the successful use of mass pressures. His methods are still used by the Washington lobby.

Wheeler's former secretary, Justin Stewart, said he "controlled six Congresses, dictated to two Presidents... and was recognized by friend and foe alike as the most masterful and powerful single individual in the United States."

Postwar Pressures. It was only in recent years that organized groups reached the numbers and the intensity at the national level that prevailed in the early 1970s.

The House Select Committee on Lobbying Activities said in a 1950 report that "the sheer weight of group pressures has increased enormously during and subsequent to the Second World War....In a very real sense, the impact of war solidly established lobbying as a major industry. Our national effort, entailing as it did far-reaching controls over the entire economy, prompted a

hitherto unequalled mobilization of group interests of every conceivable kind." *(Further excerpts from report, p. 122)*

There have been few reductions and some increases since 1950 in the Federal Government's powers to determine the fortunes of specialized interests. The Senate's Special Committee to Investigate Political Activities, Lobbying, and Campaign Contributions said in a 1957 report:

"The increasing complexity of modern life, and the consequent increase in the role of Government in the lives of all Americans have caused the pressure groups to play a more important part in our Government than was anticipated a hundred years ago."

Today hundreds of interest groups attempt to make their weight felt at selected points of government. They cover a range nearly as varied as the society of which they are a part, including commercial, industrial and agricultural interests, labor unions, ethnic and racial groups, professional organizations, cause-oriented groups and agencies of state and local government. These groups all participate in the Washington lobby.

Equally prominent among forces exerting pressures on Congress is the Executive Branch. Lambert H. Miller, senior vice president and general counsel of the National Association of Manufacturers, in 1971 described executive lobbying activities as being generally recognized as "the most pervasive, influential and costly of any such in the whole country." *(Executive Branch p. 61)*

While Senators or Representatives sometimes criticize what they regard as excessive executive pressures, they tend on the other hand to complain of a lack of leadership when executive influence is missing. The inter-branch pressure process also works in reverse. Members of Congress exert pressure on executive agencies, if only through inquiries which demonstrate an interest on the part of the body which must pass on appropriations.

Today as in the 1790s, attempts to influence the Government of the United States are not confined solely within the nation's borders. Many foreign interests—commercial, governmental, political and others—employ American agents to carry on activities similar to those of domestic pressure groups. The interest of governments and other foreign entities in U.S. Government policies kept pace with growing U.S. involvement in world affairs and commitments of American development and military funds after World War II.

More than 400 foreign employers with active U.S. representatives were listed with the Justice Department under the Foreign Agents Registration Act in the early 1970s, despite Congress' narrowing of the Act's coverage from 1966 on. Some individuals and firms represented both foreign and domestic concerns in Washington. *(Foreign Pressures p. 29)*

Origins of Groups

In its broader sense lobbying involves the attempts of pressure groups to influence the policies and actions of a government which is responsive to such pressures.

James Madison saw the origins of pressure groups, which he called "factions," as "sown in the nature of man." While liberty "is to faction what air is to fire," to eliminate faction by destruction of liberty would impose a remedy worse than the disease, he said.

Lawyers: The Major Influence Around Washington

The successful Washington lawyer is the elite of the Washington lobby, although he may never register as a lobbyist.

Like his counterparts in communities across the land, he's an expert in his chosen bailiwick. He may move in and out of high Government posts, from the Cabinet or presidential assistant level down. He is on a first-name golfplaying basis with top-rung public figures in the area of his interests.

At the highest levels of prestige and affluence, there are naturally few, and they're largely one of a kind. There is just one Abe Fortas (longtime intimate of Lyndon B. Johnson), one George W. Ball (former Under Secretary of State) and one Clark M. Clifford (former aide to Presidents Truman and Johnson and former Secretary of Defense), to cite a few, each with his contacts and experience in government and business which set him far ahead of the pack at certain times and on certain matters.

Outside the inner circle, which fluctuates with political fortunes, many other lawyers are constantly working their way through the machinery in Congress or elsewhere. The Justice Department, for example, employs hundreds of lawyers and has been called the world's greatest law office.

Lawyers probably have more to say about the laws of the U.S. Government and how they're executed than all other professions combined.

They are prominent in every phase of the governing process, from the originating of legislative proposals to their interpretation by the courts. At no point are they more in evidence than in the myriad of activities aimed at influencing legislation.

Individuals with legal training possess special advantages for lobbying, broadly defined, by virtue of their background and the outlook they hold in common with their professional colleagues throughout government.

As Charles D. Ablard said in "The Lawyer as Lobbyist" published by *ABA Journal* (1966), "there is as much need for the lawyer in the process of formulation of statutes by legislatures as there is after enactment in interpretation by the administrators and agencies to which they apply and in judicial review by the courts." Ablard has been general counsel and Congressional liaison for the U.S. Information Agency since 1969.

Every Congress has many lawyers in it. For example, in 1971 there were 301 Members—56 percent of Congress—who had gone to law school and passed a bar examination, although some had not practiced.

Most committees have staff attorneys, as do many executive agencies and departments. Their judgments are heavily relied upon.

It is not uncommon for a Government lawyer to take part in drafting a bill and getting it enacted, help interpret it for enforcement purposes and some day wind up serving private clients who are subject to the law he helped to write and administer.

Ablard gave an unusual rundown detailing a lawyer-lobbyist's techniques. This ranged from making the acquaintance of committee counsel through discussing legislation with Members and their aides—for, he said, "the assistant who favors the bill may be of great help with the Congressman."

The lawyer-lobbyist, Ablard said, should offer to help the staff prepare the committee's report. "Writing the report that creates the legislative history is often a most important part of the lawyer's role," he said, "for it prepares the basis for the later interpretation of his bill by the courts.

"Once reported favorably by a subcommittee or a committee, most bills, unless highly controversial, are passed with only minor modification by the House. Thus, getting the bill out of committee becomes of paramount importance."

Influential though some lawyers are as individuals, still more so are law firms with a roster of talented specialists with inside knowledge of the State, Treasury or Justice Departments or regulatory agencies.

Ralph Nader, whose Center for the Study of Responsive Law helped spur a trend toward public service lawyer activities, once referred to the three largest Washington firms—Covington & Burling, Arnold & Porter and Hogan & Hartson, respectively—and to "the immense power of these firms and their tailored capacity to apply know-how, know-who and other influences."

Arnold & Porter, for example, in 1970 included Paul A. Porter (chairman, Federal Communications Commission, 1944-46); Milton V. Freeman (assistant solicitor, Securities & Exchange Commission, 1942-46; administrator, Office of Price Administration, 1946); William L. McGovern (special assistant to Attorney General, 1938-45); Joseph A. Califano Jr. (special assistant to Secretary, and Deputy Secretary of Defense, 1964-65; special assistant to President Johnson, 1965-69; general counsel to Democratic National Committee in 1971); Mitchell Rogovin (Assistant Attorney General, tax division, 1966-69); Clifford L. Alexander Jr. (chairman, Equal Employment Opportunity Commission, 1967-69), and Mrs. Carolyn Agger (wife of former Supreme Court Justice and Presidential aide Abe Fortas).

Lawyers generally need not register as lobbyists or foreign agents for routine legal services such as appearing before Congressional committees or regulatory boards. Canon 26 of the American Bar Association's Canons of Professional Ethics, with which they are expected to comply, says:

"A lawyer openly, and in his true character may render professional services before legislative or other bodies, regarding proposed legislation, and in advocacy of claims before departments of government, upon the same principles of ethics which justify his appearance before the Courts; but it is unprofessional for a lawyer so engaged to conceal his attorneyship, or to employ secret personal solicitations, or to use means other than those addressed to the reason and understanding, to influence action."

Washington on Factions

George Washington warned Congress in his Farewell Address against allowing factions to circumvent the established government or the Constitution as it existed at any time, "until changed by an explicit and authentic act of the whole people." He said:

"All obstructions to the execution of the laws, all combinations and associations under whatever plausible character, with the real design to direct, control, counteract, or awe the regular deliberations and actions of the constituted authorities, are destructive of this fundamental principle, and of fatal tendency. They serve to organize faction, to give it an artificial and extraordinary force, to put in the place of the delegated will of the nation the will of party, often a small but artful and enterprising minority of the community; and, according to the alternate triumphs of different parties, to make the public administration the mirror of the ill concerted and incongruous projects of faction, rather than the organ of consistent and wholesome plans digested by common councils, and modified by mutual interests.

"However combinations or associations of the above description may now and then answer popular ends, they are likely, in the course of time and things, to become potent engines, by which cunning, ambitious, and unprincipled men, will be enabled to subvert the power of the people, and to usurp for themselves the reins of government; destroying afterwards the very engines which have lifted them to unjust dominion."

Rather, "Ambition must be made to counteract ambition." By this Madison meant that, although the Government should be given sufficient power to govern, it should itself be curbed by "supplying, by opposite and rival interests, the defect of better motives...."

Madison defined a faction as "a number of citizens, whether amounting to a majority or minority of the whole, who are united and actuated by some common impulse of passion, or of interest, adverse to the rights of other citizens, or to the permanent and aggregate interests of the community."

Under the Constitution, the lawmaking branch of the U.S. Government like those of the state governments is based on geographical representation. This leaves a natural opening for the informal and uneven growth of what students of politics often call functional representation based on the diverse interests which transcend geographical distinctions in a complex society.

The most common and lasting origins of factionalism, Madison held, involved questions of property distribution. In the twentieth century, with property issues at the heart of much public controversy and some violence, Madison's analysis still carries weight.

"...Those who hold and those who are without property have ever formed distinct interests in society," Madison said. "...A landed interest, a manufacturing interest, a mercantile interest, a moneyed interest, with many lesser interests, grow up of necessity in civilized nations, and divide them into different classes, actuated by different sentiments and views. The regulation of these various and interfering interests forms the principal task of modern legislation and involves the spirit of party and faction in the necessary and ordinary operations of government."

Bertram M. Gross, drawing on his experience as a Senate committee advisor and Presidential aide, said in 1953 it would be a serious oversimplification "to assume that all the important groups are highly organized 'classes' in the Marxist sense of the term."

In *The Legislative Struggle*, Gross noted groups' overlapping memberships and close relations with other groups, as well as a common lack of class consciousness. "Nor can the purposes of many groups be fitted into a watertight set of compartments such as economic, political, sectional, religious, or nationalistic; most of them tend to represent a combination of two or more of these," Gross said.

Pressure Methods

The Washington lobby is out to get results. It pursues them wherever results are likely to be found in the governmental process. Many organizations, directed by professionals in the art of government, focus major efforts at key points where decisions are made and policy interpreted into action. They use the methods they deem appropriate for the circumstances within the limits of their resources, group policies and ethical outlook.

If a group loses a round in Congress, it may continue the fight in the agency charged with execution or in the courts. A year or two later, it may resume the struggle in Congress. This process can continue indefinitely.

Groups' goals are as numerous and varied as the organizations themselves. Many, of course, are primarily bent on protecting or promoting their specialized interests. Some assert public benefit purposes.

A group might work, for example, for the reduction of a tax burden, the passage of a subsidy program or the defense of existing advantages against proposals to eliminate them. A competing faction might actively work against some or all of the other group's main purposes. Even so, they might find themselves on the same side upon occasion.

On a long-range basis, both groups naturally might strive through the years to build up what they consider a sympathetic or at least neutral attitude in places of power where their particular interests are affected.

These and other factors can induce some organizations not only to attempt to influence the views of Members of Congress or key executive officials on specific issues, but also to participate in the political activities which select the occupants of positions in which they are interested. *(Elections p. 35)*

There is nothing to prevent operation of groups which are primarily politically motivated. Political parties routinely set up special campaign committees aimed at segments of the electorate—the elderly, the students, the business people or ethnic groups.

Committee Emphasis. Interest groups gear their operations to the power structure and procedures of Congress. An important aspect of this is the system by which Congress divides its work up among committees which are made responsible for certain subjects.

While Members are elected to Congress from geographical areas, they are assigned to and work in committees set up on the basis of interests or functions. The committees have power which in many instances is of overriding significance.

Woodrow Wilson wrote that Congress in its committee rooms was Congress at work. Taking note of Wilson's statement, Rep. William D. Hathaway (D Maine) said in a 1970 House debate:

"The committee system is still the crux of the legislative process and is still the basis for Congressional action. Laws are not really made here on the floor of the House or on the floor of the other body. They are only revised here. Ninety percent of all legislation that has been passed was passed in the form reported by the committee to the floor."

The committee's power to prevent legislation or to determine its nature narrows down the necessary targets for the great majority of specialized interests. Their Washington representatives become experts not only in their field but also on the House and Senate committees which deal with that specialty. This focus in some cases narrows still further to certain subcommittees.

Pressure groups pay their Washington staffs to keep them abreast of developments in government which could affect their constituents. These agents make it their business to watch the work of committees in which they have an interest, to establish and maintain working relationships with key Members or staff members and to stay informed on potential or actual legislative developments. For strategic reasons they also must inform themselves on developments affecting other groups with whom they sometimes cooperate.

Many Members of Congress would probably concur with Rep. John E. Moss (D Calif.) who said in 1970 "the lobbyists know more about what goes on in the committees than any other group on the Hill, in my judgment." A parallel situation exists with regulatory agencies and departments in the Executive Branch.

Contact and Expertise. Pressure groups send representatives to testify before committees and submit prepared statements setting forth their views. In addition, their officers or lobbyists frequently discuss legislation in person with Members of Congress and with Member and committee staff personnel.

Some groups have found individual visits to a Representative or Senator by selected citizens from his home district or state effective in getting a hearing for their position. The more influential the visitor is among the Member's constituents, the greater is his suitability from the group's point of view. The visiting constituent is chosen both for reasons of expertise on a given subject and the ability to speak as a leader or typical representative of a particular group to the lawmaker.

When postal legislation was before a conference committee seeking to reconcile House-Senate differences in 1970, local, state and national officers of the United Federation of Postal Clerks from the home districts of the conferees were called to Washington "to help emphasize our legislative goals," as union spokesmen put it. The last-ditch lobbying effort, less than four months before the Congressional elections, was part of a plan in which seven postal unions cooperated in exerting pressure on members of the conference committee.

Groups sometimes employ in key posts individuals who were formerly connected with the Congressional machinery or administrative agency. These agents may be former colleagues of the incumbents with whom they must deal, perhaps having attained a first-name basis with them and their staff.

Many former Members of Congress and former officials in the Executive Branch, as well as former staff employees, go on to become spokesmen before governmental entities on behalf of interests with which they had some kind of relationship while in public office. For example, former Rep. Harold D. Cooley (D N.C.), chairman of the Agriculture Committee from 1949-53 and from 1955-66, represented the governments of Liberia and Thailand before the committee in 1971. He sought an initial sugar quota for Liberia and an increased sugar quota for Thailand. *(Sugar lobby p. 89)*

This works the opposite way also. Representatives of organized interests sometimes are elected to office or become advisers or employees on committee payrolls. Ralph E. Casey, for years a leading spokesman for shipping interests, served as special counsel to the House Merchant Marine and Fisheries Committee while it considered ship subsidy legislation in 1970. He became the Committee's chief counsel in 1971 when passenger ship legislation and appropriations to launch the 10-year ship subsidy program were among matters before the Committee. *(Maritime law p. 23, Maritime lobby p. 75)*

While the revolving door practice is found frequently, many group officials today discount the significance of the oldtime reputed "influence peddler" who worked his will with a lavish expense account and mysterious but powerful connections.

A number of group leaders have expressed views similar to those of M. R. Garstang, general counsel of the National Milk Producers Federation. He told a 1971 House hearing that years of experience by his organization had convinced him "that the most effective way to influence legislation is to develop a reasonable and just cause and support it by logical and well documented arguments." Garstang added:

"Friendly contacts with Members of Congress and their staffs are still important in the sense that they help open doors and get attentive hearings. But legislative decisions are not based on the contacts. They are based on the soundness of the arguments presented and the accuracy of the information supplied."

Garstang's comments resembled the advice given in *Trade Association Law and Practice*, a 1956 book written by George P. Lamb and Sumner S. Kittelle for trade association executives. They said:

"Effective Washington representation should be characterized by competence rather than by 'influence.' The effectiveness of 'influence' in Washington has been exaggerated. Personal acquaintance with government personnel is valuable as a time-saver—in knowing whom to see, in arranging conferences, and in recognizing important issues. Most public officials, however, and certainly the best of them, resist the blandishments of 'influence peddlers,' and rely on sound argument, not personalities, in making decisions."

Yet another viewpoint, common among legislators, is that of Rep. John H. Dent (D Pa.). Noting that he had spent 39 years in legislative bodies, Dent told the House in 1970 that "all lobbyists are not the kind and gentle

What Is A Lobbyist?

Five years before he became President of the United States, Senator John F. Kennedy (D Mass.) described a lobbyist's functions in an article for the Sunday Magazine section of the *New York Times.* Kennedy said:

"Lobbyists are in many cases expert technicians and capable of explaining complex and difficult subjects in a clear, understandable fashion. They engage in personal discussions with Members of Congress in which they can explain in detail the reason for positions they advocate.

"Lobbyists prepare briefs, memorandums, legislative analyses, and draft legislation for use by committees and Members of Congress; they are necessarily masters of their subject and, in fact, they frequently can provide useful statistics and information not otherwise available....

"Concededly, each is biased; but such a procedure is not unlike the advocacy of lawyers in court which has proven so successful in resolving judicial controversies. Because our congressional representation is based on geographical boundaries, the lobbyists who speak for the various economic, commercial, and other functional interests of this country serve a very useful purpose and have assumed an important role in the legislative process."

people that have been described here, although many of them may be. I will tell you the good lobbyists are a great aid to the legislative processes of this government. Those who know their business and give you a straight story cannot be done without, because they are a help to the legislative process. But there are those who know nothing of the subject matter....These are the kinds who destroy the writeup sessions on legislation."

Grassroots Lobbying. Pressure groups have placed increased emphasis in recent years on the use of propaganda and educational campaigns. These aim at shaping public opinion among strategic elements of the population for or against some position promoted in Congress.

A massive letter-writing campaign often follows, accompanied by an influx of delegations from back home who reinforce the telegraphed, telephoned and written expressions of sentiment with visits to individual Senators and Representatives. These occasions carry with them the implication—usually unvoiced but occasionally asserted bluntly—that voter support in the next election could hinge on the Member's position on the issue in question.

Interest groups frequently buy full-page advertisements in leading newspapers or time on television to present their views forcefully before the public in hopes of building public pressure on Congress or the President.

The precedent for indirect lobbying of legislative bodies is of long standing. For example, Madison, Alexander Hamilton and John Jay could be said to have engaged in a form of grassroots pressure tactics—at a lofty level—when they wrote scholarly newspaper articles, which became known as *The Federalist,* in-

tended to tip the scales in favor of ratification of the U.S. Constitution by the states.

The Federalist has been described by Prof. Clinton Rossiter of Cornell University as "the most important work in political science that has ever been written, or is likely ever to be written, in the United States." Its fame, he says, derives "not from the events of a single decisive year, but from the whole course of American history."

Yet the articles appeared originally under the anonymity of a pen name—a practice which Congress in recent decades has sought to discourage through disclosure legislation. Committees and Congress itself have repeatedly emphasized the right of Congress and the public to know the identities and purposes of those who try to influence public policy.

The Senate's Special Committee to Investigate Political Activities, Lobbying, and Campaign Contributions headed by Sen. John L. McClellan (D Ark.) said in its final report May 31, 1957, that all recent studies confirmed that pressure groups in recent years placed more and more reliance on mass media campaigns to stir up "inspired letter-writing campaigns" and other signs of interest among the voters.

"For example," the report said, "in 1940, 13,000 letters received by 5 Senators showed that 90 percent of the writers were opposed to the Burke-Wadsworth Selective Service Act. At the time, a private survey showed that 70 percent of the public was for the law.

"The ability of pressure groups to stir up such deluges is well known to all Members of Congress. In the absence of adequate disclosure laws concerning pressure groups, Members of the Congress can only conjecture as to whether or not direct communications they receive are spontaneous expressions of constituents' views, or strands in a net held by the unseen hand of a pressure group attempting to scoop up a vote here, a vote there."

Another viewpoint was expressed by former Rep. Carter Manasco (D Ala.), who was secretary to Speaker William B. Bankhead from 1933 until Bankhead's death in 1940 and subsequently won election to his vacated seat. After 22 years as an independent lobbyist on Capitol Hill, Manasco told a 1971 House lobby hearing that in his experience "more Congressional mail relating to legislation is stimulated by editorials, commentators, and news reports than by all the so-called pressure groups combined."

Large scale activities of the grassroots type are usually conducted by a coalition of interest groups whose leaders pool their strength for greater impact, backing and favored access to the combined memberships. Major campaigns to mobilize public opinion, such as the civil rights drives of the 1960s, the anti-war demonstrations of 1969 and 1971, and the campaigns to prevent Senate confirmation of Supreme Court nominees Clement F. Haynsworth Jr. and G. Harrold Carswell in 1969 and 1970, require considerable generalship, logistical planning and financial resources.

Thousands or tens of thousands of persons, however intensely motivated, do not descend on Congress on the same day by coincidence. A massive demonstration requires weeks or months of groundwork, planning sessions, fund raising activities, promotional and organizational efforts among many groups in many localities. These are coordinated with action in Congress.

(Continued on p. 8)

Pressure Group Tactics: Two Lobby Victories Described

Many legislative victories are the products of careful campaigns aimed at building pressures on Congress from outside while capitalizing on all possible advantages within.

This requires close teamwork between key Members of Congress and pressure groups with favored access to certain segments of the population.

Two of these pressure fights are described below.

Common Cause. Leaders of the National Urban Coalition formed a lobbying and political organization called Common Cause as the 1970s opened. Its chairman was John W. Gardner, former Secretary of Health, Education and Welfare. Common Cause reported to its members in March 1971 on its partly successful 1971 lobbying campaign to loosen the seniority system in Congress. Excerpts follow:

"We estimate that Common Cause members generated at least 10,000 letters, telegrams and phone calls to their Congressmen. Some of them made personal visits to their Representative, others talked with their Congressman's staff. All of these activities were of great help to the Common Cause legislative representatives, who discussed seniority reform with some 65 Congressmen in their Washington offices.

"...One of the reform leaders, Rep. Don Fraser of Minnesota, (outgoing chairman of the Democratic Study Group) wrote John Gardner that the substantial progress in the Democratic caucus 'was made possible in part because of the effective job of lobbying and of public education undertaken by Common Cause.'....

"When Common Cause picked seniority reform as a major lobbying issue, a decision was made to conduct the campaign on four levels: an appeal to all members for action; direct lobbying on Capitol Hill; encouraging other organizations to get active; and a telephone campaign focused on 96 crucial Congressional districts with Democratic Representatives. (With committee chairmen to choose, Democrats were the key target.)

"A group of some 20 volunteers was briefed on the issue and asked to find by telephone Common Cause members in the 96 districts who were willing to organize a concerted campaign in their area with the help of other members.

"Direct people-to-people contact was a great success. The members whom the volunteers called were enthusiastic, ready to go to work, and imaginative in their tactics. Some of the approaches used were these:

"Visits to the Congressman in his district office.

"Radio and TV discussions of seniority.

"Public meetings organized by Common Cause members.

"Press conferences and briefings.

"Discussion of seniority at church, club and political meetings—even at a Sunday School class.

"Letters to the editor.

"An open message to a Congressman, run as a newspaper advertisement by Toledo, Ohio, members.

"A sermon at church by a member-minister.

"The 'boiler-room' operation in our Washington office, using a bank of 11 telephones, was conducted entirely by volunteers with on-the-spot advice from three Common Cause lobbyists, John Lagomarcino, Peter Edelman and Jack Moskowitz." *(Coalitions p. 51)*

National Right to Work Committee. Rep. David N. Henderson (D N.C.) described a successful fight to incorporate in postal reorganization legislation which became law in 1970 a provision barring compulsory union membership among postal employees. Excerpts from his speech on April 30, 1971, to the board of the National Right to Work Committee follow:

"First of all, in a truly staggering publicity campaign, the Committee began to get press coverage all over the country and editorials in leading newspapers directing attention to and condemning the 'sell-out' by Postmaster General Blount and the Administration. Members of Congress began getting dozens of letters, telegrams, and telephone calls on the subject—many from campaign managers and other leading supporters....

"Meetings began to be held with representatives of...various organizations present for briefings on strategy and tactics and discussion of ways and means to get votes. Facing a teller vote on the floor as the first crucial test, a 'whip' system was set up to be sure that all members were reminded of the vote even though the normal party 'whip' telephone calls might not have been made.

"In all of these meetings and arrangements, the Right to Work Committee and its staff served as coordinator not only for my office and other involved legislators, but also for the other organizations participating in the fight. My legislative assistant had standing orders to coordinate all of my activities with the Committee and to keep it informed of all developments. Reed Larson (Committee executive director) and his staff, in turn, coordinated their own efforts and tactics fully with us....

"We counted votes and kept our fingers crossed... Our 'whip' system had gotten our votes to the floor and my amendment passed the House on a teller vote...We still had to face a hostile Senate, and sure enough, we lost our fight there by a narrow margin. Thus, we faced the necessity of keeping in the House amendment in a joint House-Senate Conference....

"We finally decided to bet our whole bundle on a roll-call vote on the House floor, which would direct the House conferees to insist upon the inclusion of the Henderson Amendment in the Conference report....

"...a final all-out burst of publicity and contacts by the Right to Work Committee insured that a great deal of public attention was focused on the vote and that no Member of the House would be able to nourish the hope that his vote might go unnoticed. By this time, we had full-fledged support from the U.S. Chamber of Commerce, the National Association of Manufacturers, the Farm Bureau Federation, the Associated General Contractors, and a number of other organizations...."

The House voted 225-159 to insist on the amendment, which was subsequently retained in the final version.

(Continued from p. 6)

Attention must be given by leaders to such details as the chartering of scores or hundreds of buses, arrangements for food and lodging in some cases and a timetable—fitted into Congressional activity—for briefings, calls on Members of Congress, progress reports and follow-up visits. Visiting delegations of lobbyists for a day or more are supplied packets of printed materials supporting their position, given pep talks and instructed on how to conduct themselves.

In all this activity, friendly Members of Congress—who may be carrying the ball in the legislative chambers—often give advice and loan the use of their staffs and offices. Headquarters are manned by personnel intimately acquainted with Congress and its workings. *(Box p. 7)*

Mass demonstrations sometimes are intended as much to mobilize sentiment and recruit organizers for a coming campaign as to show strength for a position at the time.

The "March on Washington for Jobs and Freedom" of Aug. 28, 1963, came after smaller demonstrations in 800 cities and towns. It brought 200,000 persons to the Lincoln Memorial. It was followed by prolonged campaigning which spanned the preliminary phases of a Presidential election and culminated in the breaking of a Senate filibuster and enactment of the Civil Rights Act of 1964. Many groups united in the drive, which produced heavy pressures on Congressional offices.

Elections and Committees

From the suggestion of future political support or opposition by a pressure group it is a short and logical step to active participation in the political process.

As the House Select Committee on Lobbying Activities put it in one of a series of reports it issued in 1950:

"The modern pressure group is as much concerned with elections as with legislative issues. A pressure group does not take a strong position on legislation and then stand idly by when its ardent sponsor or vigorous opponent is up for re-election."

Some groups have found it expedient to take part in the two-party political system, performing a role in party leadership, platform writing and the selection of candidates for Congress or the Presidency at the primary and general election stages. Others maintain a generally hands-off stance to varying degrees, although their leaders and members are free to engage in politics. Federal bans on direct political contributions by corporations, tax-exempt groups and labor unions are readily circumvented by establishment of special or "parallel" committees and by independent activities by individuals. The AFL-CIO has its Committee on Political Education (COPE), the American Medical Association its American Medical Political Action Committee (AMPAC).

One aspect of the Congressional system to which pressure groups have adjusted their strategy is that of seniority, under which Members of Congress traditionally climb with increasing tenure to favored positions of power.

Groups which help a given candidate get elected and then support him through repeated elections gain a vested interest in his seniority as he moves up to the post of committee or subcommittee chairman where he may exercise often decisive power over matters affecting their interests. Shipping interests attempt to keep individuals they favor on the maritime committees, farm groups do likewise with the agriculture committees, and organizations with heavy stakes in the tax laws keep in close touch with the Ways and Means and Finance Committees.

Some groups lean heavily to one political party or the other, but it is common for politically active groups to hedge their bets with friendly committee members on both sides of the aisle. In the 1970 general election, for example, the AFL-CIO's COPE endorsed 19 of 20 Democrats on the House Education and Labor Committee—all of whom won—and two Republican committee members, also winners.

The United Federation of Postal Clerks in 1970 successfully supported both the Democratic chairman and the ranking Republican on the Senate Post Office and Civil Service Committee. The top minority Member not only headed the nominal opposition but stood to become Committee chairman in event of a change in party control of the Senate. *(Details, p. 45, 46)*

An interdependency is built up on both sides. An interest group has a stake in keeping those it regards as friends in power posts. The Representative or Senator, on the other hand, relies on organized blocs of his constituency for re-election.

The political party machinery is of great importance in the allocation of committee assignments and leadership posts. Groups which can demonstrate apparent influence over key blocs of voters naturally tend to command inside tracks with party circles, as do those with access to the large sums of campaign contributions essential to the operations of parties and candidates alike.

Congressional investigators have repeatedly acknowledged the connection between campaign financing and lobbying. The House of Representatives recognized the link again when in 1970 it took the unprecedented step of granting its Committee on Standards of Official Conduct continuing jurisdiction over both those subjects.

Problems of Lobbying

Through the years, the role of pressure groups and lobbyists has drawn both condemnation and praise. A public controversy arose over National Association of Manufacturers lobbying in 1913 on proposed tariff regulations. Controversies also surrounded public utilities lobbying in 1928 and 1935 and maritime lobbying in 1936. *(See p. 13, 113, 115)*

President Wilson denounced lobbying on the tariff. President Truman had harsh words for the real estate lobby. President Eisenhower vetoed a bill in the 1950s because of controversy over oil and gas lobbying activities.

Former President Herbert Hoover said in 1949, "Our Representatives must run for election. They can be defeated by these pressure groups. Our officials are forced to think in terms of pressure groups, not in terms of the needs of the whole people." Rep. Wright Patman (D Texas), chairman of the House Banking and Currency Committee, long sought a Congressional investigation of the bank lobby, which he said he was convinced "is the most potent, year-round influence group" in Washington. Various other organized interests have drawn fire from time to time. *(Lobbying and the Law p. 11)*

(Continued on p. 10)

Congressional Investigations of Lobbying: 1913-1971

A capsule summary of major Congressional investigations of lobbying during 1913-71 is given below, with emphasis on the post-World War II period:

1913—A House committee headed by Rep. Finis J. Garrett (D Tenn.) investigated the National Assn. of Manufacturers. The Garrett group turned up evidence that the NAM's Col. Martin Mulhall dominated several Members of Congress, kept the chief page of the House on his payroll and influenced appointments to strategic committee posts. Following the investigation, Rep. James T. McDermott (D Ill.) resigned.

1928—A general lobbying probe was headed by Sen. Thaddeus Caraway (D Ark.), who subsequently sponsored a lobbyist-control bill which died in the House.

1928-29—At the mandate of Congress, the Federal Trade Commission investigated the lobbying activities of electric utilities and concluded that such firms spent company funds heavily propagandizing the public.

1929—A Senate Naval Affairs subcommittee looked into the activities of William B. Shearer, who represented shipping, electrical metals and machinery and firms in attempts to block limitations on naval armaments and to obtain heavy Federal appropriations for construction of ships.

1935—A fight over the Public Utilities Holding Company Act led to an investigation by a Senate group headed by Sen. Hugo Black (D Ala.) of lobbying by utilities and financial combines. The final bill contained provisions on utilities lobbying. Black's general lobbyist-control bill was passed by the Senate in 1935 and in a different version by the House in 1936.

Also in 1935, a special Senate committee headed by Sen. Gerald P. Nye (R N.D.) investigated "munitions lobby" activities in favor of high military appropriations.

1938—The Temporary National Economic Committee, set up by Congress at President Roosevelt's request, under the chairmanship of Sen. Joseph O'Mahoney (D Wyo.), included lobbying among its subjects of study.

1945—The Joint Committee on the Organization of Congress, established in 1945, studied lobbying activities along with other matters pertaining to Congress. On the basis of the Committee's recommendations, Congress in 1946 passed the Legislative Reorganization Act, which provided for the first general lobby registration law.

1950—A House Select Committee on Lobbying Activities headed by Frank Buchanan (D Pa.) investigated the lobbying of a wide range of organizations, although publicity centered on the efforts of the Committee for Constitutional Government to distribute low-cost or free "right-wing" books. The Select Committee made recommendations for strengthening the Federal Regulation of Lobbying Act of 1946, but there was no action.

1956—Following the Feb. 3 revelation by Sen. Francis Case (R S.D.) that a lawyer interested in passage of the natural gas bill had offered Case a $2,500 campaign contribution in connection with his vote in favor of the bill, two separate Senate investigations were initiated. One, conducted by a Select Committee headed by Sen. Walter F. George (D Ga.), was limited to the offer to Case. This investigation ended April 7 with a report by the Select Committee which said that the campaign contribution was not an attempt at a direct bribe of the Senator but was an attempt to influence his vote. The report recommended a thorough study of the 1946 Federal Regulation of Lobbying Act because it was "too vague and loosely defined." The two lawyers involved in the campaign offer to Case, plus the Superior Oil Co., their principal, were eventually absolved of bribery charges but pleaded guilty in Federal court to violating the 1946 lobbying law.

The second investigation was conducted by a Senate Special Committee to investigate corrupt practices involving campaign contributions, lobbying or other influences on Congress. The Special Committee was appointed Feb. 23 by Vice President Richard M. Nixon and was eventually headed by John L. McClellan (D Ark.). Following various investigations McClellan May 31, 1957, introduced a new lobbying registration law to replace the 1946 act. The bill considerably tightened the existing law by designating the Comptroller General to administer the law (the existing law had no administrator), by eliminating the "principal purpose" loophole, by requiring coverage for anyone who spent $50,000 or more a year on grass roots campaigns designed to influence the public on legislation and by eliminating the exemption available in the 1946 law for those who merely testified on legislation. The bill died.

1959—The House Armed Services Special Investigations Subcommittee held three months of hearings on influence wielded by former Army, Navy and Air Force officers who had gone to work for defense contractors.

1962—In connection with lobbying on the Sugar Act, the Senate Foreign Relations Committee began investigating foreign lobbyists.

1963—The Foreign Relations Committee probe continued and Chairman J.W. Fulbright (D Ark.) introduced a bill to tighten registration requirements under the Foreign Agents Registration Act of 1938.

Also in 1963, Robert G. (Bobby) Baker, Secretary to the Senate (Democratic) Majority, was forced to resign as a result of a probe of his activities.

1965—The Senate completed its investigation of Baker's business activities.

The Joint Committee on the Reorganization of Congress, created in 1965, studied lobby laws along with other matters pertaining to Congress. (A measure providing changes in lobby laws was reported by the Committee in 1966 and passed the Senate in 1967.)

1966—Congress revised the Foreign Agents Registration Act, narrowing its scope.

1967—Senate and House ethics committees studied the abuse of lobbying laws. (Both committees in 1968 reported code of ethics resolutions which touched on lobby activities.)

Lobby Financing

The Friends Committee on National Legislation in its 1971 appeal for financial contributions told potential givers that $5,000 would buy 1,000 hours of lobbying time on Capitol Hill.

Other items cited in its solicitation of a $210,000 budget included: $100 to finance 20 hours of testimony before Congressional committees; $25 to finance 15 hours of research; $10 to buy two hours of work with strategic coalitions, and $5 to provide one hour of constituent briefing before visiting Capitol Hill.

On the other hand, President Nixon wrote James H. Rademacher, president of the National Association of Letter Carriers, a letter dated Aug. 12, 1970, the day Mr. Nixon signed a sweeping postal reorganization bill into law. The organization's convention bulletin called the communication "one of the most extraordinary letters ever to pass between the Chief Executive of the nation and the chief executive of a labor union."

The letter, which began "Dear Jim," credited the union for the final form of the bill and the passage of a postal pay bill. "It...gives me special pleasure on this history-making day to applaud the outstanding role of the National Association of Letter Carriers, and to express my deep appreciation to you personally for generously sharing your experience, knowledge and ideas," the President said.

Mr. Nixon said he hoped Rademacher's efforts to bring about the legislation "will be fully rewarded in the years ahead, as the benefits are translated into greater well-being for your members." Many postal union workers had struck a few months earlier in support of their demands, requiring troops to take over mail delivery in New York City temporarily.

An obvious defect in the growth of pressure groups is the constant uncertainty as to whether conflicting viewpoints are adequately represented and promoted. The haphazard development of organized interests—as contrasted to unorganized ones—gives no guarantee that ambition will counteract ambition, as Madison envisioned. There have been many indications to the contrary.

The problem of over-representation of some interests and under-representation of others has caused continual concern among students of the American government.

Much evidence has been collected indicating that pressure groups can succeed in pressuring Congress into enacting legislation designed for self-enrichment or pursuit of their own goals at the expense of the general public.

The ability to build formidable groundswells of public sentiment does not depend on the validity of arguments or accurate assessment of the public good, though those may be factors. Strong opposition and effective use of proven techniques in advertising and public relations, including the use of labels and slogans to drive home a message in simplified form, can be decisive.

A group's power to influence legislation often is related to the financial and manpower resources it can commit, the astuteness of its representatives and the lengths to which it is willing to go in resorting to political coercion, misstatements of fact and concealing information.

George B. Galloway, staff director of the Joint Committee on Organization of Congress, which promoted the Federal Regulation of Lobbying Act of 1946, said the Committee reasoned that "pressure boys" spoke for only a minority of the population.

"The great majority of the American people," he said, "are not members of special-interest groups and hence are much less articulate on particular issues than are the interested minority whose affiliation with some active organization gives them a greater political leverage."

The tremendous growth of the military establishment contributed a major set of factors to the expanding Washington lobby after World War II. Defense spending, which covered a sweeping variety of items and affected many industries, for years absorbed more than half of the national budget. Companies, industries and Congressional districts relied on Federal Government contracts for their survival or prosperity.

An alliance of interests evolved among businesses interested in Federal contracts, military officers dependent in some cases on a continued high level of Government spending, labor unions in defense industries and Members of Congress whose constituencies counted on military money.

The combined effects of many individual efforts to influence policy prompted President Eisenhower to warn in his Jan. 17, 1961, farewell speech against the power and influence of what he called the "military-industrial complex." He said the impact was "felt in every city, every state house, every office of the Federal Government" and posed serious dangers for democratic government.

A complicating factor in the 1970s was the upsurge of multinational corporations, companies whose interests extended far beyond national borders. Including in their ranks some leading U.S. corporations, these concerns exerted important influences on American trade and other policies.

Three of the top five U.S. defense contractors in fiscal 1968 and fiscal 1969—Lockheed Aircraft, United Aircraft and McDonnell Douglas—were among members of the Emergency Committee for American Trade, foremost organization of multinational corporations formed in 1967. All told, 10 of the top 25 defense contractors belonged to ECAT. (*Trade lobby p. 83*)

Organizations seeking to build pressure against military spending and U.S. involvement in the Vietnam War were increasingly active from the late 1960s on. A coalition of groups waged repeated drives to force U.S. withdrawal from Indochina, defeat construction of a U.S. anti-ballistic missile system and reduce military spending. These campaigns carried over into election campaigns, where they sometimes were an important factor.

An area of uncertainty which has received only occasional notice by Congress involves the internal politics of pressure groups. While some of the larger organizations place public emphasis on democratic procedures in their policy-making, questions continue to arise over whether a group's membership actually favors the positions espoused by the group. In cases where a group's resources are committed to a legislative course, the position of dissidents within the organization may find no channel for making itself known with equal weight in official circles. The possible implications involving public policy are far-reaching.

LOBBYING AND THE LAW

Efforts to Publicize Pressure Group

Activity Result in Congressional Legislation

Sporadic controversies over activities of pressure groups or individuals lobbying Congress touched off occasional attempts from as early as 1907 to enact Federal legislation.

Eventually it was Congressional investigation into utility holding companies' lobbying on legislation to regulate them during the depression of the 1930s that paved the way for the legislation which followed. The impact persists to this day.

State legislatures, perennial targets of specialized interests, had gradually moved into the area of lobby legislation since Massachusetts set the precedent in 1890. Thirty-five states had laws covering lobbyists by the end of World War II. Their emphasis, as the *Columbia Law Review* said at the time, was on throwing "the antiseptic light of publicity on the lobby."

Congress stepped into the field on a piecemeal basis. In each case it acted, under goading by key legislators, in the wake of agitation over the activities of specific elements in the pressure picture.

On the first occasion, in 1935, it was the actions of utility lobbyists and executives that induced Congress to act. In 1936 it was the operations of shipping spokesmen, largely coinciding with the utility lobbying, that produced sufficient sentiment to result in enactment of a lobby registration requirement covering them. The provision was included in ship subsidy legislation at the end of the session under threat of a possible Senate filibuster involving that and related items. *(Maritime law, p. 23)*

In 1938, revelation of a concealed Nazi and Fascist propaganda campaign led to enactment of a law to deal with it. In the brief span of three years, Congress passed three separate laws covering the lobbyists for specified utility holding companies, certain maritime interests and foreign employers. In each case the emphasis was placed on public exposure rather than on an attempt to curtail the activities.

Congress also inserted lobbying provisions in the Revenue Acts of 1938 and 1939. The first denied tax exemption to corporations which devoted a substantial part of their activities to propaganda or otherwise attempting to influence legislation. The second disallowed income tax deductions for contributions to charitable organizations which devoted a substantial part of their activities to attempts to influence legislation.

While a number of other laws from early in the twentieth century on affected pressure groups and lobbyists to some extent, attempts to broaden the coverage and pass a law specifically covering all Congressional lobbyists were rejected until Congress enacted the Legislative Reorganization Act of 1946. Lobbying received little attention at the time, but the first general lobby registration law at the national level was rather hurriedly incorporated into the Act as Title III. Sponsors used as a model bills drafted in the heat of the investigations of a decade earlier.

In 1970 General Counsel Milton A. Smith of the Chamber of Commerce of the United States recalled "the consternation when this suddenly came up without warning" for passage in the closing days of the 1946 session of Congress.

The 40-page report of the Joint Committee on the Organization of Congress which recommended a lobby law provision devoted only three pages to the subject. The Committee expressed the view that registration of the representatives of organized groups would "enable Congress better to evaluate and determine evidence, data, or communications from organized groups seeking to influence legislative action" and thus avoid the distortion of public opinion.

The pages of the *Congressional Record* reflect the accuracy of the wry comment in the *Columbia Law Review* that "The debate on Title III in both Senate and House could hardly be characterized as penetrating."

In spite of the fact that Congress had the experience of the states to draw upon, the general lobbying law it enacted was described by many critics almost from the beginning as suffering from major shortcomings found in the state laws which preceded it.

Among the defects, it was often conceded, were loopholes in coverage, vagueness in legal language and failure to provide for adequate enforcement. *(p. 19)*

Nevertheless, more than a quarter century later the Federal Regulation of Lobbying Act of 1946 continued to stand as the only general law on lobbying of Congress. By then court rulings had whittled its coverage to the point that legal critics said the Supreme Court had saved the Act's constitutionality only by rewriting it.

While it provided some information to Congress and the public concerning the legislative interests, income and spending for lobbying purposes of many who sought to exercise their constitutional rights to influence legislation, the facts provided were frequently sketchy. Sometimes registrations were filed with Congressional officials after the lobbying reported upon had ended—even after Congress had adjourned. Financial reports were received after the time they might have provided any guidance to Members of Congress on pending issues.

Upon occasion Congressional Quarterly found that processing of lobby registrations by House officials to make them available for public inspection was set aside while other work was handled. This occurred, for example, in the closing weeks of 1970 when candidates' campaign reports took priority.

The Supreme Court had held in 1954, as House Clerk W. Pat Jennings summarized it in 1970, that "the Act covers only those whose 'principal purpose' is to influence legislation and only concerned those involved in direct dealings with Members of Congress." *(Text p. 118)*

Some major organizations, including the National Association of Manufacturers, filed no reports on grounds that lobbying was not their principal purpose and they therefore were not covered by the law. Others filed financial reports but did not register lobbyists.

"The registrations you have are the ones who are cautious enough to do so," George B. Mickum III, chairman of the committee on regulation of lobbying of the Bar Association of the District of Columbia, told a House lobby hearing in 1970. "Anyone who doesn't register, I don't think the Justice Department could get a conviction if their life depended on it. They've quit trying."

The Supreme Court's interpretation meant that the area of grassroots or indirect lobbying fell beyond the reach of the 1946 law at a time when such activities produced occasional deluges of mail and led to demonstrations in Washington by 200,000 or more persons seeking to influence Congress and the Executive Branch.

Critics of the lobby law differed as to what could or should be done to correct the situation. Some, such as the Chamber of Commerce, urged outright repeal. Others favored revision of the Act.

Still others recommended enactment of a stiff new law which would embrace groups and individuals untouched by the 1946 law as it stood and would contain much more stringent reporting requirements. Opponents criticized some of these proposals as calling for legislative overkill and unlikely to survive challenges on constitutional grounds. *(Testimony p. 22)*

The House of Representatives in 1970 gave a House committee continuing jurisdiction over both campaign financing and efforts to influence legislation. In its first report on the subjects, the Committee on Standards of Official Conduct said:

"The fact that the basic statute on one of these subjects has remained unchanged for 25 years and the other essentially so for 45 years, although admittedly both have been long-since outmoded, may be taken as an indication of the complexities involved in the attainment of needed reforms in these vital areas of law."

Through the years, Congress enacted provisions in other laws which dealt with specific types of abuses in the area of attempts to influence Government policy. Subjects involved included bribery and campaign finances. Various laws limited political contributions, provided for reports aimed at disclosing the sources of support and banned contributions for political purposes by corporations and labor unions.

However, politically-oriented groups found ways to make their weight felt if they wished, such as by working through individuals—who possessed a constitutional right to participate in the political process—or by establishing parallel organizations which fulfilled the letter of the law.

At the Federal level as at the state levels, legislation concerning pressure activities holds no immunity from lobbying. The same incentives which lead groups and individuals to try to influence other legislation apply with equal weight to bills aimed at their lobbying operations. As with other legislation, the struggle extends as circumstances warrant into the three branches of government.

Experience has shown that, in the area of lobbying law as elsewhere, getting a law on the books can be a far cry from attainment in practice of the goals expressed by the sponsors. Once Congress has acted, the burden falls on those who enforce the act. In the case of all four Federal laws dealing directly with lobbyists, enforcement has left much to be desired if publicity is the goal as stated by Congressional spokesmen.

Nicholas deB. Katzenbach, then Deputy Attorney General, testified at Senate Foreign Relations Committee hearings in 1963 that the approach in the Federal Regulation of Lobbying Act was basically similar to that in the Foreign Agents Registration Act.

"It was the intention of those who supported the Regulation of Lobbying Act to employ the glare of publicity to inform the general public and thus expose such activities to public scrutiny," he said. "I cannot honestly state that I think that act has fully achieved its purpose. Relatively little public attention is focused upon the registration statements filed."

This applies even more to the other three lobby registration provisions. There had been relatively little publicity concerning foreign agent registrations until Congressional Quarterly published the complete active list in 1970. There has been no publicity concerning the registrations of maritime and utilities representatives, and it was not until a Congressional Quarterly appeal from an adverse administrative ruling that maritime registrations were made available for public inspection in 1970.

FEDERAL LOBBY LAWS

History of Congressional Efforts to Control Lobbying

Legislators who seek to cope with lobbying abuses at the national level face these problems:
- To bring misconduct and undesirable practices into the open.
- To avoid interfering with the indispensable flow of information from specialized interests to the lawmaking branch of government.
- To avoid infringing on the Constitutional rights of free speech, press, assembly and petition.

The states, moving far ahead of Congress, uniformly based their legislation on the principle that undesirable pressure activities could be controlled better by publicity than prohibition, with certain exceptions not limited to the lobbying area such as bribery or extortion.

This principle was carried over to the sporadic efforts to legislate a law at the Federal level and was emphasized repeatedly by sponsors and Congressional committees. Exposure, rather than regulation as such, has been the expressed goal ever since. This purpose was incorporated in the title of a new Federal lobby reporting proposal in 1971, the Legislative Activities Disclosure Act.

Bills to require registration of lobbyists and the filing of reports on their employers and finances passed the U.S. House of Representatives or the Senate several times, including in 1928, 1935 and 1936, without being enacted.

The first breakthrough dealing with the Washington lobby came on a partial basis in 1935, however, amid controversy over the pressure activities of electric power holding companies and their affiliates.

In lobby supervision as in some other fields, Congressional reaction to specific events involving a relative few laid the groundwork for legislation which affected many in the long run.

For all the spirited statements at the time, however, results through the years fell short of sponsors' predictions as legislative interest slackened, responsibility shifted from legislation to little-publicized administration, and court challenges tested the legal soundness of Congress' response.

Utilities Holding Company Act

Comments by Members in 1935 suggest the temper of the times in which Congress' approach toward lobby legislation was molded. The impact fell not only on the immediate legislation—dealing only with the holding companies—but also on the Federal Regulation of Lobbying Act of a decade later which Congress would leave untouched for the next 25 years or longer.

Rep. John E. Rankin (D Miss.) told the House, concerning what he called the Power Trust: "It is the most diabolical lobby, the most powerful and the most far-reaching, that has ever attempted to influence legislation, in all the history of this Government."

Sen. Homer T. Bone (D Wash.), later a U.S. circuit judge, said in Senate debate the public utilities bill "impinges on powerful interests which have become the greatest political machine ever created under the American flag." Bone added: "Compared to them, all the so-called 'lobbyists and political fixers' of all time are as moonlight unto sunlight and water unto wine."

Sen. Hugo L. Black (D Ala.), chairman of the Senate's Special Committee to Investigate Lobbying Activities, resorted to some grassroots lobbying of his own when he denounced what he called "the insidious and indefensible power lobby" in a national broadcast while the legislation was before Congress.

To be elevated to the Supreme Court two years later, Black estimated in 1935 more than 250,000 telegrams and perhaps five million letters opposing the legislation to regulate utility holding companies were sent to Members of Congress. Nearly all, he said, were generated by holding company representatives and paid for by local power companies from funds derived from customers.

"No one single message contained any information to the Congressman or Senator that the message was conceived by a holding company beneficiary, actually written by a subordinate of this beneficiary, and actually paid for by a local power company," Black said. He said of the power lobby:

"Contrary to tradition, against the public morals, and hostile to good government, the lobby has reached such a position of power that it threatens government itself." (Speech excerpts, p. 113)

The House Rules Committee which investigated the 1935 lobbying said in a report that "the campaign to influence utility holding company legislation was probably as comprehensive, as well managed, as persistent and as well financed as any in the history of the country...." (Report excerpts, p. 115)

In enacting the Public Utilities Holding Company Act of 1935, Congress incorporated its first direct venture into lobby law—a provision requiring registration of lobbyists in that field.

Section 12i of the Act, 15 USC 79 1(i), required anyone employed or retained by a registered holding company or a subsidiary to file reports with the Securities and Exchange Commission before attempting to influence Congress, the SEC or the Federal Power Commission. It remained on the books thereafter.

Merchant Marine Act

Legislation to provide the first direct ship subsidy program in U.S. history was before Congress at the same time as the utility holding company bill. The ship bill asked by President Franklin D. Roosevelt, however, was held over until 1936.

The activities of shipping representatives aroused controversy rivaling that surrounding the utilities spokesmen. This, too, had both an immediate and a

Types of Legislative Influence

Activities designed to influence legislation or which have the effect of doing so cover a wide range. This variety complicates the task of drafting law to disclose or prevent abuses while avoiding infringement on constitutional rights of free speech, press and petition.

The Senate's Special Committee to Investigate Political Activities, Lobbying, and Campaign Contributions divided such activities into seven categories. Its 1957 report said it would "facilitate a better understanding of the manifold problems" involved if the types and patterns of activities were classified separately. The report listed:

"Group 1.—Direct contacts with Congress to influence legislation by a person who has been employed or retained for such purpose.

"Group 2.—Direct contacts with Congress to influence legislation by a person employed or retained by a trade association or other membership group to devote a part or all of his time to legislative matters, where such activities form only a part of the association's work. (These are often referred to as multipurpose organizations.)

"Group 3.—Occasional direct contacts with Congress to influence legislation by an officer or employee of a business firm or labor union who devotes the major portion of his time to the regular business of the firm or labor union.

"Group 4.—Direct contacts with Congress to influence legislation by any other individual not covered by groups 1, 2 or 3.

"Group 5.—Campaigns addressed to the public through newspapers, magazines, television and radio containing explicit appeals to the public to contact Congress to influence legislation.

"Group 6.—Campaigns addressed to the public through newspapers, magazines, television, or radio containing implicit appeals to the public to contact Congress to influence legislation.

"Group 7.—The preparation and distribution of books, pamphlets, or data by research groups, which might influence legislation, but without any intent to produce legislative action.

"Also of significance are activities by the executive branch to influence legislation, and contacts with the executive branch for such purpose.

"With the exception of group 1, there are conflicting views as to whether the foregoing activities are subject to the registration and reporting provisions of the present Federal Regulation of Lobbying Act, as well as differences of opinion as to whether they should be made subject to reporting."

delayed-action effect on Congressional legislation covering lobbyists and pressure groups.

A special committee headed by Black investigated ocean and air mail contracts. A committee report in 1935 criticized what it called "the concerted and arrogant action" of certain Government officials and shipping interests to bypass the required competitive bidding on mail contracts.

The report said that while ocean-mail contractors were delinquent in their obligations to the Government, "excessive salaries, fees, commissions, and expense accounts have been paid to officers, agents, and high-powered 'fixers' plying their art in Washington." One steamship company president, it said, had expenses in Washington averaging more than $1,000 per day in 1928-29 when maritime legislation was pending before Congress.

"The shipping interests have operated through many agencies without disclosing their activities to the general public," the Black committee report said. "They have extended financial aid to numerous associations and organizations...." The report referred to their activity as "insidious propaganda."

In its second move to expose to public view the activities and backing of certain groups and individuals attempting to influence Government policy, Congress approved a lobby provision (Section 807) in the Merchant Marine Act of 1936. It was closely patterned after the utilities provision of the preceding year.

The new provision, 46 USC 1225, required representatives of subsidized shipping and shipyard interests and their employers to file specified information on their lobbying interests and finances with the Secretary of Commerce. *(Maritime law, p. 23; lobbying, p. 75)*

Foreign Agents Registration Act

In 1938 the disclosure that Nazi and Fascist propaganda was getting distribution in the United States by means of hidden identities led to still another piece of lobby legislation, though powerful opposition in the House Rules Committee delayed action. *(Box p. 32)*

As with the utilities and maritime lobby provisions, Congressional action on foreign agents stemmed from attention raised by specific episodes involving their attempts to influence public opinion and legislation.

The Foreign Agents Registration Act of 1938, as amended, 22 USC 611 et seq., required anyone representing a foreign government or other foreign employer, within the definitions of the Act, to register and file reports.

"We believe that the spotlight of pitiless publicity will serve as a deterrent to the spread of pernicious propaganda," said a report by a special committee headed by Rep. John W. McCormack (D Mass.), the future Speaker. "We feel our people are entitled to know the sources of such efforts, and the person or persons or agencies carrying on such work in the United States."

The Act originally required agents to register with the State Department. This was soon shifted to the Justice Department amid complaints of a lack of enforcement. The complaints recurred later.

The Act was amended several times, including in 1939, 1942, 1946, 1950, 1956 and 1961, without changing its broad purposes. In 1966 Congress narrowed the scope of the Act and made changes which the Justice Department's top internal security official said in 1970 had had "a hampering effect" on enforcement. *(For details, see p. 29.)*

1946 Lobbying Act

Attempts were made in both houses of Congress in 1935 and 1936 to enact broader legislation covering lobbying in general. Sponsors included Black in the Senate and Rep. Howard W. Smith (D Va.) in the House. Their bills contained registration and reporting requirements.

"What I want to do is to expose to the pitiless light of publicity all these activities and put these reports where they can be seen, both in the Senate and the House, as well as with the Federal Trade Commission," Black testified in 1935. The Senate passed a substitute for his bill (S 2512) that year.

The House Rules Committee in recommending passage of Smith's bill (HR 11223) in 1936 said in its report that Congress and the public "have a right to know by whom and in whose interest such appeals are made, by whom these movements are financed, and the manner in which money is expended.... If it cannot stand publicity, it should not be permitted to exist."

The House Judiciary Committee quoted at length from the Rules Committee's report in submitting a new substitute (HR 11663) based on amendments to the Smith bill. The Judiciary report said "Congress should know the background and sources from which emanate organized efforts to control legislation.... The sole purpose...is to shed the light of day upon their activities...."

The House passed HR 11663 in 1936, but a conference committee failed to reconcile differences between the Senate and House versions.

In 1946, Congress passed a general lobbyist registration law, the Federal Regulation of Lobbying Act, as part of the Legislative Reorganization Act of 1946 (S 2177—PL 79-601). There was little debate on the lobbying provisions at the time. The lobby law was never subsequently amended, and only four sets of prosecutions had been brought for violations through the end of 1970. *(Box p. 17)*

The Act drew heavily from the Black and Smith bills in their varied versions of a decade earlier. It began to receive criticism almost at once. For example, two law journals published critical reviews in January 1947. Many of their points have been reiterated through the years. *(See box this page for provisions.)*

An unsigned *Columbia Law Review* article spoke of "the carelessness with which the entire act was drafted...." It said "the act was neither carefully drafted nor fully considered. Its ambiguous terms encourage evasion, and, in providing for enforcement, Congress has failed to draw upon the experience of the states...."

A writer in the *Yale Law Journal* said the bill "was hurriedly drafted and modeled on anachronistic precedent." He said: "The unfortunate identity of language between the instant Act and the Black and Smith bills is not solely explicable in terms of Congressional intent; it is attributable largely to the speed which marked the drafting of the Reorganization Act, the indifference with which legislators regarded the lobbying provisions, and the political expediency of avoiding too sharp a break from past attempts."

George B. Galloway, staff director of the Joint Committee on the Organization of Congress whose recommendations led to inclusion of the lobby law in the Reorganization Act in 1946, said in 1956 "there is widespread agreement that the act suffers from defective draftsmanship and has given rise to many interpretive difficulties." He added:

Who Must Register

The 1946 Federal Regulation of Lobbying Act requires paid lobbyists to register with the Clerk of the House and the Secretary of the Senate and to file quarterly financial reports with the House Clerk.

However, large loopholes in the law exempt many interests from registering. The law requires registration only by persons paid to lobby for someone else. They must report how much pay they receive and from whom.

Organizations not employed as lobbyists for someone else must file financial reports but do not need to register.

Section 307 of the Act requires registration by any person "who by himself, or through any agent or employee or other persons in any manner...solicits, collects or receives money or any other thing of value to be used principally to aid...the passage or defeat of any legislation by the Congress."

The Act does not seriously limit the activities of lobbyists, especially the large number of interest groups whose lobbying activities do not fall under the narrow definitions of the law. For example:

• Many large organizations such as the National Association of Manufacturers do not register as lobbyists because they contend that lobbying is not the principal purpose for which they collect or receive funds.

• Groups or individuals who spend their own funds on lobbying do not have to register.

• Courts have interpreted the 1946 Act to mean that lobbying efforts are not covered unless a lobbyist contacts Members of Congress directly. Thus lobbyists who generate grass roots pressure on Congress are not covered.

• Testifying before Congress or preparing such testimony does not fall under lobbying activities, according to the Act.

• Some lobbyists contend that their contacts with Members of Congress are designed to inform—not influence—and thus don't constitute lobbying.

• Individuals and groups decide entirely for themselves what percentage of their budgets to attribute to lobbying activities.

• The Act does not require the Clerk of the House and the Secretary of the Senate to investigate lobby registrations and financial reports for their truthfulness. Nor can they require individuals or groups to register as lobbyists. The Justice Department can prosecute lobby act violators but does not investigate reports and acts only when it receives a complaint. There have been only four prosecutions and a test case since 1946.

"As to information required, the act fails to require (what the LaFollette-Monroney Committee recommended) that registration statements include information as to the size of groups that lobbyists claim to represent, how the membership decides its lobbying policy, and by what right the lobbyist speaks for the groups."

The 1946 Act also had its defenders. The House Select Committee on Lobbying Activities in its report

Legislative Activities Disclosure Act

A proposed "Legislative Activities Disclosure Act" drafted as a possible replacement for the Federal Regulation of Lobbying Act of 1946 (2 USC 261 et seq.) was the subject of hearings in 1971 by the House Committee on Standards of Official Conduct. *(Testimony, p. 22)*

The bill (HR 5259) stemmed from exploratory committee hearings in 1970. It was patterned after a bill with the same title recommended by the Special Committee to Investigate Political Activities, Lobbying, and Campaign Contributions in 1957. The 1971 proposal was broader, however.

The bill declared as its purpose "to provide for the disclosure to the Congress, to the President, and to the public, of the activities, and the origin, amounts, and utilization of funds and other resources, of and by persons who seek to influence the legislative process."

The proposal transferred administration to the Comptroller General, avoided such words as "regulation" in favor of disclosure, and eliminated the controversial "principal purpose" test of the 1946 Act.

It required registration of persons defined as falling within the measure's provisions and required detailed reports of receipts and expenditures every six months. Lawyers said coverage was considerably broadened from the 1946 law.

Among those covered was anyone who urged others to influence legislation if the solicitation reached or could be expected to reach at least 1,000 persons or if the solicitation was made to at least 25 persons paid or promised payment for their efforts to influence legislation.

The Comptroller General was empowered to prepare regulations which would take effect unless disapproved by the specified House or Senate committee within a prescribed time.

A criminal penalty of up to $10,000 fine or one-year imprisonment, or both, for failure to file was provided.

argued the Act's constitutionality and said it "found much that is very sound" in a *Federal Bar Journal* review by Norman J. Futor, then with the Justice Department. Chairman Frank Buchanan (D Pa.) placed Futor's article in the March 27, 1950, *Congressional Record*. The article, supporting the Act's constitutionality, detailed the contributions of the Black, Smith and other bills to various sections of the Federal Regulation of Lobbying Act.

Supreme Court Opinion

The 1946 Act did not in any way directly restrict the activities of lobbyists. It simply required any person who was hired by someone else for the principal purpose of lobbying Congress to register with the Secretary of the Senate and Clerk of the House and file certain quarterly financial reports so that his activities would be known to Congress and the public. Organizations which solicited or received money for the principal purpose of lobbying Congress did not necessarily have to register, but they did

have to file quarterly spending reports with the Clerk detailing how much they spent to influence legislation. In 1954, in the Harriss case, the Supreme Court, 5-3, upheld the constitutionality of the 1946 lobbyist law. *(Text of Court opinion and dissenting views, p. 118)*

Loopholes. The Court said that the law applied only to groups and individuals which collected or received money for the principal purpose of influencing legislation through direct contacts with Members of Congress. This interpretation, based upon the Court's reading of the legislative history, contained several major loopholes or vague areas permitting various organizations and individuals to avoid registering and/or reporting on spending under the 1946 law.

The first involved collection or receipt of money. Under the language of the law as interpreted by the Court, groups or individuals that merely spent money out of their own funds to finance activities designed to influence legislation apparently were not covered by the law unless they also solicited, collected or received money for that purpose.

The second involved the term "principal purpose." A number of organizations argued that since influencing Congress was not the principal purpose for which they collected or received money, they were not covered by the law regardless of what kind of activities they carried on. This argument was used both by the National Association of Manufacturers and the Chamber of Commerce of the U.S. as a basis for refusal to report any spending as an organization under the lobbyist law. The Chamber later started reporting.

Still a third loophole was the Court's holding that an organization or individual was not covered unless the method used to influence Congress contemplated some direct contact with Members. The significance of this interpretation was that individuals or groups whose activities were confined to influencing the public on legislation or issues (so-called "grass roots" lobbying) were not subject to the 1946 law.

A fourth weakness in the law was that it left vague precisely what kind of contacts with Congress constituted lobbying subject to the law's reporting and registration requirements. The language of the law itself specifically exempted testimony before a Congressional committee, and in 1950, in the Slaughter case, a lower Federal court held that this exemption applied also to those helping to prepare the testimony. Other direct contacts presumably were covered, but a whole gray area soon emerged, with some groups contending that their contacts with Members of Congress were informational and could not be considered lobbying subject to the law.

Still a fifth weakness was that the law left it up to each group or lobbyist to determine, more or less for himself, what portion of his total expenditures need be reported as spending for lobbying. As a result, some organizations whose budgets for their Washington, D.C., operation ran into the hundreds of thousands of dollars reported only very small amounts for spending on lobbying activities, contending that the remainder of their spending was for general public information purposes, research and other items. Other organizations, interpreting the law quite differently, reported a much larger percentage of their total budgets as being for lobbying. The result was that some groups which year after year re-

Lobbying Act: Federal Court Cases Since 1946

Five Federal court cases have involved the Federal Regulation of Lobbying Act of 1946. Following are summaries of the five cases.

NAM Test Suit. The National Association of Manufacturers Jan. 28, 1948, brought a test suit challenging the validity of the lobbying law. On March 17, 1952, a Federal court in Washington, D.C., ruled that the law was unconstitutional. It held that definitions in the law were too "indefinite and vague to constitute an ascertainable standard of guilt." Eight months later, on Oct. 13, 1952, the U.S. Supreme Court on a technicality reversed the lower court, leaving the 1946 law in full force but open to further challenge.

Harriss Case. The Government June 16, 1948, obtained indictments against several individuals and an organization for alleged violations of the registration or reporting sections of the 1946 lobbying law. It was charged that, without registering or reporting, New York cotton broker Robert M. Harriss had made payments to Ralph W. Moore, a Washington commodity trader and secretary of the National Farm Committee, for the purpose of pressuring Congress on legislation and that Moore had made similar payments to James E. McDonald, the agricultural commissioner of the state of Texas, and Tom Linder, the agricultural commissioner of the state of Georgia. A lower court ruling Jan. 30, 1953, by Judge Alexander Holtzoff held the lobbying law unconstitutional on grounds that it was too vague and indefinite to meet the requirements of due process, and the registration and reporting requirements violated the First Amendment (freedom of speech, assembly, etc.) and that certain of the penalty provisions violated the constitutional right to petition Congress. Holtzoff's ruling was appealed by the Government to the Supreme Court. On June 7, 1954, in a 5-3 decision, the Supreme Court reversed Holtzoff and upheld the constitutionality of the 1946 lobbying law, though construing it narrowly.

In upholding the validity of the lobbying law, the Supreme Court sent the cases of the individual defendants back to the lower court for a decision on whether the individuals involved were guilty. The ultimate result was that none of the defendants was found guilty. The case against Harriss was dismissed on grounds that the lobbying law, as construed by the Supreme Court, applied only to those who solicited or received money for the purpose of lobbying, whereas Harriss was charged merely with paying money to Moore. The case against Linder was dismissed on grounds he was exempt from the lobbying law under a specific provision exempting public officials. The charges against McDonald were dropped because of his death earlier in the case. The charges against Moore were dismissed Nov. 2, 1955, and the lower court Nov. 2, 1955, acquitted the National Farm Committee.

The importance of the *Harriss* case lay not in the decisions on the individual defendants but in the Supreme Court's ruling that the 1946 lobbying law was constitutional.

Savings & Loan League. A Federal grand jury in Washington, D.C., March 30, 1948, indicted the U.S. Savings and Loan League for failure to comply with the 1946 lobbying law. However, the case was dismissed April 19, 1949, by a Federal district court.

Slaughter Case. On Nov. 23, 1948, ex-Rep. Roger C. Slaughter (D Mo. 1943-47), a bitter political foe of then-President Truman, was indicted on charges he had lobbied for the North American Grain Assn. without registering under the lobbying act. Slaughter's defense was that he had merely acted as an attorney and had helped prepare testimony for witnesses. On April 17, 1950, Slaughter was acquitted, with the judge holding that the specific provision of the lobbying act which exempted persons who merely testified before a Congressional committee applied, also, to those who helped such persons prepare testimony.

Natural Gas Case. On Feb. 3, 1956, Sen. Francis Case (R S.D.) announced on the floor of the Senate that he would vote against the natural gas bill because an out-of-state lawyer who was interested in passage of the bill and who had learned that Case was favorably inclined to the measure, had left a $2,500 campaign contribution for the Senator. (Case had refused the contribution.) As a result of this incident, President Eisenhower Feb. 17 vetoed the natural gas bill on grounds the attempted contribution to Sen. Case was an "arrogant" effort by agents of a natural gas producer to influence legislation with a campaign contribution. John M. Neff of Lexington, Neb., the man who had offered the contribution to Sen. Case, July 24 was indicted on charges of violating the Federal Regulation of Lobbying Act. Also indicted were Elmer Patman of Austin, Texas, and the Superior Oil Co. of California. Both Neff and Patman were attorneys for Superior Oil. In a Senate investigation and at court proceedings, Neff and Patman said the $2,500 offered to Case came from the personal funds of Superior Oil President Howard B. Keck. The money was given by Keck to Patman, who in turn gave it to Neff. Neff then offered it to Case. The accused denied any attempt at bribery and said the purpose of the offer was to aid Senators they believed to be of the economic school of thought that would favor the natural gas bill, which exempted producers from certain Federal regulation.

On Dec. 14, 1956, both Neff and Patman pleaded guilty of violating the lobbying act by failing to register although engaged in lobbying the natural gas bill. They were fined $2,500 each and given one-year suspended sentences by Federal District Judge Joseph C. McGarraghy in Washington, D.C. Superior Oil was fined $5,000 on each of two counts of aiding and abetting Neff and Patman to violate the lobbying law. Bribery charges arising from the case were dropped. The convictions of Neff, Patman and Superior Oil were the first (and through 1970 only) convictions ever obtained under the 1946 lobbying law. There was never any suggestion that Senator Case had either sought the campaign contribution or had accepted it or had in any way acted improperly.

"How to Be Heard"

The American Civil Liberties Union (ACLU) in 1971 urged members to join in enlisting public opinion in support of legislation on Federal employees' rights. To "help turn our lobbying effort into a victory," the ACLU advised use of what it called "the proven techniques below":

"1. Write your senators and congressman, asking them to reply with statements of their positions. *Let the ACLU's Washington office...know what views they express.*

"2. Get to know the staff people in your senators' and congressman's home offices. Tell them your views. They're an important channel.

"3. Take advantage of weekends and congressional recesses to visit your senators or congressman while they're home from Washington.

"4. Enlist friends and major supporters of your senators and congressman to urge their support for the bill.

"5. Write letters to the editor of your local newspaper—an oft forgotten *free* forum.

"6. Urge local newspapers, television and radio to give editorial support to the bill.

"7. Interest reporters and columnists in the problem in general and the bill in particular.

"8. Form coalitions with other interested groups. For this bill start with local branches of federal employee unions; the American Federal Government Employees and National Federation of Federal Employees have already endorsed the bill.

"9. Get these and other community groups to issue statements endorsing the bill. Send this statement to your senators and congressman. Ask them to read the statements *and* to insert them in the *Congressional Record.* Bring them to the attention of the press.

"10. Urge your friends and associates, as well as your local ACLU affiliate, to join you in any or all of these steps."

Mrs. Hope Eastman, acting director of the ACLU's Washington office, urged special attention to members of the House Post Office and Civil Service Committee, its Employee Benefits Subcommittee and the Senate Judiciary Committee, whose names she listed.

---

ported a large portion of their budgets gained reputations as "big lobby spenders" when, in fact, they simply were reporting more honestly and fully, at least under a different view of the law, in comparison with other groups spending just as much.

Another weakness in the lobbying law was that it applied only to attempts to influence Congress, not administrative agencies or the Executive Branch where a considerable amount of legislation was generated which was later enacted by Congress, and where many decisions and regulations similar to legislation were put into effect under administrative rule-making and quasi-judicial powers.

Finally, reinforcing all the other weaknesses was the fact that the 1946 law did not designate anyone to in-

vestigate the truthfulness of lobbying registrations and reports and to seek enforcement. The Clerk of the House and Secretary of the Senate were to receive registrations and reports but were not directed or empowered to investigate reports or to compel anyone to register. Since violation of the law was made a crime, the Justice Department had power to prosecute violators, but no mandate was given it to investigate reports.

Despite the many loopholes and despite the absence of any active enforcement agent, many groups and individuals which might have contested or evaded their obligation to register or report as lobbyists voluntarily did so.

Nevertheless, the inadequacies and vagaries of the law reduced its effectiveness in presenting to Congress and the nation a true picture of what lobbyists and pressure groups were doing and spending in the nation's capital. The registrations and quarterly spending reports gave an incomplete picture.

These problems led to many proposals, from time to time, both to close the loopholes in the existing law and possibly to impose some direct curbs on the types of lobbying activities that were permissible. But no amendments to the 1946 lobbying law were enacted through the end of 1970, despite a major effort in 1967 backed by President Johnson. A new effort was launched in the House in 1971. *(Box p. 16, testimony p. 22)*

Reporting Issue

One controversial aspect is whether interest groups and lobbyists should be required to report compensation. Some have opposed this requirement as useless or an unnecessary intrusion on business privacy. Lambert H. Miller, the National Association of Manufacturers' general counsel, in 1970 testimony questioned "whether it serves any valuable and worthwhile purpose for the Congress to seek to collect voluminous statistics about the expenditures of such organizations" as the NAM and whether it actually indicated the extent of lobbying. He said it was immaterial for Congress to know whether a lobbyist made $10,000 or $70,000, since two such lobbyists could be equally effective.

On the other hand, Sen. J. W. Fulbright (D Ark.) said at a 1963 foreign agents hearing: "...if a man gets $100,000 for a couple of months' work, that arouses my curiosity more than if he got $100 or $200."

In a test case *(Security and Exchange Commission v. Morgan, Lewis and Bockius, 113 Fed. Sup. 85)* U.S. District Judge Allan K. Grim upheld the SEC lobbyist requirement as including lawyers' fees and expenses. Later upheld on appeal, Grim wrote (June 3, 1953):

"...Congress utilized the technique of disclosure as a deterrent to aspects of lobbying which were regarded as involving too subtle an abuse to be dealt with effectively by...prohibition.... It is evident that payment of a fee higher than and unrelated to the value of legitimate legal services conceivably could involve payment for influence or supposed influence or a payment subject to the understanding that the recipient would make ostensibly on his own behalf, but really on behalf of his holding company client, the type of political contribution which his client is prohibited from making.... Furthermore, the expenses of an attorney might include expenditures... which could be regarded as improper attempts to influence administrative or legislative activity."

LOBBY LAW INADEQUACIES

1946 Act Described by Witnesses as 'A Sick Statute'

The Federal Regulation of Lobbying Act, battered and buffeted in the quarter century since its enactment, underwent further criticism before the House Committee on Standards of Official Conduct in October 1970. Three witnesses, two of them attorneys for major business groups, said the law should be changed. They expressed divergent views on what the solution should be or whether one was feasible.

The witnesses variously described the Act as "incomprehensible and unworkable," "vague and ambiguous" and "seriously deficient in many ways." They said it lacked definition, contained reporting requirements that were "simply a nightmare" and was "a sick statute" which posed "an almost insurmountable problem" for those seeking to comply with it.

Despite similar criticism of the Act from the time of its passage in 1946, the law was not modified through 1970. As all the witnesses emphasized, the Supreme Court narrowed its scope considerably in 1954. The dissenting views of three Justices who would have held the Act unconstitutional at that time were quoted frequently to the Committee.

The hearing was the first held on the subject since the House approved a resolution (H Res 1031), in July 1970, which gave the Committee continuing jurisdiction over lobbying and campaign financing matters. As the first standing House committee to receive continuing lobby jurisdiction, it was authorized to investigate at its own discretion and to recommend any needed changes in lobby law. Rep. Melvin Price (D Ill.) heads the Committee of six Democrats and six Republicans.

Although the Committee was instructed to make its first report in 1970, the approaching adjournment of Congress made it certain that no new lobby legislation was enacted before 1971.

In a report at the end of 1970, the Committee said the 1946 Act "has without exception been described to the Committee as a thoroughly deficient law." It proposed replacement of the Federal Regulation of Lobbying Act with a new "Legislative Activities Disclosure Act" which drew partly from a bill offered by a 1957 Senate committee. *(Box p. 16)*

Witnesses

Testifying at the Oct. 1 hearing were George B. Mickum III, chairman of the Committee on Regulation of Lobbying of the Bar Association of the District of Columbia; Lambert H. Miller, senior vice president and general counsel of the National Association of Manufacturers (NAM) and Milton A. Smith, general counsel for the Chamber of Commerce of the United States.

All three witnesses strongly criticized both the existing law and the legislative remedies proposed in the past, all based on amending the 1946 Act. A new approach suggested by the bar association drew objections in turn. The attorneys for the Chamber of Commerce and the NAM both questioned whether the subject of lobbying could be suitably dealt with by general legislation without infringing on constitutional guarantees. Miller said:

"Certainly we have no quarrel with the right of Congress to know about activities designed to influence legislation. I might say, however, that I don't envy the Committee its job in seeking solutions to this very difficult problem touching so closely as it does the constitutional protection of free speech, free press and the right to petition."

The NAM counsel added: "...A fair case can be made for the proposition that a reporting and disclosure statute will for the most part obtain information from the honest and forthright organizations and individuals who have nothing to hide and that the sinister or corrupting influences, if any, will continue to function notwithstanding the requirements of reporting and disclosure."

Chamber of Commerce counsel Smith, when asked if he felt there is a need for legislation to clarify the existing law, said, "If you don't repeal the present law outright, my answer would be yes." He said, "Within existing constitutional limitations, I doubt seriously whether any useful legislative purpose is served by anything along the lines of the existing law."

Smith said he was with the Chamber before the 1946 Act was passed. He recalled "the consternation when this suddenly came up without warning" for passage in the closing days of the 1946 Session of Congress.

Mickum Testimony

Mickum said: "The basic position of the Bar Association is that the difficulty with existing law and all current proposals is that lobbying is not defined. Yet what constitutes lobbying is pivotal in determining who must register....The existing Act, as well as the proposed amendments, say in essence that a person does not have to register as a lobbyist unless his activities and expenditures are of a level that is ill-defined. The existing law characterizes this level as 'principal' and in the (proposed) amendments it is labeled 'substantial.' These are words of ambiguity which make it virtually impossible to ascertain with reasonable certainty whether or not registration and reporting are required."

Mickum predicted that the Supreme Court would eventually declare the 1946 Act unconstitutional. Referring to the Court's ruling in *United States v. Harriss* (June 7, 1954), he said: "The Supreme Court attempted to save the law by rewriting it—there's no question about that." A law clerk at the Court that year, Mickum said he was convinced the reason the Court did not strike the law down was that the majority felt Congress would not enact another in its place.

"The present law is not administered," Mickum said. "The only information anyone can get is what appears in Congressional Quarterly." He said if someone

Many Lobbyists File Insufficient Data With Congress

More than half of the financial reports filed by Congressional lobbyists for the second quarter of 1970 were rejected as containing insufficent information. Fewer than half of the lobbyists whose reports were returned to them by the Clerk of the House complied with his request for revision.

Those who either failed to resubmit the reports or sent them back without including the requested additional information comprised almost 28 percent of all who had filed the original quarterly statements required by the Federal Regulation of Lobbying Act of 1946.

W. Pat Jennings, Clerk of the House, told the House Committee on Standards of Official Conduct in 1970 that this was among significant findings of an indepth review of the reports sent in by pressure groups.

Jennings, a former Representative (D Va. 1955-67), testified at hearings by the Committee which in 1970 was given unprecedented continuing jurisdiction over lobbying and campaign financing matters. The Committee was scheduled to hold separate hearings later on campaign financing, though the link between that and lobbying received some attention at the hearings Oct. 7 and 8.

Another witness, Sen. Robert Dole (R Kan.), urged the Committee to consider ethical questions raised by participation of Members of Congress in activities aimed at building pressure on their colleagues.

Dole said sponsors of a telecast May 12, 1970, on which several Senators solicited money to develop public expressions of sentiment for an amendment offered by Senators Mark O. Hatfield (R Ore.) and George McGovern (D S.D.) to shut off funds for the Vietnam war, "broke new ground in the field of lobbying."

Deficient Reports

The Federal Regulation of Lobbying Act requires covered lobbyists to register with both the Clerk of the House and the Secretary of the Senate and to file spending and financial statements with the Clerk of the House. The reports, which reflect only part of the over-all spending to influence Congress, listed a total of $5.1 million in 1969.

Jennings testified that he received 1,331 reports for the second quarter of 1970. "Of these, 706 or 53 percent were returned for revision and resubmission prior to publication in the *Congressional Record,*" he said. "To date, 347 of the returned reports have been resubmitted with all but eight complying."

He was asked, "What do you do about the balance?" Jennings replied, "Just note them."

"I have no enforcement powers," he said. "There is nothing in the present Act that would give me the authority to question anyone who doesn't file." At another point, he said, "If they don't file—" and completed the sentence with a shrug. "I'm convinced some of those we're sending forms back to are saying to heck with it and throwing them in the wastebasket."

The Supreme Court in 1954 held that the Act covers only those whose "principal purpose" is to influence legislation and only those involved in direct dealings with Members of Congress. Jennings recommended replacing the "principal purpose" criterion with a "dollars-and-cents" standard applicable to both direct and indirect or grassroots lobbyists.

Jennings said he was not able to advise pressure groups properly under the 1946 Act as to whether they were required to register and report. For example, he said, "I cannot interpret this Act as to what is substantial." The question of direct contact also posed uncertainties.

Jennings suggested changing the title to "Federal Disclosure of Lobbying Activities Act," authorizing the Clerk to make audits and field investigations and to enforce the requirements with civil injunction proceedings. He said administration of the law should remain with the Clerk's office.

Lobbying by Members

Dole enlarged on criticism he expressed on the Senate floor Aug. 21, 1970, concerning the May televised appeals by Senators who asked letters, petitions and financial contributions supporting their drive for what was called the "Amendment to End the War." Quoting four appeals in the telecast, Dole said:

"So with two swift strokes, these Senators wrote a new chapter in the book of Congressional comity and conduct. Not only did they actively solicit and seek to stimulate public pressure on their colleagues, but they sought funds with which to further increase and generate such pressure."

He said millions of pieces of mail on the amendment "flooded Washington" afterward "and thousands of people came to discuss it with their elected representatives." More than a half-million dollars in contributions was raised, which he said was used to open "a massive, nationwide advertising campaign...to further pressure Members of the House and Senate on this spurious, illusory and misleading amendment."

Dole said the advertising "asked the American people to pressure Senators, and members of the (sponsoring) committee, when they discussed the issue, were in effect, lobbyists." Dole said the case raised a question as to what limits were proper.

"There is more at stake here than merely the passage or defeat of individual pieces of legislation," he said. "At stake is whether the House of Representatives and the Senate are to remain deliberative bodies or become merely the bases of operations for 535 elected lobbyists."

Rep. Melvin Price (D Ill.), chairman of the Committee on Standards of Official Conduct, said after Dole's testimony that the subject of participation by Members of Congress in lobbying activities "might well be something we should give some attention to."

fails to register under the Act, "I don't think the Justice Department could get a conviction if their life depended on it. They've quit trying."

Mickum said the bar association proposed legislation requiring that anyone who fell within the definition of lobbying must register and file reports, with specific exceptions. "Lobbying, as we see it, includes contact with a Member, his staff or the staff of a committee for pay....It encompasses any activity seeking to change the substantive content of a bill, resolution, amendment, nomination, or other matter which is before Congress...."

He said lobbying also includes "the act of any person who with someone else's money attempts to induce the general public, or segments thereof, to communicate with Members of Congress for the purpose of influencing the legislative process." Among those who would be exempted, Mickum said, would be a person spending only his own money, a person communicating with a Member of Congress at the Member's request, committee witnesses and news media. Federal employees acting in the course of their duties also would be exempted.

"Congress must take a radically different approach to regulating lobbying if it wants to do so," he said.

Miller Testimony

Miller said "the basic difficulty with the Federal Regulation of Lobbying Act has always been lack of definition as to what is meant by the term 'to influence directly or indirectly the passage or defeat of any legislation by the Congress of the United States.' Until the Congress can describe more precisely what is meant by this language, anyone seeking to comply with the Act will have an almost insurmountable problem, even with the best will in the world, in knowing what, if anything, must be reported in order to avoid the potential criminal penalties provided."

Miller, who had held his NAM post for 21 years, said that in *United States v. Harriss* "the Court substantially rewrote the Act by eliminating entirely the language involving 'indirect' efforts to influence legislation. Had this not been done, even the Court majority apparently would have found difficulty in upholding this Act as being constitutional. Three judges of the Supreme Court (Justices Black, Douglas and Jackson) would have held the Act unconstitutional in any event for, as Justice Douglas stated in his dissent, the lobbying law 'either forbids or requires the doing of an act in terms so vague that men of common intelligence must necessarily guess at its meaning and differ as to its application.'"

Miller said that in attempting to rewrite the law Congress faced "a very difficult area" due to First Amendment problems. He expressed doubts that the Bar Association approach would stand up in court.

Miller said various bills introduced in the current session of Congress were generally similar to Title V of a bill (S 355) passed by the Senate March 6, 1967. He cited several specifics which he said "indicate that the changes incorporated in S 355 to amend the Federal Regulation of Lobbying Act do nothing to correct or improve the basic shortcomings and deficiencies of the existing law. A prospective registrant is still left without guidance as to what activities are or are not covered by the Act. Notwithstanding, an effort must be made to determine whether or not such undefined activities are 'substantial'

as opposed to being a 'principal purpose' and failure to guess right can lead to criminal prosecution."

The NAM counsel said there is "nothing sinister, corrupt or deceptive" about the activities of the average business association. "It seems to me there is a real question as to whether it serves any valuable and worthwhile purpose for the Congress to seek to collect voluminous statistics about the expenditures of such organizations and whether or not, once collected, this information would prove meaningful to the Congress or to the public as an indication of the extent of so-called lobbying activities."

Smith Testimony

Smith, the Chamber of Commerce counsel, said "a faulty approach" has led to failure of all past proposals to revamp the 1946 Act. "Typically, the approach has been to try to graft on an already incomprehensible and unworkable criminal statute even more impracticable, unnecessary, and burdensome requirements," Smith said. He continued:

"The starting point, unquestionably, is recognition that the present Act needs substantial revision, if it is to be a useful, workable statute to supplement other laws specifically directed toward corrupt practices, without subjecting individuals and organizations who openly and lawfully exercise rights of free speech, assembly and petition to constant uncertainty and hazard of criminal prosecution....

"Instead of being vague and ambiguous, the law should clearly define and be limited to the corrupt and improper practices which are sought to be barred. Specific exemptions or exclusions should be carefully spelled out. There should be eliminated record-keeping or reporting requirements that are needlessly detailed, burdensome, and overlapping or with which literal compliance may be impossible as a practical matter."

Smith said, "Adherence to the sound view of the Supreme Court that a lobbying registration and reporting statute must, to keep within First Amendment bounds, not extend beyond so-called 'direct lobbying', will help in drafting a new law that avoids the defects and pitfalls of the present one."

The chamber official said he heartily endorsed a statement in the minority report of the House Select Committee on Lobbying Activities (H Rept 3239, Jan. 3, 1951) which said:

"We doubt whether the so-called indirect lobbying, which on the surface at least, is no more or less than constitutionally protected freedom of speech, can, or should be, regulated by the Congress. We do feel that those individuals whose principal purpose is to attempt to persuade individual Members of Congress to follow a certain course of action might well be required to identify themselves and their source of support. Whether any lobbying statute should go further than this is seriously open to question." *(Committee report, p. 122)*

Smith said, "To impinge in any way upon the right of America's voluntary business organizations to speak for their members or to publish their side of the case on important national issues would be to give aid and comfort to forces that would extend Government intervention and control of the economy and of individual action."

The House committee made its first attempt to draft a new Federal lobby law in 1971. That effort touched off criticism from interest groups matching that leveled earlier against the 1946 Act itself. The NAM, Chamber of Commerce and bar association all challenged the bill on constitutional grounds.

1971 Lobby Law Proposal

"This is the most far-reaching proposal of its kind ever introduced in Congress," Smith testified of the Committee's bill in March 1971. He said it would impose "an intolerable and unjustified burden...on thousands of persons and organizations" through its broadened reporting and recordkeeping requirements.

Provisions aimed at disclosure concerning the origins of grassroots attempts to influence Congress through massive mail and communications campaigns were among points criticized by several witnesses.

"Personally, I don't think it does any better at getting rid of vagueness and ambiguities than the present Act," Miller said.

The Legislative Activities Disclosures Act (HR 5259) was introduced by Committee Chairman Price and ranking minority member Jackson E. Betts (R Ohio).

The bill, identical with minor exceptions, was published as a "preliminary draft for discussion purposes only" in the Committee's Dec. 31, 1970, report to the House. The report said the draft sought to avoid the defects "of what has without exception been described to the committee as a thoroughly deficient law...." Court opinions were drawn from extensively, the report said, particularly in considering First Amendment rights of free speech, assembly and petition.

Several witnesses said, nevertheless, that they considered those rights jeopardized by the bill as drafted. Mickum, for the District bar association, criticized the proposal as providing overkill.

"At times, the bill's requirements seem to us to abridge or suppress basic constitutional rights and, in some of its aspects, we fear that it will impair the ability of Congress to acquire information appropriate to its legislative function," Mickum testified.

He said "some provisions of the bill require much more than the Congress needs to have under its 'right to know' and in imposing formidable burdens of record-keeping, reporting, and filing statements may be inconsistent with the First Amendment."

Chamber of Commerce. Smith said the "very sweeping scope of the reporting requirements" in the proposal would require examination "of literally thousands of communications" involving the nationwide activities of chamber affiliates to ensure compliance with the law.

"We would have to ride herd over (all the communications and published materials) to make sure that hour by hour, day by day, we had a record of every communication with a Member of Congress," he said.

Smith noted that the bill was patterned closely after a bill by the same title submitted in 1957 by Sen. John L. McClellan (D Ark.), who then headed a special Senate lobbying investigating committee. The scope and impact of the 1971 bill were broader than the McClellan bill, Smith said.

Noting that criminal prosecution could follow failure to comply with the new law or regulations issued under it by the Comptroller General, Smith said it could take years to settle constitutional questions.

"Meanwhile," he said, "one more Federal agency will be empowered to conduct investigations and make compliance examinations. Even though an organization may consider that it has no registration or reporting responsibility, it will be exposed to investigation at all times. This exposure, of course, will extend to myriad individuals who may have some interest or activity with respect to legislation."

In addition to the many additional persons or organizations falling within the new definition of paid "legislative agent," Smith said, "anyone who, in the course of his employment at any time, on any four different days in a calendar half-year seeks to influence legislation would be covered. Any telephone call or a letter or telegram to a Congressman, a Congressional committee, or a Congressional staff member, if construed as constituting a covered 'solicitation' would have to be counted, along with any 'solicitation' to any Federal agency, department or other instrumentality, or any officer or employee thereof. Presumably, even a response by a constituent to an inquiry by his Representative or Senator would have to be accounted for, if it could be construed as an effort to influence pending or proposed legislation."

National Association of Manufacturers. NAM counsel Miller said: "The coverage is, of course, of the broadest magnitude and as a result, in my judgment, raises numerous questions of a constitutional nature, to say nothing of inflicting most burdensome registration and reporting requirements on individuals and organizations with very imprecise guidelines as to whether various activities or functions are covered."

Miller said he knew of no reluctance in the business community to make whatever disclosure was proper to enable Congress to know about activities designed to influence legislation, though he said this would be rather limited in extent.

Yet the bill as written, he said, "would at best provide volumes of information of questionable relevance to the problem at hand and, at worst, would serve to inhibit the submission of views or information which might be useful in the legislative process, or circumscribe the free exercise of rights protected by the First Amendment."

Opposition to the draft proposal also came from officers of the National Association of Home Builders and the National Milk Producers Federation, as well as from a spokesman for both the National Tax Equality Association and the National Association of Businessmen.

Builders. Herbert S. Colton, general counsel to the National Association of Home Builders, said definitions and provisions were so broad they "would impose well nigh impossible burdens on the Association" and its local and state groups. Hundreds of members and employees, he said, would be subjected to record-keeping and filing requirements which "are onerous in the extreme."

Former Rep. Carter Manasco (D Ala. 1941-49), while opposing the 1946 Act as "a reflection on the integrity of the Congress," said he could see requiring campaign contributors to report whether gifts were voluntary or solicited. "You'd be surprised at the number of requests the lobbyists get for campaign contributions," he said.

MARITIME LOBBY LAW

Publicity Goals of 1936 Statute Never Realized

When Congress enacted legislation in 1936 requiring regular reports from Government-subsidized maritime interests, sponsors expressed hopes that the public's knowledge concerning efforts to influence government would be increased.

The action came amid controversy over lobbying activities. As with other Congressional legislation dealing with various segments of the Washington lobby, the expressed purpose was to publicize, rather than attempt to restrict, the activities of persons and organizations aimed at influencing legislative and executive policies.

Section 807 of the Merchant Marine Act of 1936 (46 USC 1225) required representatives of ship companies and shipyards receiving subsidies to file monthly statements on their income, expenses and interests. It also required reports from their employers.

Though publicity was the goal proclaimed in Congress, results over the next quarter-century were far different than predicted. The reports not only drew no publicity but were barred from public inspection.

When Congressional Quarterly sought access in 1970 to statements filed by certain maritime spokesmen and their employers, it was denied.

Secretary James S. Dawson Jr. of the Maritime Administration and Maritime Subsidy Board said he was aware of no previous instance in which the statements had been made available to non-official parties. He ruled the reports were internal memoranda containing confidential business information and not subject to public inspection.

Upon appeal under Section 3 of the Administrative Procedure Act (PL 89-487), the Public Information Act of 1966, the denial was reversed by Robert J. Blackwell, Acting Maritime Administrator. The records then became available upon request for specific items and payment of the stipulated fees, for what officials said they believed was the first time.

Preliminary examinations of items extracted from the voluminous files dating back many years showed that some leading trade associations had been exempted by executive ruling from filing statements. On the other hand, a great deal of detailed information was available from individual companies and their Washington representatives.

Salaries shown for company presidents ranged up to $60,000 a year plus profit-sharing bonuses and expenses. One company's Washington representative listed expenses ranging from $400 to $1,100 a month and averaging about $707 monthly in 1958, $475 monthly in 1965 and $450 monthly in 1966, his final year.

Among organizations which were prominent when Congress considered a new Federal subsidy program to rebuild the U.S. merchant fleet and which Maritime Administration officials said were exempted from filing were the American Institute of Merchant Shipping, the Shipbuilders Council of America and the American Maritime Association.

"Our position is that they register under the Federal Regulation of Lobbying Act," Dawson said in 1971.

He noted that similar reports of income and spending were not required from non-subsidized companies. Members of the trade associations who are subsidized, on the other hand, were also required to file annual accountings with the agency's finance office.

"Most attorneys dealing with us aren't trying to influence legislation," Dawson said. "Those that do that are mainly company presidents and officers and so on who have to register under the lobby act up there (in Congress)." He said his office gets "a better insight" on the activities of shipping spokesmen from their annual reports of expenditures, salaries and legal fees to the finance office under another provision of the law.

The reports to the finance office are not subject to public inspection, officials said.

Background

The Merchant Marine Act of 1936 (46 USC 1101), which was to stand as the most significant maritime legislation enacted by Congress until at least 1970, was aimed at aiding U.S. ship operators to compete with foreign shipping. *(Shipping Lobby, p. 75)*

It centered around payment of Government subsidies to qualifying American shipping interests to offset the lower construction and operating costs of foreign competitors on trade routes held essential to the national interest.

The Act was passed amid major controversy on at least three fronts:

• Scandals turned up by Congressional and executive investigations of ocean mail hauling contracts, highlighted by the activities of shipping lobbyists and their relationships with key Government officials.

• Scandals over the pressure activities of public utility holding companies. *(p. 113)*

• The respective merits of private versus Government ownership of the merchant marine or sizable parts of it. The dispute was stimulated by the depressed economic conditions as well as by reports of profiteering and inside maneuvering.

A factor in the landmark victory for advocates of private ownership was Congressional approval of a provision in the 1936 Act affecting lobbyists. For the first time, it required spokesmen for subsidized maritime interests to file monthly reports on their finances. It also required their employers to report. Two Senators cited that among reasons for their decision against a filibuster attempt.

Black Probe. As in the case of the Public Utility Holding Company Act of 1935, Sen. Hugo L. Black (D Ala. 1927-37) was prominent in investigating shipping pressure activities and promoting legislation to disclose them. He headed a Special Committee to Investigate Ocean and Air Mail Contracts.

In a report June 18, 1935, the Committee noted that Congress in 1928 had specified competitive bidding on mail contracts and said: "In fact there was no competitive bidding. Officials and contractors combined to and did prevent it." It said the Act had been "flagrantly maladministered."

"Holding companies, subsidiaries, associates, affiliates, and whatnots have been used by shipping companies for the uniform purpose of siphoning the income of subsidized operating companies into the pockets of individuals," the report said.

Black testified before a Senate Judiciary subcommittee April 16, 1935, in support of his proposed general lobby registration bill (S 2512), which though rejected became a source for the Federal Regulation of Lobbying Act of 1946.

Among practices he said his committee had found involving shipping interests: "The evidence shows there were frequently efforts made to have chairmen named on various committees in the Senate, and to have particular men assigned to consider particular legislation....

"From the investigations with which I have been connected," Black continued, "...I am absolutely convinced that our Government has lost hundreds of millions of dollars which it should not have lost and which it would not have lost if there had been proper publicity given to the activities of lobbyists...."

Black said evidence showed that some lobbyists were on "the most intimate personal terms" with people with whom they did business.

"Frankly," Black said, "I do not see any reason why men in the department...should get on those intimate terms and go into the employment of those people when they have passed upon the transactions involved. I have no sympathy with that kind of thing at all. However, it seems to be customary...."

Reporting Provision. On June 19, 1936, the day the Senate by voice vote passed the Maritime Act, Black said:

"...Section 807 is a new section which has been added and which gives the Maritime Commission the right to regulate lobbying. It is copied from the holding-company measure."

Section 807 of the Merchant Marine Act of 1936 made it unlawful for a representative of a shipbuilder or operator holding or applying for a subsidy contract to discuss specified shipping matters before Congress or maritime officials unless the employer had previously filed a statement showing his interest, the nature of his employment and his compensation.

The section also required maritime representatives to file monthly statements of their expenses and compensation.

The record suggests that Members of Congress viewed shipping lobbyists in the same light as those for other specialized interests. Black, in a Senate speech concerning the 1936 Act, said:

"...it also contains provisions which for the first time require that the lobbyists for the shipping interests, many of whom perhaps are in the galleries now, as they usually are, shall register and reveal how much they receive. So far as this bill and the present system are concerned, there can be no question that the bill is an infinite improvement over the present system."

Government and Interests

"Hello, Ralph." "How're you doing, Jim?" Thus did the top officer of a major shipping organization and the chief counsel of the House committee which handles shipping legislation greet each other as a 1971 hearing ended.

In doing so they unconsciously pointed up some of the complexities in the relationships of government and private interests. Moments earlier this alignment existed:

Presiding at the hearing was Chairman Edward A. Garmatz (D Md.) of the Merchant Marine and Fisheries Committee. At his elbow was Ralph E. Casey, general counsel.

Testifying was Andrew E. Gibson, as Assistant Secretary of Commerce and Maritime Administrator the Government's top maritime official. Looking on was James J. Reynolds, president of the American Institute of Merchant Shipping (AIMS).

All were highly respected, praised by colleagues and by occasional political opponents as honorable and devoted to the public good.

Slightly more than a year earlier, Reynolds and Casey had been colleagues in AIMS, holding the top two positions as president and executive vice president, respectively. Casey became special counsel for the Committee at the start of 1970, the year Congress enacted the most significant shipping legislation in 34 years. All interested parties agreed it was urgently needed.

In a way their roles were reversed from most of the 1960s when Reynolds was on the side of the Government and Casey spoke for shipping.

A former member of the National Labor Relations Board, Reynolds in the 1960s was Under Secretary of Labor for labor-management relations. As the second-ranking official in the Labor Department, he was the Government's key official in negotiating maritime labor disputes.

Casey at the time was president of the American Merchant Marine Institute (AMMI), a major predecessor of AIMS, and the industry's chief spokesman in some of the dock difficulties. Now he was back in the legislative job he left in the 1950s to join AMMI. *(Box p. 76)*

Gibson was a senior vice president of Grace Lines before his appointment. Garmatz' election campaigns were heavily financed by shipping interests. *(p. 80)*

Similar circumstances may be found in other parts of Congress, dealing with various fields. They suggest the extent to which the public relies on the character of those involved and the difficulties of attempting to cope with occasional abuses through legislation.

Sen. Joel Bennett (Champ) Clark (D Mo. 1933-45) said: "I think the Senator from Alabama is entirely correct, and it is for that reason that I do not intend to pursue my opposition to the measure and kill it by talking it to death."

Black replied: "I think the views of the Senator from Missouri and mine are very much in accord. If those who favor a subsidy are not willing to pass the bill with these provisions, I am sure the Senator agrees with me that the time would be here to attempt to defeat ship-subsidy legislation and see if it is possible for us, when Government money is being spent, to have the Government own the ships which are built."

Later that day when postal appropriations were before the Senate, Black referred to the new provision. He said: "The bill which passed the Senate this morning limits the profits, limits the salaries, limits the bonuses, limits the securities, provides safeguards for labor, requires that the new authority created shall promulgate rules and regulations regarding the registration of every lobbyist who comes to Washington or who resides in Washington and who seeks to influence legislation or seeks to influence Government contracts."

Administration

Among the most publicized ship lobbyists at the time was Ira A. Campbell, counsel to the American Steamship Owners Association and the leading lobbyist for ship interests. After the 1936 Act went into effect, he suggested that his organization did not fall within the reporting requirements of Section 807.

Max O'Rell Truitt, general counsel of the Maritime Commission, wrote Campbell Sept. 15, 1937. He said he felt "the Association should be considered as a 'person employed or retained,' even though the employment was by ship operators as a group, rather than by any ship operator individually. When the Association advocates or opposes matters in the interest of the members, it comes within the provisions of Section 807 notwithstanding the fact that a particular ship operator may not be affected in any given instance. Any other view would result in saying that when shipbuilders or ship operators act jointly, instead of individually, they avoid the provisions of Section 807."

Truitt said the statute was "intended to reach the act of opposing or advocating matters which affect shipbuilders or ship operators, regardless of the particular form of the representation by the person so acting or the relationship between the person so acting and the shipbuilder or ship operator whose interests are affected." He asked for information covering the matter. The file does not indicate it was submitted.

Nine months later, on June 30, 1938, the founders of the American Steamship Owners' Association incorporated the American Merchant Marine Institute with the same purposes, president (Frank J. Taylor) and initial members. John J. Burns, general counsel, told Secretary W. C. Peet Jr. of the Maritime Commission in 1939 he did not consider the AMMI subject to Section 807. Pressed by Peet, he submitted the requested memorandum and a membership and dues list. The files made available to Congressional Quarterly contained no indication of further filings under the provision.

In 1953 Francis T. Greene, within weeks after leaving his post as general counsel of the Maritime Administration, filed a form covering his activities in November 1953 as the new executive vice president of the AMMI. He wrote:

"In view of the fact that it has not yet been settled whether or not trade associations and their officers are required to register under Section 807 of the Merchant Marine Act, 1936, I am filing the enclosed statement without prejudice." He soon registered under the Federal Regulation of Lobbying Act.

Ralph E. Casey, chief counsel to the House Merchant Marine and Fisheries Committee in 1955-56, joined AMMI and registered as a Congressional lobbyist in 1957. He was AMMI's president through most of the 1960s. The Maritime Administration said Casey and the AMMI were among those exempted from registering under Section 807.

On Jan. 1, 1969, the American Institute of Merchant Shipping (AIMS) was formed by 38 companies which formerly composed AMMI, the Committee of American Steamship Lines and the Pacific American Steamship Association, among others. Albert E. May, vice president, who formerly was an executive of the Committee of American Steamship Lines, on March 20, 1969, wrote Dawson referring to several discussions they had had on Section 807:

"...While some of these companies have contracts under the provisions of the 1936 Act the majority do not. One of our functions is to represent the group interests of these companies before government agencies and the Congress. Because of the group aspect of our work and because of the legal opinions filed with your agency some years ago by one of our predecessor organizations, the American Merchant Marine Institute, we have concluded with your concurrence that AIMS does not come within the purview of Section 807...."

May said the group would "be happy at any time to file any reports or information, including Section 807," requested by the Maritime Administration. He and other AIMS officers registered and reported under the Federal Regulation of Lobbying Act.

Foreign Flags

Elements of organized labor and management have staged a running battle for years over the operation of foreign-flag ships by some U.S. owners. Oil interests with their large fleets of oceangoing tankers figure prominently in the shipping industry in this connection.

The National Maritime Union has repeatedly criticized what it calls "runaway-flag" ship operations. By arrangement with Panama, Liberia and Honduras, since 1955 ships registered under their flags but having more than 50-percent ownership by U.S. citizens have been considered subject to the "effective control" of the United States in event of an emergency.

"The big runaway flag operators—the ones responsible for the 'effective control' hoax—are such corporate giants as Esso, Gulf Oil, Texaco, Alcoa, U.S. Steel, Mobil, etc.," Joseph Curran, president of the union and co-chairman of the Labor-Management Maritime Committee, said in 1970.

The American Committee for Flags of Necessity in a *New York Times* ad (June 21, 1961) said:

"The bulk of these so-called 'runaway ships' was built abroad and manned with foreign crews for exactly the same reason that other U.S. corporations, with Government encouragement, have built plants in other countries: to compete on an equal basis in international trade."

The group said American seamen's wages were three to five times as high as those of foreign seamen.

CONGRESSIONAL ETHICS

Accusations of Wrongdoing During 91st Congress

In their dealings with the many specialized interests which surround them, many Members of Congress find it a delicate matter at times to draw the line between proper and questionable behavior.

While cases which result in criminal prosecution are few in relation to the numbers involved, many other instances arise which produce controversy over possible breaches of ethical conduct. Both the House and Senate have acknowledged this by establishing special committees to conduct official inquiries into allegations of improper relationships between Members and outside interests.

Scandal reached into the office of the Speaker of the House of Representatives in 1969, involving charges of influence peddling reminiscent of earlier disclosures concerning the top staff echelon in the Senate. In each case the top aide to the leadership was convicted of criminal misconduct.

McCormack, Sweig, Voloshen

A grand jury investigation in Baltimore involving criminal conspiracy and perjury charges resulted in the indictment and perjury conviction of the top staff member of Speaker John W. McCormack (D Mass.).

Martin Sweig, 48, former administrative assistant to McCormack, was convicted of perjury by a Federal jury in New York City July 9, 1970. He was acquitted on five other counts and one count of conspiracy. He was given a 2½-year prison sentence and fined $2,000 Sept. 3 by Federal Judge Marvin Frankel. The judge said that the trial had disclosed "a picture of corruption of a very profound kind."

"I am convinced this is a grievous case of perjury," Judge Frankel said, adding that it was linked to "an abuse of Government trust."

Nathan M. Voloshen, New York City lawyer and long-time friend of Speaker McCormack, pleaded guilty June 17, 1970, to charges of conspiring to use the Speaker's office to influence matters before Federal agencies. Voloshen, 72, also pleaded guilty in New York Federal Court to three counts of lying to a grand jury about the charges. Sweig had been charged with having misused his position on the Speaker's staff by pressuring Federal agencies on behalf of clients represented by Voloshen. Voloshen's guilty plea came at the start of the trial for the two men.

Voloshen was fined $10,000 and given a suspended one-year prison sentence Nov. 24, 1970, in Federal court in New York. Sweig, who appealed his sentence, was hired Dec. 1, 1970, by Rep. Robert L. Leggett (D Calif.) as a staff assistant. He was expected to remain on the payroll for several months until he became eligible for Congressional pension.

The one perjury count of which Sweig was convicted concerned his denial to a grand jury in October 1969 of knowing anything about efforts made from the Speaker's office to obtain a hardship discharge from the Army for Pvt. Gary Roth, son of a New York client of Voloshen. Roth received the discharge. The court heard testimony that calls were made to Ft. Jackson, S.C., in the draftee's behalf, including one call from a person identifying himself as McCormack.

During the trial, McCormack testified he had no knowledge of his aide's activities or dealings with regulatory commissions, Government departments, the Selective Service System or business firms. He said he was "not an inquiring fellow." McCormack announced May 20, 1970, he would retire at the end of the 91st Congress.

Baltimore Grand Jury

The names of four Members of Congress and one former Senator came into a year-long investigation of a Baltimore contractor accused of trying to defraud the Federal Government. A grand jury in Baltimore alleged in its presentment that Victor H. Frenkil, a wealthy Maryland contractor and head of the company that built the parking garage for the Rayburn House office building, tried to use threats and political influence to win approval for a $5-million claim against the Government.

The grand jury and two successive U.S. attorneys recommended the case be prosecuted but Attorney General John N. Mitchell, citing lack of evidence, refused to authorize signature of the formal indictments.

Most of the investigation was conducted by Stephen H. Sachs, former U.S. attorney in Baltimore. Sachs' term expired in early June 1970 and he left office. On June 24, his successor, George Beall, was told by the Justice Department to review the entire case. Beall is the brother of Sen. J. Glenn Beall Jr. (R Md.).

The New York Times reported June 21, 1970, that Sen. Russell B. Long (D La.) and former Sen. Daniel B. Brewster (D Md. 1963-69) were said to have been offered bribes of up to $125,000 each. The *Times* said there was no evidence that they accepted the offer or received any money.

A summary of the grand jury's presentment was made public June 22, 1970, at the order of Chief Judge Roszel Thomsen of U.S. District Court in Baltimore. The summary said Frenkil's firm remodeled at a cut-rate price the Bethesda, Md., home of Rep. Hale Boggs (D La.), House Majority Whip, in the hope of getting his aid. The report said Frenkil promised employment advances to Congressional employees concerned with the claim in return for favorable action and threatened them with the loss of their jobs if the claim was disapproved. Boggs denied he received special favors.

Two other House Members were mentioned as urging a speedy review of the contractor's claim. Democrats Samuel N. Friedel and Clarence D. Long, both of Maryland, said subsequently that they had only made inquiries for a constituent about the case.

Mail Order Firm Bribes

A Federal grand jury Dec. 1, 1969, indicted Brewster on charges that he violated Federal bribery laws. Also charged were Spiegel Inc., a Chicago-based mail order firm, and its registered Congressional lobbyist, Cyrus T. Anderson. The indictment charged that Brewster received $24,500 from Spiegel and Anderson to influence his vote on postal rate legislation.

The five-count indictment against Brewster was dismissed Oct. 8, 1970, by a Federal judge. The ruling said Brewster was protected under the Congressional immunity clause of the Constitution. The case was appealed by the Justice Department Nov. 30, 1970, to the Supreme Court.

Automobile Leases

The Ford Motor Company for the past 10 years had been leasing insured Lincoln Continental sedans to key lawmakers for $750 a year, it was reported Aug. 3, 1970, by United Press International. At least 19 House and Senate Members, all but two of them committee chairmen or ranking minority members, accepted the offer.

Among the committees whose top members enjoyed the favorable lease arrangement with Ford were those responsible for auto safety and highway, consumer and tax matters that frequently are of interest to the auto industry.

A Ford spokesman said that 12-month Continental leases comparable to those made available to the top committee members can be obtained by private individuals in the Washington, D.C., area for an average of about $290 a month (about $3,480 a year). Ford said its offer was open only to committee chairmen and senior Republican Members, that in no case was it initiated by Ford, and that the cars were made available only upon request. The arrangement followed a Ford policy of placing cars in the hands of prestigious drivers, including sports and entertainment figures, the company said.

Confirming that they leased Continentals under the special Ford offer at the time the UPI report was made were these Democratic House committee chairmen:

W. R. Poage (Tex.), Agriculture; Thomas E. Morgan (Pa.), Foreign Affairs; Samuel N. Friedel (Md.), House Administration; Harley O. Staggers (W.Va.), Commerce; Edward A. Garmatz (Md.), Merchant Marine; Thaddeus J. Dulski (N.Y.), Post Office; George H. Fallon (Md.), Public Works; William M. Colmer (Miss.), Rules; and George P. Miller (Calif.), Science and Astronautics.

Those who leased Continentals in the Senate were Democratic Chairmen Russell B. Long (La.), Finance, and James O. Eastland (Miss.), Judiciary.

Also on the Continental list were these ranking Republican House Members: Representatives Frank T. Bow (Ohio), Appropriations; Leslie C. Arends (Ill.), Armed Services, and Robert J. Corbett (Pa.), Post Office.

Ranking Senate minority Members with Continentals were Senators Norris Cotton (N.H.), Commerce; Winston L. Prouty (Vt.), District of Columbia, and Roman L. Hruska (Neb.), Judiciary.

In the House, Democratic Whip Hale Boggs (La.) had a leased Continental. Sen. Robert P. Griffin, the GOP Whip in the Senate, used a leased Continental.

In addition to those legislators to whom new Continentals were supplied at the start of each model year,

four chairmen or ranking Members elected to take another Ford luxury car, the Thunderbird, also at $750 a year, or the Mercury, at $600.

House Armed Services Committee Chairman L. Mendel Rivers (D S.C.) chose the Thunderbird. So did Rep. William C. Cramer (R Fla.), senior Republican member of the Public Works Committee and a candidate for the Senate in Florida in 1970. Rep. Olin E. Teague (D Texas), chairman of the Veterans' Affairs Committee, used a Mercury as did Sen. Alan Bible (D Nev.), chairman of the Select Small Business Committee.

The Senate ethics committee Aug. 24, 1970, unanimously recommended that Senators quickly terminate the low-cost automobile leases. Chairman Stennis said that the Committee had decided "Senators should not accept any favorable terms and conditions that are available to them only as Senators."

Justice Department Investigations

The Tillman Act, which became law in 1907, prohibits corporations and national banks from contributing to election campaigns. This prohibition was extended to labor unions by the Taft-Hartley Act of 1947.

Until 1969, these statutes were rarely enforced. Only three prosecutions were undertaken from 1907 through 1968. However, in 1969 and 1970 the Justice Department under the Nixon Administration indicted 17 corporations, banks and labor unions under Title 18, Section 610 of the United States Code. Fourteen of the defendants pleaded guilty or did not contest the indictments. One was acquitted, and two awaited trial.

Others brought to trial by the Justice Department in 1970 on charges of making illegal campaign contributions were International Latex Corporation of Wilmington, Del., and Guaranty Bank and Trust Co. of Alexandria, La. The companies paid fines of $5,000 and $15,000 respectively. A court proceeding against Pine Telephone Company of Muskogee, Okla., ended in acquittal.

In most instances, the Justice Department does not release names of Members of Congress who receive illegal loans or contributions. A Department spokesman said the reasoning behind this policy is the belief that most candidates do not know where specific campaign funds originate and to connect a candidate's name with unlawful practices would be "patently unfair."

Among the more recent indictments brought by the Justice Department against corporations and unions were two in California, one in New York and one in North Dakota.

One was a case involving two Federally subsidized shipping companies, American President Lines Inc. and Pacific Far East Lines Inc., both of San Francisco. The firms were fined $50,000 each after they pleaded guilty to making illegal campaign contributions. *(Maritime lobbying p. 26, 77)*

The Associated Press Sept. 9 reported the names of 16 Senators and Representatives who had received illegal contributions in varying amounts from the shipping companies. The largest sum of $1,500 went to Rep. Edward A. Garmatz (D Md.), chairman of the House Merchant Marine Committee. A total of $1,000 was given for Sen. Warren G. Magnuson (D Wash.), chairman of the Senate Commerce Committee. Both Committees control the flow of Federal subsidies to the shipping lines.

Other Members who were listed by the AP as having been given contributions from the companies, and the amounts they received, included:

House Republican Leader Gerald R. Ford (Mich.), $100; House Democratic Whip Hale Boggs (La.), $200; House Republican Whip Leslie C. Arends (Ill.), $100; Rep. William S. Mailliard (R Calif.), ranking Republican on the House Merchant Marine Committee, $1,000; Rep. John J. Rooney (D N.Y.), $800; Rep. Frank T. Bow (R Ohio), $800; Rep. Elford A. Cederberg (R Mich.), $300; Rep. Robert L. F. Sikes (D Fla.), $500; former Senators Daniel B. Brewster (D Md.) and Thomas H. Kuchel (R Calif.), $500 each; Representatives Thomas L. Ashley (D Ohio) and Jack Edwards (D Ala.), $100 each; and the late Rep. Glenard P. Lipscomb (R Calif.), $500.

Also mentioned by the press report was Rep. L. Mendel Rivers (D S.C.), chairman of the House Armed Services Committee, who was listed as receiving $300 from the firms although his check was not included in the court case.

Contributions made by the two San Francisco firms totaled at least $8,500 and were made in the 1966 and 1968 Congressional campaigns.

Two other cases involved:

• The Seafarers International Union of Brooklyn, N.Y., indicted June 30, 1970, by a Federal grand jury on charges of making illegal campaign contributions to Republicans and Democrats. The indictment said the union had conspired to contribute $750,000 between 1954 and 1968.

• The First Western State Bank of Minot, N.D., indicted July 31, 1970, by a Federal grand jury on charges of conspiring to make political contributions from bank funds during the years 1964 through 1969. The seven defendants named in connection with the case were prominent in Democratic party activities in the area, including the Hubert H. Humphrey for President campaign in 1968.

The investigations followed the 1968 convictions of officers of St. Louis, Mo., Pipefitters Local 562 for illegal campaign contributions. Many of the violations came to light during an unrelated examination of the books of several unions and firms by the Internal Revenue Service.

'Bobby' Baker

Robert G. "Bobby" Baker, former secretary to the Senate Democratic Majority, Jan. 14, 1971, began serving a one-to-three-year prison term at Lewisburg Federal Penitentiary in Lewisburg, Pa.

Baker, who resigned from his Senate post in 1963, was turned down by the Supreme Court Dec. 21, 1970, in his effort to obtain a review of his 1967 conviction for tax evasion, conspiracy and theft.

Baker, 41, was indicted in 1966 on charges that he understated his income on Federal tax returns, conspired to avoid paying taxes on legal fees, and retained for his own use about $100,000 in campaign contributions he was expected to give to his superiors in the Senate.

Background. The indictment followed a series of investigations which began in 1963 with the disclosure that Baker had become a millionaire while serving in his $19,000-per-year Senate job.

He resigned on Oct. 7, 1963, after being accused of using his position to advance his business interests. He has continued to insist that he is innocent of any wrongdoing.

In his years as Senate Majority Secretary, Baker's investments included a vending machine company, a Wisconsin mortgage insurance corporation, land in Florida and a bank in Tulsa, Okla.

A civil suit filed Sept. 9, 1963, charged Baker with using his position in the Senate to obtain defense contracts for his vending machine firm, Serv-U-Corp, and with accepting $5,600 to secure a defense contract for a rival vending machine company, Capitol Vending Co. The suit, filed by Capitol, was settled out of court for $30,000.

Following Baker's resignation, Sen. John J. Williams (R Del.) launched a personal investigation of Baker's activities and was successful in persuading the Senate Rules and Administration Committee to open an investigation. Minority Members later alleged a whitewash.

Baker's 1966 trial featured testimony by two California savings and loan executives that they contributed $66,000 to eight Democratic Members of Congress through Baker in 1962. Two Members testified they received none of the funds, and the defense stipulated that none of the other six had done so.

As majority secretary, Baker kept track of the leadership position on votes, informed Senators about pending business and views of the leadership and participated in fund-raising activities. He worked directly for Senate Majority Leader Lyndon B. Johnson.

FOREIGN PRESSURES

Nazi Tactics Led to 1938 Foreign Agents Statute

On the eve of World War II, disclosure that Nazi and Fascist propaganda was being circulated in the United States through concealed identities led Congress to enact what was then called the "McCormack Act" requiring agents of foreign principals to register.

The Foreign Agents Registration Act of 1938, which former Chief Justice Harlan Fiske Stone called "a new type of legislation," was intended—in the words of two Congressional committees—to throw "the spotlight of pitiless publicity" on sources of foreign propaganda in this country. With a few exceptions, the publicity has fallen considerably short of that despite the accumulation of bulky and informative files.

On two occasions when the subject was explored, Congressional investigators reported lack of vigorous enforcement, first under the State Department, then under the Justice Department. Justice officials protested the allegation.

In 1966, the Act underwent important revision, with a change of emphasis and significant narrowing of scope. New registrations almost halved in the following four years, compared with the four years previous. As former Attorney General Ramsey Clark explained the changes in his report for 1967:

"The net result of the 1966 amendments was, to a large extent, to remove the applicability of the Foreign Agents Registration Act from the so-called subversive area and place primary emphasis on the protection of the integrity of the decision-making process of our Government as well as on the right of the public to the identification of the sources of foreign political propaganda."

Spokesmen for the Justice Department opposed some provisions of the Act as passed in 1966, though they supported the legislation in general.

Background

The use of agents to influence policies of other nations has been a two-way street for the United States. Former Under Secretary of State George W. Ball said in 1963 that in the early 1840s President Tyler and Secretary of State John Calhoun sent newspaper editor Duff Green to France. His assignment was to promote opposition and sentiment against the Anglo-French Anti-Slave Trade Treaty.

Twenty years later, Secretary of State William Seward sent an archbishop and two companions to European capitals where they sought to influence opinion in favor of the Union cause in the Civil War.

The United States was on the receiving end, as well. "Certainly foreign interests have over the years sought to influence the U.S. Congress," Ball testified at hearings on foreign agents. The Reciprocity Treaty of 1854 concerning U.S. relations with Canada, for instance, "is reputed to have been lobbied through the Congress," Ball said. He added that "the State Department itself

employed a lobbyist to spend considerable sums in securing Canadian support" for the treaty.

When the United States bought Alaska, Ball said, the Russians hired an ex-Senator for $30,000 and spent much more "to lobby through the passage of the appropriations bill providing for the payment of the $7,200,000 purchase price."

Impact of War. Upheavals during and after World War II, accompanied by U.S. prominence in world affairs, brought a sharp upsurge on both counts. Nicholas deB. Katzenbach, Deputy Attorney General (1962-1964), said in 1963 that in the preceding 15 years "there has been a tremendous increase in the activities of Americans representing foreign governments and foreign interests...." He noted involvement by other countries in aid, trade and tariff programs of the United States after the war and the impact which U.S. policies had on those nations' domestic economies.

"Therefore, they are intensely interested in the decisions made by those who administer our laws, and by those who enact them or otherwise influence their administration," Katzenbach said. "These countries have a major incentive, therefore, to engage in activities similar to those engaged in by domestic interests in the United States such as trade associations, labor unions, farmers, municipalities, public utilities, and others whose economic welfare is directly and importantly affected by governmental decision."

Katzenbach said that with increasing U.S. world involvement, "the interest of these other countries in what we do will become ever more pervasive."

Registrations

The first move to identify agents of foreign powers active in the United States resulted from hearings started in 1934 by a special committee headed by Rep. John W. McCormack (D Mass.), the future Speaker. Concern over activities of Nazi and Fascist agents led to enactment June 8, 1938, of the Foreign Agents Registration Act. Both the House and Senate committee reports cited publicity as the goal. The House report said:

"We believe that the spotlight of pitiless publicity will serve as a deterrent to the spread of pernicious propaganda. We feel our people are entitled to know the

Purpose of Foreign Agents Act

Congress declared the policy and purpose of the Foreign Agents Registration Act of 1938 as being "to protect the national defense, internal security, and foreign relations of the United States by requiring public disclosure by persons engaging in propaganda activities and other activities for or on behalf of foreign governments, foreign political parties, and other foreign principals so that the Government and the people of the United States may be informed of the identity of such persons and may appraise their statements and actions in the light of their associations and activities."

sources of such efforts, and the person or persons or agencies carrying on such work in the United States."

Enforcement was placed in the State Department's Division of Controls. Criticism followed: Less than four months before Pearl Harbor, Rep. Jerry Voorhis (D Calif. 1937-47) inserted in the *Congressional Record* (Aug. 14, 1941) a report by a lawyers' group called Institute of Living Law, which said:

"...The first action that might be expected would be the preparation of a list of the registrants....No such thing has been done...." It said objective analysis "must convince any unprejudiced observer that the act has been rendered a dead letter, of no practical importance in exposing the propaganda activities it was designed to expose...." It laid the chief responsibility for this on the State Department.

Enforcement was switched to the Justice Department in 1942 and has remained there. By the end of 1959, 1,320 registrations had been filed, with a record high of 434 then active. In addition, 2,023 short-form registrations had been filed by individuals.

The Act was amended frequently—for example, in 1939, 1942, 1946, 1950, 1956 and 1961—without changing its broad purposes. Since 1950, the Justice Department has issued an annual booklet listing registrants and their foreign principals. The booklet carried much more detail in the 1950s than later.

Revision of Act

The stated goal of publicity notwithstanding, Chairman J.W. Fulbright (D Ark.) said in opening 1962-63 Senate Foreign Relations Committee hearings: "Little, if any, precise detailed information has been available up to now on what nondiplomatic agents do or how they do it." The hearings developed hundreds of pages of testimony on actions by persons representing foreign interests in the United States. Prominent were activities of a sugar lobby and study of political campaign contributions related to a Philippine claims bill enacted in 1962. *(Sugar lobby, p. 91)*

A Committee staff study issued July 22, 1962, said the Justice Department had "only sporadically enforced" disclosure requirements under the Act, with strict enforcement limited to agents of Communist countries. Fulbright said there had been "an increasing number of incidents involving attempts by foreign governments or their agents, to influence the conduct of American foreign policy by techniques outside normal diplomatic channels."

A bill (S 2136) sponsored by Fulbright and Sen. Bourke B. Hickenlooper (R Iowa 1945-68) provided the basis for eventual revision of the Act with enactment in 1966 of S 693 (22 USC 611).

Fulbright told the Senate June 21, 1966, in urging adoption of the conference report: "Foreign and domestic affairs are so interrelated today that the political and propaganda efforts of foreign agents ultimately affect every American. Both Government officials and the public need to—and have a right to—know more about the objectives, tactics, finances, and general mode of operations of those who seek to influence Government policies for foreign interests."

While the 1966 changes were described as bringing the Act up to date and tightening the requirements, they reduced the scope of the Act. The Justice Department supported the legislation, but the final version contained several provisions the Department opposed as weakening the Act or placing undue burdens on the Government. The Attorney General's reports for 1964-65 when the Act was pending made no mention of objections.

Rep. John J. Rooney (D N.Y.) called the Act inconsequential, likening it to "issuing motor vehicle licenses." The number of registrations fell off from 1966 on, largely because of changes in definitions specifying who and what were covered. Among these were narrowing of the definition of an agent, requiring proof of a clear agency relationship in enforcement plus engagement in "political activities" as defined in the Act. Attorneys were given new exemptions in routine legal functions.

One firm availing itself of the lawyers' exemptions was Covington & Burling, whose partners included former Secretary of State Dean G. Acheson. Nathan B. Lenvin, former chief of the Internal Security Division's registration section, on July 9, 1968, exempted Covington & Burling from reporting for nine foreign clients, including the governments of Venezuela, Pakistan, Iran, Canada and Colombia.

Initial registrations are required of those who meet the Act's definitions, with supplementary reports every six months. Individuals within registered firms who handle the specified activities file short-form statements which stand until changed or terminated.

Hampering of Enforcement

Some of the changes which Congress made in the 1938 Foreign Agents Registration Act in 1966 had "a hampering effect" on its enforcement, according to the Justice Department's top internal security official.

Though the bill containing the revisions was supported by the Department, certain changes were enacted over Department objections with little or no floor discussion. One change cited as hampering enforcement efforts, on the other hand, exactly followed a compromise suggested by the Department after it protested that the original proposal posed "a serious problem not heretofore faced" in enforcement.

The Foreign Agents Registration Act was enacted with the purpose of requiring public disclosure by persons engaging in propaganda activities and other activities on behalf of foreign principals. It underwent broad revision in 1966, following a series of hearings by the Senate Foreign Relations Committee concerning the activities of nondiplomatic representatives of foreign interests in the United States.

Registrations have fallen off since revision of the Act as a result of broadened exemptions, as anticipated. The Government's burden of proof was substantially increased by redefinitions of who and what were covered by the Act. A gap was to some extent created in anti-subversive law, said Assistant Attorney General J. Walter Yeagley in charge of the internal security division.

In addition to items covered by Yeagley in response to specific written questions, a provision enacted in 1966 over Justice Department objections three years earlier exempted certain political propaganda from the labeling and reporting requirements. The new wording was somewhat reminiscent of the Act's provisions in that respect before 1942. The Justice Department and Supreme Court subsequently used the term "halfway measure" in referring to it in that period.

There were other 1966 changes in the law which enforcement officials viewed favorably. One of these authorized the Justice Department to use injunctive and intermediate procedures to obtain compliance. This eliminated the earlier reliance solely on criminal proceedings to force compliance, which Yeagley said in most instances were "tantamount to overkill." There have been no prosecutions nor injunctions sought since the change.

But the frequently expressed primary goal of publicizing the identities and interests of persons seeking to influence U.S. actions on behalf of foreign principals continued as elusive as ever, for the most part. The Justice Department itself seemed to vary through the years in its aggressiveness in attempting to overcome this factor.

The Justice Department in the past decade has ceased to cross-index foreign agent registrants in its annual published reports to Congress. It is therefore no longer possible to ascertain from the report on administration of the Foreign Agents Registration Act the foreign principals of an individual. To do so requires additional background information or inquiry at the Justice Department's registration section.

No up-to-date index listing the principals, registrants or individuals for whom records are maintained is made available to the public. The Department also has stopped its previous practice of filing propaganda submitted under the Act for public display at the Library of Congress.

Effects of 1966 Changes

From the standpoint of enforcement, Yeagley cited both adverse and favorable effects of the revision of the Foreign Agents Registration Act in 1966. Among these, he told Congressional Quarterly in 1970 a few months before President Nixon appointed him a Federal judge, were:

• A "hampering effect" on enforcement through narrowing of the definition of "political activity." This meant "that some activities previously covered were beyond the reach of the Act," Yeagley said. Left out by the 1966 amendments were elements included under an earlier administrative ruling pertaining to intelligence, military activities and reporting of restricted information relative to national defense.

• A "hampering effect" on enforcement through the addition of an extra element of proof—that of the existence of an agency relationship—required of the Government, combined with the reduction of categories of activities subject to the registration requirements. As a result,

Yeagley said, "many persons formerly subject to the registration provisions of the Act are no longer reached."

• Creation to a certain extent of a gap in antisubversive law through a change in the emphasis of the Act along with deletion of the element of "collecting or reporting information to a foreign principal" from the definition of an agent.

Congress changed the emphasis of the Act from subversive activities to exposure of attempts to influence Government decisions. In doing so, Yeagley said, "Congress was merely recognizing a change which had already taken place with regard to the character of persons who were registering under the Act."

The Senate Foreign Relations Committee in its report on the 1966 amendments said "the place of the old foreign agent has been taken by the lawyer-lobbyist and public relations counsel whose object is not to subvert or overthrow the United States Government, but to influence its policies to the satisfaction of his particular client...."

Yeagley said the changes have "resulted in the fact that any person, including a subversive who collects or reports, for example, nonclassified strategic information to a foreign government, cannot now be charged with an obligation to register under this Act. To this extent, a gap has been created."

• Authorizing the Department to use measures short of criminal proceedings to enforce compliance with the registration requirements. Yeagley called this helpful.

In brief, Yeagley said, "the scope of the Act has been narrowed and the standard of proof has been increased which, of course, has the effect of limiting the statute's reach." *(Full text of Yeagley comments p. 33)*

The 1966 changes brought a reduction in the number of attorneys registered as agents of foreign clients. They were once the second most numerous type of registrant, just below public relations specialists. The Act exempted attorneys in the course of normal legal activities, in accord with recommendations of the American Bar Association. The ABA's Robert Dechert said in 1965:

"It would be naive to believe that our political life is not affected by foreign influence.... The danger occurs when undisclosed foreign principals act through deceptive agents in an attempt to change the course of our national life for their best interests."

Nazi Propaganda

Findings of the House committee headed by Rep. McCormack in the 1930s were succinctly summarized in a dissent to *Viereck v. United States* (318 U.S. 236) in 1943. Associate Justice Hugo L. Black, joined by Justice William O. Douglas, said the Committee had found—as Black put it—that "business enterprises had been utilized as a means for propagandizing, and that many persons...had published articles in various magazines, concealing their identity behind pseudonyms. The purpose of these activities, the Committee found, had been to influence 'the policies, external and internal, of this country, through group action. They were employing the same method that they had employed in Germany for the purpose of obtaining control of the government over there'."

Agent-Principal Relationship

The relationship of an agent with his foreign principal, a hard-fought battleground in the past, was a crucial but little-debated factor in the 1966 revision of the Foreign Agents Registration Act, which passed the Senate by voice vote and the House by a 285-0 roll-call vote.

By inserting the words "at the order, request, or under the direction or control, of a foreign principal" in the definition of an agent, Congress increased the Government's burden of proof considerably. A parallel raising of the proof burden resulted from the insertion at several points in the propaganda section of the Act of the words "for or in the interests of such foreign principal."

Both Yeagley and Nicholas deB. Katzenbach, then Deputy Attorney General, at different times recommended against one or the other of these changes.

Under the 1966 law, an agent was required to file with the Department a report on each item of political propaganda disseminated "for or in the interests of any of his foreign principals," as the Department rules interpreting the law put it. Two copies of the propaganda also were required. Katzenbach told the Senate Foreign Relations Committee Nov. 19, 1963:

"...Under the present law, any political propaganda disseminated by an agent of a foreign principal must be labeled and filed. These revisions would have a real and significant narrowing effect upon the obligations of an agent. They would open the door for an agent of a particular foreign government or foreign political party to disseminate unlabeled political propaganda favoring that country or political movement under the claim that it is in his own behalf and an expression of his own personal views."

Yeagley on Feb. 16, 1965, testified: "The proposed redefinition of the term 'agent of a foreign principal' poses a serious problem not heretofore faced by the Department in its administration of the Act. Under existing law an agency status is created whenever a person acts or agrees to act on behalf of a foreign principal. For example, it suffices to prove that a person collects or reports information to, accepts compensation from, solicits or disburses money for, a foreign principal. We believe the new definition adds a new requirement that may at times be difficult to prove."

In a subsequent letter to Sen. J.W. Fulbright (D Ark.), chairman of the Committee, Yeagley suggested a rephrasing of the definition proposed by Fulbright, saying "the difficulty that the Department has with this part of 1 (c) might be alleviated" thereby. The rephrasing was adopted in the final version.

Agency Relationship

The agency relationship figured heavily in a case lost by the Government in 1951. U.S. District Judge Matthew F. McGuire, the second-ranking official in the Justice Department in 1940-41 and a special assistant to the Attorney General in 1934-39, granted acquittal of an indictment against the Peace Information Center and five individuals in connection with the circulation of the Stockholm peace appeal. The appeal was branded by Secretary of State Dean Acheson as a "propaganda trick" in a spurious Russian peace offensive a few months before Korea was invaded.

Resistance to Disclosure

Since the 1930s, when Nazi and Fascist agents were disseminating propaganda in the United States, efforts to disclose publicly the identities and activities of persons or groups representing foreign interests in this country have been marked by resistance.

Rep. John W. McCormack (D Mass.), who sponsored the original "McCormack Act" as the Foreign Agents Registration Act was known, told the House as Majority Leader in 1942—in urging tightening of the 1938 law:

"When I introduced the bill as a result of the recommendations of the special committee, we had powerful opposition. It took quite a long while to get that bill through. The Committee on the Judiciary reported it out in one Congress and we could not get a rule out of the Rules Committee. I know because I tried. I could not get a rule from the Rules Committee. I could not get a hearing. That shows how much opposition there was to the bill that is now on the statute books...."

The House Judiciary Committee report recommending passage of the Act in 1937 (H Rept 1381, 75th Congress, 1st Session) said:

"Incontrovertible evidence has been submitted to prove that there are many persons in the United States representing foreign governments or foreign political groups, who are supplied by such foreign agencies with funds and other materials to foster un-American activities, and to influence the external and internal policies of this country, thereby violating both the letter and the spirit of international law, as well as the democratic basis of our own American institutions of government."

The Rules Committee chairman from 1932 through 1938 was the late John J. O'Connor (D N.Y.), a New York City lawyer later described by *The New York Times* as "the leading spokesman in Washington for Tammany Hall" during his 16 years in the House of Representatives. O'Connor was opposed by President Franklin D. Roosevelt in the 1938 elections, largely because of his opposition to Roosevelt's plan to enlarge the Supreme Court. O'Connor failed to get the Democratic nomination for re-election, then obtained the Republican nomination but was defeated. He afterward practiced law in Washington and New York, specializing in shipping litigation, and registered as a Congressional lobbyist in 1947 for the Society of Marine Inspectors and in 1958 for Isbrandsen Co. Inc., a shipping concern.

The judge upheld the defense contention that the Center would have had to act under control or through a consent to be classified as publicity agent for the Committee of the World Congress of the Defenders of Peace, the principal for which the Government charged the defendants failed to register the Center.

Chief defense counsel Vito Marcantonio (U.S. Rep. R N.Y. 1935-37, ALP N.Y. 1939-51) argued that the Center had acted in its own behalf and not as the representative of any other group. The star witness for the Government was O. John Rogge, Assistant Attorney General in charge of the criminal division in 1939-40 and special assistant to the Attorney General in 1943-46. Listed as a vice president of the Committee of the World Congress of the Defenders of Peace, Rogge testified that the organization and its subsidiaries including the Peace Information Center actually became an agency for the foreign policy of the Soviet Union. He was quoted by reporters as saying his break with the World Congress became final after Korea was invaded.

The acquittal came after Jean Gabriel Laffitte of France, secretary of the World Congress, swore in an affidavit that the organization's governing committee never consented to the Peace Information Center's acting as its agent.

The 1951 annual report by the Attorney General said of the case: "The defense motion upon which the judge ruled was based upon a case decided under the Foreign Agents Registration Act prior to the 1942 amendments, in which the court had held that it was incumbent upon the Government to establish the agency relationship as defined by the Re-Statement of the Law of Agency in order to sustain a conviction for failure to register. It is the Government's contention that the Foreign Agents Registration Act as amended in 1942 has substituted the statutory definition for the common law definition of the term 'agent'." The Peace Information Center was defunct by the time the case was heard, and there was no further action.

A few years earlier, Chief Justice Harlan Fiske Stone touched on the point in an opinion for the Supreme Court in *Viereck v. United States (318 U.S. 236)*. Stone wrote March 1, 1943:

"The Government argues that the statute would have been a 'halfway measure' had it not required, or at least authorized the Secretary (of State) to require, the registrant to reveal the propaganda which he put out other than on behalf of his foreign principal. Congress itself has recognized that the legislation was in this sense a halfway measure when in 1942 the Act was amended so as to require both original and supplemental registration statements to contain a 'comprehensive statement of the nature of registrant's business,' together with other specifically required information as to the character of registrants' activities." Stone said in a footnote that the chief of the special defense unit of the Justice Department "had a large share in drafting the 1942 legislation." Stone said the House and Senate Judiciary Committee reports recommending the 1942 legislation "reveal a clear purpose to make the registration requirements of the new Act extend to all his activities. We think that in this respect the new Act extends beyond the old...."

Justice Department Views

While declining to discuss the subject orally, Assistant Attorney General J. Walter Yeagley responded to written questions submitted by Congressional Quarterly. The questions dealt with the impact of the 1966 amendments to the Foreign Agents Registration Act so far as enforcement is concerned.

The complete text of Yeagley's replies to each question follows. In some cases the questions have been reworded, without changing their sense, in the interests of clarification. The replies were given in 1970.

Question: *The 1966 amendments narrowed the scope of "political activities" embraced by the law. Katzenbach said this could "seriously hamper" enforcement. Has it hampered enforcement?*

Answer: Prior to the passage of the 1966 amendments, the only definition of "political activities" appeared in the former Rule 100, the principal purpose of which was to aid in determining the availability of the Section 3 (d) exemption from registration. The current statutory definition of the term "political activity" includes only those elements of former Rule 100 pertaining to the dissemination of political propaganda and to activity seeking to influence official and civilian opinion within the United States. The former Rule 100 also included elements pertaining to intelligence and military activities and the reporting of restricted information relative to the National Defense which have not been incorporated in the new definition.

The present definition of "political activity" appears to be an expression of Congressional intent concerning the types of activities which should require an agent of a foreign principal to register. "Political activities" is one category of activity in the definition of "agent of a foreign principal" that would require registration; the narrowing of the definition of "political activity" has therefore resulted in a hampering effect to the extent that some activities previously covered are now beyond the reach of the Act.

Question: *The 1966 changes, through narrowing of the definition of "agent of a foreign principal," require the Justice Department to establish an agency relationship to enforce registration requirements. Katzenbach called this "an unreasonable burden to impose upon the Government." How has this affected enforcement?*

Answer: Under the former definition of "agent of a foreign principal" it was necessary to prove only that a person engaged or agreed to engage in certain described activity. The 1966 amendments, in Section 1 (c) (1) of the Act, require that the government prove in each case the existence of an agency relationship between the registrant and the foreign principal. Therefore, under this part of the present definition, a person to be constituted an agent of a foreign principal must not only engage in the specific activity referred to but must do so as an agent, representative, employee, or servant, or by acting "at the order, request, or under the direction or control of a foreign principal."

The addition of an extra element of proof for this portion of the definition has, of course, increased the government's burden of proof. This fact, together with the reduction in the categories of activities which would give rise to an obligation to register, can be said to have a hampering effect on enforcement in the sense that many persons formerly subject to the registration provisions of the Act are no longer reached.

It should also be noted that the new amendments retain in Section 1 (c) (2) that part of the old definition which recognizes the creation of the necessary agency relationship whenever an individual is "purporting to act as" or whenever he "holds himself out to be" an agent of a foreign principal, whether or not pursuant to a contractual relationship. However, the applicability of this portion of the definition has also been restricted since the "purporting to act" must be with respect to the activities set forth in Section 1 (c) (1).

Question: *What has been the impact in the broadening of commercial exemptions under the 1966 amendments? Yeagley testified in 1965 that "the legislative history of the proposed amendments makes clear that normal commercial activities are to be exempt."*

Answer: Private and nonpolitical commercial activities have always been exempt under this Act. Broadening of this exemption by the recent amendments extended the benefit of this exemption to a United States organization with international affiliates even if it engages in political activity within the United States, provided this activity does not serve a "predominantly foreign interest."

Unlike other changes brought about by the 1966 amendments discussed herein, we do not feel that the enlarging of the Section 3 (d) exemption has had any adverse effect with respect to enforcement of the Act.

Question: *Congress in 1966 granted exemption from registration for attorneys in the course of normal legal activities involving foreign clients. What has been the impact and what are the Department's views on this exemption?*

Answer: Prior to the 1966 amendments, acting as an attorney was an activity spelled out in the definition of an agent which would constitute an individual an "agent of a foreign principal." However, attorneys representing private foreign principals in normal legal activities of a nonpolitical nature were entitled to an exemption from registration under Section 3 (d) of the Act since their activities would be both private and nonpolitical. But an attorney who represented a foreign government in any capacity other than in "housekeeping activities" (purchase, lease, rental, of embassies, etc.) would be engaging in nonprivate activity and required to register.

The 1966 amendments pertaining to the definition of an agent of a foreign principal and the exemptions for attorneys in Section 3 (g) have resulted in a decrease in the number of registered attorneys. Under the present amendments, for an attorney to be required to register, in addition to showing the attorney-foreign client relationship, it must also be shown that the attorney engages in one or more of the four categories of activity and that he does not come within the exemptions.

The amendments pertaining to attorneys seem to be consistent with the normal activities of an attorney in the usual public forums. It is to be noted that the appearance of an attorney before courts and agencies of the government requires open disclosure on his part as to the identity of his client and the purpose of his appearance. This area of activity of an attorney is exempt under the new amendments. However, where the activities of the attorney for a foreign client go beyond the limits established by the exemption, such as lobbying or public relations activity, he does not have the benefit of the exemption and must register therefor.

Question: *The 1967 Attorney General's report on administration of the Foreign Agents Registration Act said the 1966 amendments had changed the emphasis of the Act from subversives to attempts to influence Federal Government decisions. Has this been reflected in the types of persons who register? Does this leave a gap in antisubversive laws?*

Answer: The change in the emphasis of the Act by Congress has not resulted in any noticeable change in the types of persons who have registered since the effective date of the new amendments. In changing the emphasis of the Act, Congress was merely recognizing a change which had already taken place with regard to the character of persons who were registering under the Act. As the Senate Committee on Foreign Relations stated in their Report on the 1966 Amendments (Senate Report No. 143) "the place of the old foreign agent has been taken by the lawyer-lobbyist and public relations counsel whose object is not to subvert or overthrow the United States Government, but to influence its policies to the satisfaction of his particular client,"..."One of the major purposes of this bill is to reaffirm the change in focus of the act to place primary emphasis on protecting the integrity of the decision-making process of our Government and the public's right to know the source of the foreign propaganda to which they are subjected."

This change in the emphasis of the Act, together with the removal of the element of "collecting or reporting information to a foreign principal" from the definition of an "agent of a foreign principal," has resulted in the fact that any person, including a subversive who collects or reports, for example, nonclassified strategic information to a foreign government, cannot now be charged with an obligation to register under this Act. To this extent a gap has been created.

Question: *What is the budget of the Registration Section? How many are on its staff—how many lawyers and clerical workers?*

Answer: There is no specific budget allocation as such, for the Registration Section. This Section is a part of the Internal Security Division of the Department and is included in the Division's over-all budget which in Fiscal 1970 amounts to $1,458,000.

Currently, the staff of the Registration Section consists of nine attorneys, including the chief of the Section, one political analyst and five clerical employees.

Question: *How would you summarize the net impact of the 1966 amendments in the field of enforcement?*

Answer: In brief compass, the scope of the Act has been narrowed and the standard of proof has been increased which, of course, has the effect of limiting the statute's reach. Compliance with the provisions of the Foreign Agents Registration Act is, with rare exception, accomplished through normal administrative procedures. Prior to the 1966 amendments, however, our only means of ultimate enforcement was in the institution of criminal proceedings. As was recognized not only by this Department but also by the Congress, less stringent means of effecting compliance were indicated as the criminal proceeding in most instances was tantamount to overkill. Therefore, injunctive remedies as well as intermediate procedures involving the issuance of Notices of Deficiency as reflected in Sections 8 (f) and (g) respectively were enacted. While a suitable test vehicle for the injunctive remedies has not as yet presented itself, a substantial employment of Notices of Deficiency has been very salutary in accomplishing compliance with tardy registrants. Other means of achieving compliance have been utilized to good advantage, such as an increased use of the influence and general assistance of the Department of State with registrants directly tied in with foreign governments having diplomatic representatives in Washington, D.C. The regular administrative procedures coupled with Section 8 (g) have been very helpful in achieving compliance with the Act.

LOBBIES AND ELECTIONS

Special Interests and Candidates

Barter Support at the Polls for Backing in Office

The Washington lobby swings its greatest weight in connection with elections.

Elective officials and interest groups operate in the constant awareness of elections past and future. This knowledge, with all it implies, injects an underlying factor into every major pressure confrontation in Congress or the Executive Branch.

Lobbying and party politics often become interlaced in the jostling for position before elections. That is when leaders of specialized interests seek to exert top leverage, using the prospect of support or opposition at the polls as their weapon.

Political strategists gear their campaigns heavily to blocs of voters in whatever constituency is involved. The support of a major organization can provide a running start toward victory; its opposition can mean an uphill battle at best and perhaps make the difference between victory and defeat.

U.S. Representatives must run for re-election every two years—a fact which leads to the frequent statement that they are always campaigning. Senators face the voters every six years, thus receiving a breathing spell between elections. In every election, however, one-third of the Senate is up for election.

The major cost of campaigning alone forces candidates to take organized groups into account. As former Rep. Thomas B. Curtis (R Mo. 1951-69), chairman of a "Task Force on Financing Congressional Campaigns" established by the Twentieth Century Fund, said in 1970:

"Political campaigning has become an extremely expensive undertaking. Its high cost threatens to eliminate from political life all but those who have personal wealth or who have access to personal funds."

A pressure group with money, voting power and organization has much to offer a candidate for major office. Such a group is in a position to exert influence on the political party power structures themselves and may have much to do with party positions.

Campaign Financing

A candid demonstration of the interrelationship between campaign financing and lobbying came in the 1957 hearings of the Special Committee to Investigate Political Activities, Lobbying, and Campaign Contributions headed by Sen. John L. McClellan (D Ark.). Hoyt S. Haddock, executive secretary of the AFL-CIO Maritime Committee, was questioned by Chief Counsel George Morris Fay and McClellan. Following are excerpts from the hearing:

Fay: "Now, Mr. Haddock, as a registered lobbyist it is your responsibility and duty to actually contact the representatives of the different committees before whom legislation is pending in which your union is interested?"

Haddock: "That is correct; it is."

Fay: "So that in your particular case, you are in the position of on the one hand seeking assistance for the support of legislation, and on the other hand in a campaign, in a general election, in a position of giving support to those from whom you sought support."

Haddock: "That is right."

Fay: "Is that a practice that is common to the unions or is that just a practice as far as Maritime is concerned; do you know?"

Haddock: "I would say it is common to unions, to the best of my knowledge." (*Haddock said that other organizations followed similar practices.*)

McClellan: "I wonder if that is a wholesome thing... Is that something that is inextricably associated with democracy in our system of government, that the men who come to us and plead with us to try to persuade us to become their friend and think their way—if so you can get a contribution in the next campaign, and if you don't the contribution may go against you to your opponent. I am wondering if that is a wholesome thing? I think it prevails, and I am trying to determine whether if it is not a wholesome thing, it should not be condemned. If it is unwholesome in American political life in our system of government, how can we prevent it by law? Can you give us any enlightenment on that?"

Haddock: "I can only give you my own opinion, sir.... Separating myself from my job as a lobbyist for a moment, and becoming a citizen, I would make political contributions to candidates who I wanted elected who voted the way I thought they ought to vote. And the way I let them know I think they ought to vote."

McClellan: "You do that as a citizen, as a private citizen?"

Haddock: "Yes, and so what I do as a lobbyist is actually no different from what I do as a citizen. I cannot see that there is anything unwholesome about it. I think it is a part of democracy."

Group Campaign Logic

After leaders of the United Mine Workers of America were charged with making illegal contributions in the 1970 general election, editor Justin McCarthy outlined the union's position in the official *United Mine Workers Journal.* He wrote in 1971:

"...This union, down through its history has done the best it could to help elect its friends and defeat its enemies for political office. That's a long-standing policy of all organized labor....

"Petitioning the government in Washington today consists of letting one's Representatives and Senators and the White House and the various government agencies know where one stands on the vital issues of today.

"Coal miners petition their government through their union, the United Mine Workers of America and its parallel organization, Labor's Non-Partisan League. All of us in the Washington headquarters of the union at one time or another have personal contact with government people. We tell them what our members, the coal miners, want. We hope they listen to us....

"Now Senators and Representatives and party candidates to the top jobs of President and Vice President have to be elected. And to be elected today one has to work very hard to get what is known as 'public exposure.' All kinds of people, including members of labor unions—the AFL-CIO organizations, the railroad brotherhoods, etc., help candidates get 'public exposure'....

"Doctors also have all kinds of ways of working in behalf of their favorite political candidates, as do Texas oil millionaires, the National Association of Manufacturers, the Chamber of Commerce, the coal operators and so forth. All of these require a lot of effort by the members who belong to these organizations."

Fifty of the 55 candidates in Congressional elections endorsed by the mine union in 1970 won their elections.

In 1971 M. A. Hutcheson, general president of the United Brotherhood of Carpenters and Joiners of Amer-

ica, told members: "We in the building trades need to mobilize our political strength more effectively than we ever have before. It is in the political arena that most of our future battles lie."

Congress-Election Repercussions. Illustrative of the range of potential election repercussions which can exist in Congressional issues was the situation facing Rep. Wilbur D. Mills (D Ark.) during preliminary maneuvers for the 1972 Presidential campaign.

Mills, chairman of the House Ways and Means Committee, was a key figure in two major legislative controversies: foreign trade and health insurance. Both had far-reaching effects on millions of American citizens, in one case affecting their jobs and in the other their finances. Strong pressures were at work on both sides of the issues, demanding or opposing new legislation dealing with those subjects.

Meanwhile, a movement aimed at winning the Democratic nomination for President for Mills got under way at the same time his Committee considered what to do about trade and national health insurance. On Mills' actions the support, opposition or neutrality of such groups as the AFL-CIO and other elements of organized labor, the American Farm Bureau Federation, the American Medical Association, and major business and oil interests on opposing sides of the trade issue, could depend.

Goals. Many interest groups aim at specific targets in Congressional positions where their own interests are handled. Some go a step further, attempting to provide a "mandate" from the voters which might influence both houses of Congress in the direction of their particular philosophy. Two organizations which attempt this are Americans for Democratic Action (ADA) and Americans for Constitutional Action (ACA), opposing each other on what are commonly called liberal and conservative lines, respectively.

The *ADA World* noted that the Administration would be watching the 1970 vote in mapping its "war-peace strategy." The publication editorialized: "We cannot hope to reorder American priorities until we demonstrate through votes at the polls that this nation is in fact determined to take the road to peace."

An ADA staff study cited among consequences of a "liberal victory in the Senate" in the 1970 elections:

Strengthening of Senate Democratic leaders "in their efforts to push Senate Democrats to a more liberal line"; increased pressure on Senate Republican leaders "to pursue a liberal strategy rather than a purely Administration strategy"; strengthened liberal representation on the Senate Foreign Relations and Appropriations Committees, "perhaps even the Finance and Armed Services Committees"; strengthened liberal representation on the Senate Democratic Steering Committee.

ACA President Charles A. McManus told his trustees at about the same time that in many respects "the direction of Administration policy, as well as the composition of the Congress, is at stake" in the elections.

McManus said "each conservative seat held and gained will mean not just one vote in the Congress, but a stronger conservative mandate to the full legislative body, both national parties, and the presidency. Hence the stakes are far higher than the surface members involved, and may well affect the historic thrust of the Nixon Administration in every critical field."

ELECTIONS: THE STAKES

Lobbies Deeply Involved in Political Campaigns

The pressure group battles of a given Congress begin before it exists, amid the disputes of the Congress preceding it. In the ceaseless struggle among competing interests, each session of Congress provides an anvil on which election issues are hammered out and an arena in which issues and candidates vie for attention.

Emotional disputes which affect key segments of the population are the grist from which factions hope to snare votes in the succeeding elections. In the 91st Congress, for example, there were heated clashes over postal employees' pay, education funds, tax laws, two Supreme Court nominations and defense spending.

In each case, organizations involved on various sides employed high-powered advertising methods and modern communications techniques to persuade target constituencies of their personal stakes in the outcome. The groups sought at the same time to identify their particular viewpoints as being in the public interest.

The groups' intent often is the same, though their goals may differ widely. The basic purposes behind some of their election year activity: Ease tomorrow's lobbying efforts for themselves by using today's as a springboard from which to elect Members of Congress and other public officials who are sympathetic to their views. Not only was immediate control of Congress at stake in the 1970 elections, but reapportionment of House seats would affect future House makeup.

A large-scale grassroots lobby campaign can create through involvement in the governmental process sizable groups of motivated political workers, an essential ingredient of successful election campaigns. This may contribute to election victories while establishing political debts to be paid by the winners.

Even a temporarily losing lobby battle, such as the education coalition's 1970 attempt to override President Nixon's appropriations veto, holds a potential of affecting key Congressional races one way or another. The coalition's instructions given to hundreds of local educators in Washington for "Operation Override" advised them in visiting their Representative to "tell him that you and your associates will do everything you can to assist him locally"—provided they received a favorable response.

George Fisher, president of the National Education Association (NEA) which forged the coalition in 1969 from dozens of specialized interests, said, "We want to beat five or ten Congressmen who switched their votes and upheld the veto." After the NEA's tax-exempt status was questioned on the House floor, Fisher said he spoke in general terms rather than in specific reference to NEA's campaign role.

Illustrative of the revolving door between pressure groups and government was the fact that the coalition, called the Emergency Committee for Full Funding of Education Programs, was headed by former Health, Education and Welfare Secretary Arthur S. Flemming, included former HEW Secretary Wilbur Cohen and was

Lobby Groups and Elections

The House Select Committee on Lobbying Activities, then headed by Rep. Frank Buchanan (D Pa. 1946-51), said in its 1950 report following extended hearings:

"This committee is convinced that most lobby groups of any consequence are to some extent involved in influencing elections. Today's legislative stakes are too high for such groups to abstain from working for the election of candidates most likely to favor their demands. This positive participation in influencing elections is an important consideration often ignored by political scientists. More important, however, is the negative participation of pressure groups in elections. The very essence of a pressure group is that it is a body of people who want something. If the present object of their pressure does not give them what they want, they may turn to another candidate at the next election....

"Each Member of Congress has this basic truth in his mind in all of his dealings with pressure groups and their members. He knows that each pressure group believes its program to be meritorious, and in the public interest. It is only logical to assume that they may oppose him at the next election if he does not vote in accordance with their views."

directed by Charles W. Lee, former aide to the Senate Labor and Public Welfare Committee.

The coalition crossed party lines. The lobbying was on both sides of the issue, sparked protests from each about the tactics of the other and was climaxed by the President's resort to an unprecedented veto on television. Some have contended through the years, normally from the outside, that the Executive Branch wields possibly the most powerful lobby in Washington. (Executive Branch lobbying, p. 61)

An ever-present factor in the figuring of farsighted political strategists, within lobby groups as elsewhere, was the Presidential election of 1972 with its primaries and another Congressional campaign.

Attempts to make political capital which might ensure greater lobbying success in the future stem similarly from nonlegislative events, such as executive actions in school integration or law enforcement.

The push and pull of conflicting interests in a nation of more than 200 million people ranges across the three branches of the Federal Government. Group leaders are well aware that the areas of law-making, law-executing and law-interpreting all pack an impact on their interests. This also applies at many levels of state and local governments, particularly with prospects—as in 1970—of an increasing flow of Federal money and authority to states and cities in connection with block grants and revenue-sharing.

Lobbying and Politics

Congressional struggles related to elections are both a cause and an effect of what a House Select Committee on Lobbying Activities in 1950 called "this growing and inevitable juncture of lobbying and politics."

While the Constitution provides for membership in Congress on a geographical basis, pressure groups are set up on the basis of functional representation—that is, on the basis of common interests, whether economic, ethnic, ideological or some other. They cross, disregard or straddle political party lines in many instances, sometimes providing significant bridges between the parties. On the other hand, some interest groups tend to be closely aligned to one of the two major national parties in a marriage of convenience for both sides while nominally adhering to a nonpartisan stance.

"...At bottom, group interests are the animating forces in the political process; an understanding of American politics requires a knowledge of the chief interests and of their stake in public policy," V.O. Key Jr. said in *Politics, Parties & Pressure Groups.*

Federal law prohibits corporations, labor unions and tax-exempt organizations from engaging in partisan political activities. However, the lines are hard to draw and there are many ways around the restrictions. These include establishment of political action branches and individual political activities of leaders.

Although the laws often have been criticized, sporadic attempts to change them have met insuperable obstacles. Besides difficulties arising under constitutional guarantees of free speech and free petition, the barriers unquestionably have included adversary interests.

Lobby laws in general, at Federal and state levels, are evidence that legislation which directly affects lobbies holds no immunity from lobbying. Supreme Court Justice Hugo L. Black spoke of this when as a Senator (D Ala. 1927-37) he headed a Special Committee to Investigate Lobbying Activities. He investigated lobbying by public utilities and shipping interests. As a result, lobby registration laws covering both were enacted and are still on the books. Black told a Senate Judiciary subcommittee April 16, 1935, concerning his efforts to publicize shipping representatives' activities:

"Everything that has been proposed, every legislative proposal that has been made, every effort to protect the rights of the Government, has met with opposition. They have had their representatives here secretly more than openly...." Black said the shipping representatives waved the flag of patriotism, "when all...they were interested in was the flag of dollars...."

Lobby legislation touches the foundations of the political support of many Members of Congress. Where elections are concerned, it involves the interest group's ultimate weapon: Support or opposition for re-election. Questions of self-interest, even political survival, can arise for politically vulnerable lawmakers.

1970 Elections

Politically involved organizations keep a close eye on the performance of Members of Congress and other public officials. Among those which measure Members' performance on selected votes each year are the liberal Americans for Democratic Action (ADA) and the Committee on Political Education (COPE), the AFL-CIO's political arm. Their 1970 election outlook, not uncommon, highlighted the close relationship between lobbying and politics.

The *ADA World* said editorially in January 1970: "ADA's 1969 voting record underscores the significance of the 1970 elections." A few weeks later (Feb. 19) its lead story began:

"Participation in 1970 election campaigns—primaries and finals—is now ADA's most important task, officers and members of the national board agreed...."

COPE Director Alexander E. Barkan told his membership early in 1970, referring to the 91st Congress: "In a sense, the story of the importance of the 1970 elections to workers and their unions can be found in the voting records carried on these pages." The ratings listed Members as voting "right" or "wrong" on certain issues.

The Chamber of Commerce of the United States, with grassroots strength based on state and local businessmen's organizations, like organized labor, wields an implicit though often once-removed lever in coming elections.

"Our putting the heat on a Congressman to vote a certain way is only part of the job, and he knows it," *Dun's Review* quoted an unidentified chamber official as saying late in 1969. He added, "Our most effective weapon is getting the local chambers in his district to go to work on him." The official said the tactic did not always work "because the AFL-CIO and the farm organizations are doing the same thing. But on certain issues with certain Congressmen, it can be decisive."

Members of Congress protest at times that group ratings influence constituents to support or oppose them on the basis of 12 or 18 votes rather than on their total performance. They consider this unfair. The American Political Science Association in 1945, after a four-year study on how to reorganize Congress, listed among eight factors handicapping Congress "the importunities of special-interest groups which tend to divert legislative emphasis from broad questions of public interest." The importunities often fail to counter-balance each other.

Some groups saw greater significance than usual in the 1970 elections, although road-fork analyses are standard campaign rhetoric. The division between a Republican President and a Democratic Congress was a factor, with but a few switches required to shift both houses of Congress to Republican control for the first time in years. Organized factions can tip the balance in close contests.

Both group and individual lobbyists' interests are at stake when political power swings to new hands. Lobbyists' fortunes ride with every reversal of the "ins" and "outs" in the legislative and Executive Branches. Contacts built up over years can be involved.

From a pressure group standpoint, the "liberal-conservative" tug-of-war holds greater relevance than political affiliations in some instances. An opinion frequently expressed from the civil rights camp was this by Roy Wilkins, executive secretary of the National Association for the Advancement of Colored People (NAACP) and chairman of the Leadership Conference on Civil Rights, in a 1970 funds appeal: "Much of the progress achieved in civil rights during the past decade is on the verge of extinction" because of a seeming swing of the country toward a more conservative point of view.

From another sector in the political spectrum, the conservative Americans for Constitutional Action (ACA) expressed disappointment at liberal-conservative trends it found in 1969 Congressional performance, especially among Republican Members who formerly rated higher by the ACA's standards. "Their voting records in 1969 reveal support of some liberal Kennedy-Johnson Administration programs continued by the Nixon Administration," ACA President Charles McManus said.

Significant in pressure group strategists' thinking was the likelihood that circumstances of age and physical vigor would necessitate appointment of a majority of Supreme Court Justices in the 1970s. Mr. Nixon's appointments, as pledged in his 1968 campaign, of persons he described as "strict constructionists" of the Court's role under the Constitution produced two of the most heated lobby battles of his Administration. The opposition in 1969 and 1970 was headed by a coalition of ADA, civil rights and organized labor forces.

The 1970 elections determined 35 U.S. Senate seats—a factor of paramount importance in future Supreme Court confirmations alone. This point was abundantly emphasized by opponents of the Nixon Administration. The elections also determined all 435 House seats, 35 state Governorships and control of 45 state legislatures.

Political patronage and campaign machinery hinged on the outcomes, paving the way for the 1972 elections. Special interest groups—whether based on business, labor, farm, ideological or some other common purpose—have much riding on these elections with their repercussions at all levels of government in nation and state. A group's interest often involves not only positive goals but also the

prevention of governmental action, as in regulation or controls over capital or unions. Students of government say the prevention of action often is more readily achieved. The occupants of key posts are all-important.

An analysis of 1970 election stakes by *ADA World* was applicable to factions across the board. Noting the seats to be filled, it said in an editorial:

"...Add to these an abundance of local contests, and you have a national referendum of giant proportion. 1970 elections will have a direct impact on the Administration. There is great potential here, an opportunity to influence government decision-making profoundly....

"Should the political pendulum swing right next fall, the Administration and Congressional conservatives will have added strength to more effectively push policies hardly to the liking of liberals." Noting that state legislatures elected in 1970 would reapportion House districts on the basis of 1970 census figures, the ADA publication said "if a state legislature happens to be preponderantly conservative, reapportionment will reflect conservative needs....All in all, liberals have more than usual riding on the 1970 outcome."

Barkan said the story told by COPE's voting studies "is one of attempted retreat from social welfare responsibility by the conservatives in Congress, and a counter-pull by Congressional liberals in their effort to retain or expand the gains of recent years in many areas of American life—education, voting rights, urban aid, war on poverty." In common with other union spokesmen, he predicted "a far broader attack on the labor movement should conservatives gain control as a result of next November's elections."

The COPE director, too, called attention to the redistricting of House seats in 1971. "Thus, the legislatures will have a decisive impact on the makeup of Congress for the next 10 years," Barkan said.

Alliances between legislative candidates and organized interests at local and state levels often persist and take on increasing importance as an office-holder moves upward. A mutual dependence can result, varying widely with the faction and the individual, with their fortunes sometimes tending to be intertwined as he builds seniority and attains key committee positions—a prime objective of interest groups because of the power to promote or retard legislation affecting them.

Pressure Groups and Voters

The wide involvement of pressure groups in political activity is considered an inevitable feature of the U.S. political-governmental system by some students of the subject. They hold that the movement into political arenas from early days of the country is a natural outgrowth of the democratic structure and, indeed, preceded adoption of the Constitution.

This movement stems, by this view, from the same factors which lead to lobbying of the Legislative and Executive Branches. Contributing to this process of political involvement at the national level in the mid-twentieth century are:

• The continuing expansion of the Federal Government and its far-reaching powers to affect specialized interests, backed by unprecedented political power and enormous financial resources.

• The high cost of running for public office, making it imperative for candidates to have organized backing.

Labor and Politics

A labor union official outlined the growing trend toward political involvement by organized labor in the AFL-CIO's magazine *The American Federationist.*

Gus Tyler, assistant president of the Ladies Garment Workers, said (January 1970), "the mainstream of American labor has been flowing into ever widening political channels ever since Samuel Gompers, in the first decade of the 20th century, launched a national campaign to elect a Congress to amend the Sherman Act."

He predicted the trend would continue in the 1970s, adding: "Attempts to curb unions, especially in public employment, will make politics a prime line of battle."

Tyler said the pre-nomination support of Hubert H. Humphrey, Democratic candidate for President, in 1968 "marked a new level of political involvement by American labor." From 1900 to 1936 the AFL had avoided formal endorsements of Presidential candidates of either major party, but the AFL backed Robert LaFollette's third-party candidacy in 1924.

In 1952 the AFL backed Adlai Stevenson. The AFL-CIO later backed John F. Kennedy and Lyndon B. Johnson. All three were the Democratic nominees.

"...But the AFL-CIO has stayed neutral before conventions in the choice of candidates, whatever its behind-the-scenes role may have been," Tyler said.

• What some describe as the inherently expansive nature of pressure groups, which provides a built-in momentum toward activity offensively or defensively in any arena which holds prospects for benefit or injury to the interests involved. Corresponding motivations exist at state and local levels, varying with powers and funds which provide the target.

If the political arena is indispensable to key interest groups as a locale in which to pursue their ambitions, the organized factions are equally essential to public figures dependent on the political process. Frequently a question could be raised as to which was predominant— the political or the special interest motivation. Many individuals operate in both areas.

Besides providing a base of dependable support and a potential recruiting ground for campaign workers, a pressure group frequently permits a campaigner superior access to public exposure in an age when the competition for publicity is a major consideration.

In its general interim report issued Oct. 20, 1950, the House Select Committee on Lobbying Activities of the 81st Congress said: "...The pressure group cannot be satisfied. If it fails to achieve its aim at once, it keeps fighting to achieve it. If it gets what it wants, then with very few exceptions it wants something more....

"But lobbying is inherently expansive in an even more significant sense. We refer to the fact that modern pressure politics is not and cannot be confined to legislative policy alone. One of the oldest textbook truisms about lobbying is that it is nonpolitical in the sense that pressure groups are interested only in issues and not in men. We think, however, that our investigation provides evidence to the contrary; a majority of the groups which we investigated were in some degree engaged in influencing the outcome of elections."

Suggestive of the sensitivity of the subject, the report itself drew criticism as attempting to influence an election. It was signed by the Committee's four Democratic members. A minority report by the three Republican members said "the whole tenor of the general interim report was designed to cast reflections on those groups within the economy which would be inclined to support antiradical candidates in the November election."

The minority report said that "by a great coincidence" the interim report was made public two weeks before the 1950 election, preceded two days earlier—"by an equally odd coincidence"—by a document labeled "Expenditures by Corporations to Influence Legislation." A similar publication entitled "Expenditures by Labor and Farm Groups to Influence Legislation," the minority said, was issued only after the election. *(Appendix, p. 123)*

A later Congressional investigating committee, which included a future Democratic President and a future Republican Presidential candidate, also took note of pressure groups' attentions to voters as the power behind Congress. This was the Special Committee to Investigate Political Activities, Lobbying and Campaign Contributions in the 85th Congress. Headed by Sen. John L. McClellan (D Ark.), it numbered among its members Sen. John F. Kennedy (D Mass. 1953-60) and Sen. Barry Goldwater (R Ariz.). The Committee's final report released May 31, 1957, said:

"All recent studies confirm that the emphasis of pressure groups has changed in recent years, from the old style of 'buttonholing' legislators in the Halls of Congress to new techniques. The hearings of this Committee, as well as the hearings of prior studies of the activities of pressure groups, indicate that more and more reliance is being placed on mass media campaigns, which result in inspired letter-writing campaigns and other manifestations of interest in legislation by the voters."

Like other probe units, this Committee also had its differences. Senators Kennedy, Albert Gore (D Tenn.) and William A. Purtell (R Conn. 1952-59), while upholding much of the Committee report, said in separate views that "sound considerations of public policy require the enactment of realistic and enforceable limitations upon both campaign expenditures and campaign contributions."

The Committee's proposed legislation failed to do so, they said. "Instead of improving present law," they said, the proposed solution "would provide a legal loophole of more immense proportions than those contained in the existing and hopelessly inadequate Corrupt Practices Act which it is our duty to correct."

Goldwater, with Sen. Styles Bridges (R N.H. 1937-61) concurring, also objected to the bill while supporting much of the Committee report. Goldwater said:

"It is obvious to us that under the name of 'education' the unions of America, as well as corporations, are spending vast sums of money that are not being reported as political expenses.... It seems to us that there can be no effective legislation written covering elections without explicit concern for some of the enormous loopholes presently existing and, in particular, the use of such devices as the terms 'educational' and 'citizenship' to describe massive political expenditures in such a way as to avoid public scrutiny or public responsibility. The second device being used, apparently on a gigantic scale, is the use of paid political manpower which also seeks by calculated indirection to avoid public scrutiny or public responsibility."

Shaping of Issues

The laws still hold glaring gaps, rendering difficult or impossible attempts to pinpoint all that special interest groups are spending or doing in hundreds of political arenas across the land with incalculable impact on future government.

That business, labor and other factions are active is evidenced in countless ways—as in statements by their leaders, activities by their conventions or policy bodies, group publications for general or special-audience consumption, political orientation or "education" meetings at the nation's grassroots, communications to Congress and to some extent in the limited financial reports filed with Congress or with officials in the states.

Pressure groups derive from their basic nature as a collection of people with one or more common interests one of their greatest attractions for political campaign purposes: A presumed dual capacity to speak both to and on behalf of their constituencies. They thus become a crucial link in communication between office-holders or aspirants and key blocs of voters.

In the contest for the public's mind—the struggle to influence opinions, to shape issues and their priority in the voters' view—pressure groups are hard at work in the months preceding the next elections. One prominent aspect of this is the effort to dramatize issues, and to narrow their focus to a scale individuals can grasp.

ELECTIONS: THE STRATEGY

Lobby Officials Drive to Mobilize Memberships

During the debates which preceded adoption of the Constitution, Alexander Hamilton took issue with what he called "visionary or designing men" who said "the spirit of commerce has a tendency to soften the manners of men...." These men argued, he wrote in what became *The Federalist,* that "Commercial republics, like ours...will be governed by mutual interest, and will cultivate a spirit of mutual amity and concord..." Upon which Hamilton asked:

"Has it not, on the contrary, invariably been found that momentary passions, and immediate interest, have a more active and imperious control over human conduct than general and remote considerations of policy, utility, or justice?" Shortly afterward James Madison said:

"As long as the reason of man continues fallible, and he is at liberty to exercise it, different opinions will be formed. As long as the connection subsists between his reason and his self-love, his opinions and his passions will have a reciprocal influence on each other; and the former will be objects to which the latter will attach themselves."

Nearly two centuries after the Declaration of Independence, opinions and passions sway Americans' conduct as strongly as ever. In the formation of those opinions and in the whetting of passions, organized interest groups play a leading role. This is a continuing process which can peak before an election.

Communication Problem. With the United States more than 50 times as populous as when Madison and Hamilton wrote, the communication of ideas—upon which opinions and passions are based—has become a gigantic task. In complex modern society with its quickened pace accompanying technological advances, few individuals other than the President can reach the mass audience with any consistency.

That audience, however, consists of innumerable smaller audiences with specialized interests. Here the groups organized around those interests are in their element. They possess a unique power in many cases to facilitate or retard the exchange of ideas and information between their constituents and public officials or candidates.

This power over communication can be used to the advantage or detriment of given individuals, offering possible leverage in the pursuit of group goals before elections. The exercise of this power within the interest group is vested in a few policymakers and executives. The public has no guarantee that a group's policies invariably reflect the sentiments of its members. *(Box, p. 42)*

A spokesman for one major organization touched on the significant role of a key individual in communication between group members and the Government. Mark E. Richardson, assistant counsel of the National Association of Manufacturers, told a Washington legal symposium Feb. 25, 1965:

"...As our society becomes more intricate, the need to communicate the ideas of the various elements in that

---

Election Year Emphasis

Every election year lobby groups are found busily driving home political messages to their own members with an eye on Congress at the same time.

Factions' communication facilities which regularly barrage Congress on behalf of group interests are then trained on group members as well, translating lobby goals into political terms.

Typical election year rhetoric among pressure group spokesmen was that of Grand Chief Engineer C. J. Coughlin, chairman of the Brotherhood of Locomotive Engineers' national legislative board. Coughlin said in a statement for *Locomotive Engineer* (May 1, 1970):

"I would remind every member of this organization that only by electing sympathetic Congressmen and Senators can we expect to realize the goals we have set for the men in engine service."

Interest groups seek to influence the opinions of target blocs of voters and arouse them to action. Group strategists strive for increased access and influence at power centers in Congress and the Executive Branch by demonstrations of real or apparent power at the polls.

In the process, they may try to use election year leverage to achieve legislative goals. In 1970, for example, this was a factor in Federal employee pay raises, attempts to change the electoral college system and anti-war protests.

Group campaign activities range from backing of a handful of key Congressional committee members to carefully coordinated drives to influence public opinion across a broad front. Much of the action falls within the "educational" realm, broadly construed.

(For pressure group results in the 1970 elections, see next chapter p. 45.)

---

society becomes more apparent, and lobbyists more essential....The lobbyist acts as a conduit for the two-way flow of ideas between the elected and appointed officials who constitute 'the government,' and those elements of 'the governed' which, in total, constitute our society."

The interest group's publications, like its lobbyists, are a communication link between political figures and a bloc of voters. The potential impact of a publication with favored access to a certain segment of the electorate is accentuated by the flood of printed matter available. Most people are exposed to a small fraction of the total outpouring. As Congress itself has recognized in various lobbyist registration laws, the sources to which individuals turn for information affect their opinions. Not only

Group Decision-Making: Democracy or Oligarchy?

Organized groups adopt positions on public issues in varying ways according to their constitutions and leadership. Formal machinery often is similar to the republican principles of the American political system, in some cases antedating that system and based at the grassroots.

Delegates chosen by local members represent them at a broader level, where a few may be selected for the next higher level and so on, culminating perhaps in a national convention or in special policy-making bodies.

The basic stance of some major groupings has become fairly predictable with the accumulation of vested interests through prolonged political involvement. Prof. V. O. Key Jr. said in *Politics, Parties and Pressure Groups:*

"The partisan orientation of large groups with a varied membership becomes more noticeable as these groups move from the advocacy of the narrow interests of their membership toward an attempt to represent the views of their members on almost the whole range of public questions."

Organized labor has generally shown a national affinity for the Democratic party, major business organizations for the Republican party. Farm interests have been split. The American Farm Bureau Federation frequently is found on the Republican side, the National Farmers Union and the National Grange on the Democratic side. State and community circumstances create many divergencies.

In some cases the party label is less significant than "liberal-conservative" differences centering partly around the question of a greater or lesser Federal role in social matters. The Americans for Constitutional Action, for example, supports Republicans or Democrats it describes as conservatives; the Americans for Democratic Action supports those it deems liberals, most of them northern Democrats.

Challenges are sometimes made as to whether the positions presented to Congress and to the public by spokesmen for organized factions reflect members' views.

The relationship between group advocacy and member opinions was questioned at hearings by the Joint Committee on Organization of Congress which led to enactment of the 1946 law requiring lobbyists to register. George H. E. Smith, an associate of historian Charles A. Beard and research assistant to the Senate Minority Leader, testified in 1945.

Smith said he thought lobbies should be required not only to register but also to certify that a majority or two-thirds vote of the membership authorized presentation of a given position to Congress.

"In many cases," Smith said, "these representatives have not submitted that position to the membership at all, it is merely a direction from a small group, a board of directors or council, and they presume to speak in the name of 3 million members or 5 million members, but those members have very, very little knowledge of what has been authorized or of the position being taken by the directors of their national group."

Some organizations are meticulous in explaining officers' precautions to ensure democratic procedures. There are many indications, however, that Smith's words still apply in some cases. The democratic process faces the same hazards within pressure groups as without, including apathy and ignorance. Congress has enacted no provision like that proposed by Smith, but labor law specifies procedures to protect members' rights in labor unions.

Controversy has arisen from time to time over the Labor Department's enforcement policies. Major conflict involved the United Mine Workers of America (UMWA) before and after Joseph A. Yablonski was murdered Jan. 5, 1970, a few weeks after losing an election for the union presidency. Yablonski, chief lobbyist for the Coal Mine Health and Safety Act of 1969 (PL 91-173), became a harsh critic of union leadership after years of union service. UMWA's District 50, which said it had grown larger than the UMWA itself, seceded in 1970 charging, in the words of President Elwood Moffett, "tyranny and villainy." UMWA President W.A. Boyle contended the union was "the victim of a journalistic lynching bee."

what they read but also what they fail to read influences their outlook.

Political interest groups are virtually unanimous in regarding "educational" activities among their primary responsibilities. Their policies and methods in this regard vary as widely as their publications, which range from factual reporting to open propagandizing.

Many action groups are well aware of the potent weapons which modern mass communications provide for the shaping of opinions and the whetting of passions. Like the candidates or officeholders with whom they often closely work, groups turn to specialists in the use of those weapons. Publicity and image making or breaking are important aspects of some organizations' operations. The dramatizing of immense issues by focusing attention on a few charismatic individuals was effectively used by the civil rights movement with the late Martin Luther King Jr. in the spotlight.

1970 Campaign Activities

Special interest groups were especially active in at least three areas leading up to the 1970 elections:

- Shaping of issues.
- Promotion of issues and candidates.
- Financing of campaigns.

Business, labor and citizens' organizations were among those which staged voter registration drives and held "citizenship" meetings or seminars featuring candidates or discussions of campaign issues and tactics.

Much of the activity was conducted under nonpartisan banners, but in practice the degree of impartiality varied with the leadership. There were many opportunities for departure from neutrality, and politically involved leaders frequently made their opinions abundantly clear at the expense of supposed nonpartisanship.

Not all such departures were as apparent as the contradiction in terms presented by the Machinists Non-Partisan Political League of the International Association of Machinists and Aerospace Workers, AFL-CIO. The League supported for re-election 42 U.S. Representatives—all Democrats.

The Chamber of Commerce of the United States, which again in 1970 was sponsoring practical politics courses and seminars on management of political campaigns, said in a question-answer booklet for businessmen: "Q: How do labor unions view corporate sponsored 'good government' programs? A. Some with skepticism, others with mild cooperation." This would apply in many parts of the political spectrum, in various directions.

With important elections hinging on a handful of votes, perhaps less than one vote per precinct, voter registration and get-out-the-vote efforts by partisan groups naturally were aimed at increasing the vote in support of their cause. Aside from the many nonpartisan civic programs at community levels, it would be unrealistic to expect a group having major interests and goals at stake to concentrate such efforts where they would merely increase the opposition's voting strength. The internal politics of pressure groups poses important questions concerning members' self-interest here which have received sporadic and indecisive attention.

Motivation. A heavy percentage of pressure group activity before elections falls within the realm of "education" in a broad sense. Politically active factions as part of the nation's political process are out to motivate target blocs of voters to act in a certain way—to give higher priority to some issues than to others; to favor candidates or incumbents largely as a result of those priorities; to support them with campaign work or money, and to vote for them. All this has much to do with opinions, but it goes beyond that.

Many group leaders would echo the sentiment given election year prominence in the Liberty Lobby's *Liberty Letter:* "Education without Action availeth Naught." To induce action among constituents, some groups draw no discernible lines between informing and the whetting of passions.

Liberty Letter, issued by a group calling itself "America's largest independent political organization," told readers (May 1970) the Administration's welfare bill (HR 16311) was "a frightfully destructive outrage which threatens the total destruction of what remains of American life." Enactment would open a door, it said, "for demagogues to campaign on promises of stupendous handout increases, making the bread and circuses of ancient Rome look like comparative arch-conservatism! Taxes could sky-rocket, until those who work are totally pauperized!" By contrast, the National Chamber of Commerce expressed its opposition to the bill far more dispassionately. The bill ran into trouble in the Senate.

"We don't try to control votes," AFL-CIO President George Meany told newsmen in February 1970. "Our COPE (Committee on Political Education) activities are designed on two principal lines: one, to get our people to vote; two, to provide them with information, from the record, on which they can base their vote and on which we hope they will exercise their right of voting, in a manner which would be beneficial to the workers of the country as a whole. Of course, this would mean that we hope they would cast their vote along the lines indicated by the

Key Points of Power

Those interest groups which restrict their Congressional activities to selected areas, as contrasted with the society-wide operations of some large organizations, can focus their election attentions on a few friends or foes in Congress, if they choose.

With their legislative fortunes intentionally somewhat independent of normal political trends, those groups have no need for a large number of Members sympathetic to their views. They simply require one or two Members with great influence on the lawmaking machinery at the proper spot.

Edward Schneier in *The Annals* of the American Academy of Political and Social Science called attention in 1970 to a tendency among Members of Congress to rely on certain colleagues for guidance on topics within their respective competence. Schneier referred to this as a two-step flow of information and said:

"...If there is a two-step flow of information in the legislature, it takes only one strategically placed member to insert a 'Louis B. Mayer' amendment, only one small clique to ensure a protective tariff for glass, only one cotton-oriented subcommittee to draw up the cotton-subsidy program and push it through."

Other factors may, of course, lead a group with limited interests to cooperate as a link in a broader movement of allied groups similar to the coalitions sometimes found in direct legislative lobbying. Here again the validity of the group's internal politics can be a factor.

voting records of the candidates which we present to them."

Neither the AFL-CIO's political education arm nor those of other groups leave it to chance that followers will draw the correct conclusions. How bluntly the message is put depends on the audience.

Business-Labor

Heated exchanges in the 1970 campaign between some factions illuminate a perennial battleground fought over for a century by groups representing organized business and labor. The nature of the debate points up the carry-over of unfinished business from one Congress to the next in the never-ending contention for access to governmental power.

"It's a Neck-Tie Party...Yours!" said the opening headline on *Memo from COPE* dated April 13, 1970. *Memo* called the 1970 Congressional elections "the most important non-Presidential year contests in recent times." It predicted "a public hanging" for workers and unions in 1971 "if conservatives capture the Congressional and Senatorial elections next November."

Other headlines said "The Anti-Worker Noose Is Ready," "Labor-Busting Laundry List" and "Anti-Labor Drive Hinges on Election." *Memo* told readers the Chamber of Commerce of the United States and its allies in and out of Congress "want trade unions reduced to impotence." It listed 22 "anti-worker bills" with their sponsors—11 Republicans and two southern Democrats.

One of the bills (S 3526), an Administration measure introduced by Sen. Robert P. Griffin (R Mich.), provided for compulsory arbitration in transportation disputes under certain conditions. It was partly reproduced on the cover of *International Teamster* (April 1970), which calls itself "the largest labor publication in the world" with an estimated 5 million readers. The caption said, "This Bill Will Destroy Collective Bargaining." The Teamsters Union helped form the labor coalition Alliance for Labor Action outside the AFL-CIO in 1969.

From many quarters of organized labor have come similar comments, such as this by the Brotherhood of Locomotive Engineers' Grand Chief Engineer C. J. Coughlin (May 1970):

"Organized labor today is in a bitter struggle against those forces in this nation which seek to destroy the unions and strip away the gains that have been made over the years by virtue of hard work and sacrifice on the part of organized labor."

Union spokesmen find a counterpart in the National Right to Work Committee, their foe in bitter legislative battles since its formation in 1955 as "a single-purpose citizens organization devoted to the concept that no individual should be compelled to pay money to any private organization as a condition of employment." The Committee led a coalition of business and employer-oriented organizations which successfully blocked union attempts in the mid-1960s to repeal Section 14(b) of the Taft-Hartley Act, which permits states to enact laws banning the union shop. That struggle resulted in two Senate filibusters by Republicans and southern Democrats.

The Committee in 1969 set up a Legal Defense and Education Foundation to lead a drive "to end the use of tax-exempt compulsory union dues for politics," as Information Director Hugh C. Newton put it. Newton in February 1970 expressed the hope "that public awareness of the problem of compulsory unionism will grow by leaps and bounds...and result in a greater demand on Congress to end the practice."

The Committee spoke of Congressional inertia which it attributed to this factor: "Too many Senate and House Members owe their souls to the union officials for their campaign financing....By the use of the union member's dues—without his advice and consent—the bosses gain the allegiance of the legislators."

Broader Divisions

Political confrontations between pressure groups involve broader issues than those of labor-management relations, important though they are. Some major groups take part in political coalitions, though others remain aloof.

The AFL-CIO, for example, called the Congress of 1965-66 "the most outstanding Congress in our history," almost entirely because of enactments of President Johnson's "Great Society" social legislation rather than labor legislation. A coalition of organized labor, civil rights and liberal-intellectual forces largely descended from New Deal days participated in that effort. The general alignment of those factions, and of their opponents, over the next few years was largely determined in advance, though there were conflicting reports of their status going into the 1970s.

In 1969 and 1970 opponents of President Nixon's Republican Administration found a rallying point in his Supreme Court appointments, starting with their successful drive to block Senate confirmation of Clement F. Haynsworth Jr. On the national stage provided by the Senate, they focused attention on issues of race, labor relations and ethics within the symbolic figure of one man.

"The fight against Judge Haynsworth is important because he makes us remember what we sometimes forget—that whatever differences we may have among ourselves, we have a lot more in common. For one thing, we have enemies in common." Thus did Bayard Rustin, key strategist of the civil rights movement since he coordinated the big March on Washington in 1963, size up the struggle to the AFL-CIO biennial convention Oct. 3, 1969. Rustin headed the executive committee of the Leadership Conference on Civil Rights and said he was a socialist.

Gus Tyler, assistant president of the Ladies Garment Workers Union, said "it was labor that gathered the facts, made the case, lobbied the Senate and watered grass-roots sentiment" in the Haynsworth battle. But it was significant, he said, that "labor won as part of a broad coalition." *(Labor-civil rights coalition, p. 57)*

The coalition also defeated Mr. Nixon's next nominee, G. Harrold Carswell, which led the President to say that the Senate as then constituted would refuse to confirm a southerner for the Court. The statement brought denials. For better or worse, the two Supreme Court fights left their imprints on the opinions and passions of blocs of voters who a few months afterward faced decisions at the polls.

Election Leverage

Pre-election months are viewed by pressure groups as a fertile period in which to pursue their legislative objectives. The Chamber of Commerce of the United States, for example, was among groups which in 1969 lobbied for replacement of the electoral college system by a form of direct popular election of the President. It favored either a district or direct popular vote plan.

Others favoring direct elections included the AFL-CIO, League of Women Voters, American Bar Association and National Small Business Association.

The House on Sept. 18, 1969, passed a measure (H J Res 681) calling for a constitutional amendment abolishing the electoral college. The Chamber's *Public Affairs* marked the event by publishing a picture of two lobbyists and three House leaders—the Chamber's public affairs manager and the Bar Association's Washington director, standing with Speaker John W. McCormack (D Mass.), Chairman Emanuel Celler (D N.Y.) and ranking minority member William M. McCulloch (R Ohio) of the House Judiciary Committee.

Early in 1970, however, the Chamber saw a dimming of chances for a change in the voting system before the 1972 Presidential election. *Public Affairs* urged more letters to Senators. "An aroused citizenry in an election year like 1970 can be most effective," it said. The viewpoint expressed in its elaboration on that point casts light on the reasoning of many interest groups on a broad range of issues. It said:

"If the people want electoral reform, an election year is an ideal time to gain the type of reform most desired; or if this proves impossible, then to learn which candidates for public office are opposed to giving the voting public a greater voice in the election of the President."

1970 ELECTION RESULTS

Pressure Groups Count Election Wins, Losses

Organized labor, which had described the 1970 Congressional elections as a crisis for the future of labor unions, scored notable successes at the polls Nov. 3.

Several other national pressure groups also had reason for satisfaction with many of the results, both in terms of numbers and in relation to key contests involving Congressional leadership posts holding particular significance for specialized interest groups.

Many factors may complicate a group's decisions on whether or not to take public positions or engage in active campaigning in specific races. Results frequently cannot be taken at face value in attempting to assess a group's influence on the outcome. Endorsements sometimes are withheld where the result is considered certain. At other times a candidate may refuse endorsement by a given group on grounds that it could damage his chances.

Factions commonly seek to convince officeholders of their power at the polls and for that reason may endorse candidates who are considered probable winners in any event, thus creating presumed political debts and enhancing their performance record.

Election of endorsed candidates ranged as high as 91 percent in the case of the United Mine Workers, which saw 50 of its 55 endorsed candidates elected. Other groups which endorsed a large number of successful candidates for House and Senate seats included Americans for Constitutional Action (ACA) with 83 percent and Americans for Democratic Action (ADA) with 64 percent.

By far the most successful in terms of numbers of endorsed candidates who won was the AFL-CIO's Committee on Political Education (COPE). Its state councils endorsed 361 House and Senate candidates, of whom 219—or 61 percent—were elected. COPE endorsed 330 candidates in the House, winning 200. Of 31 COPE endorsements in the Senate, 19 won.

Committee Posts. Of greater significance than numbers in many cases were the committee assignments involved in pressure group activities. COPE endorsed 19 of 20 Democrats on the House Education and Labor Committee, including the chairman and all subcommittee chairmen. They all won.

COPE backed John F. Seiberling Jr., the Democratic opponent of Rep. William H. Ayres (R Ohio), highest ranking Republican on the Committee who was defeated. COPE also supported two winning Republican Committee members, Alphonzo Bell of California and Ogden Reid of New York, while losing on opponents of eight other Republican members.

In the Senate, COPE endorsed successful Harrison A. Williams Jr. (D N.J.), third-ranking Democrat on the Labor and Public Welfare Committee who was in line to become chairman. Sen. Ralph Yarborough (D Texas), the chairman, was defeated in the 1970 primaries in what was considered a serious blow by organized labor. Sen. Jennings Randolph (D W.Va.), second-ranking Democrat, was chair-

Key Legislators

		ACA [1]	ADA [2]	NCEC [3]	SANE [4]	FOE [5]	IAM [6]	UMW [7]	EA [8]
Muskie (D Maine)	+			√			√		
Hart (D Mich.)	+		√	√		√	√		
Symington (D Mo.)	+		√	√			√	√	
Mansfield (D Mont.)	+			√			√	√	
Williams (D N.J.)	+		√	√	√		√		
Gore (D Tenn.)				0	0		0	0	
Moss (D Utah)	+			√			√	√	
Jackson (D Wash.)	+						√	√	
Hartke (D Ind.)	+			√	√		√	√	
Price (D Ill.)	+							√	
Adair (R Ind.)		0							√
Bray (R Ind.)	+	√						√	
[1] Philbin (D Mass.)				√	√	√			
Fulton (R Pa.)	+							√	

+ —Winning candidates
√ —Victory for group
0 —Defeat for group
1 —Defeated in primary

man of the important Public Works Committee. COPE also endorsed Edward P. Kennedy (D Mass.), the only other Democrat on the Committee up for re-election. He also was a winner.

Among Republicans, COPE supported opponents of all three Committee members running. Winston L. Prouty of Vermont won, but George Murphy of California and Ralph T. Smith of Illinois were defeated.

The UMW successfully backed Sen. Frank E. Moss (D Utah), chairman of the Interior and Insular Affairs Minerals, Materials and Fuels Subcommittee, and Sen. Henry M. Jackson (D Wash.), the Subcommittee's second-ranking Democrat. In the House, the UMW's successful endorsements included Rep. Ed Edmondson (D Okla.), chairman of the Interior and Insular Affairs Mines and Mining Subcommittee, and two other Subcommittee members—James Kee (D W.Va.) and Joe Skubitz (R Kan.).

The defeat of Sen. Albert Gore (D Tenn.) represented one of the relatively few election setbacks in a key Congressional post, with many groups having a stake in that outcome. Gore was third-ranking Democrat on the Finance Committee and chairman of the Foreign Relations Arms Control, International Law and Organization Subcommittee. He also was second-ranking Democrat on the Foreign Relations Economic and Social Policy Affairs Subcommittee, where he would have been in line for the chairmanship with the Nov. 3 defeat of Chairman Thomas J. Dodd (D Conn.).

Gore had been endorsed by COPE, UMW, National Committee for an Effective Congress (NCEC), International Association of Machinists (IAM) and SANE. Other groups with which he ranked highly on the basis of vote ratings included the Teamsters Union, National Education Association (NEA), National Farmers Union (NFU) and United Federation of Postal Clerks (UFPC). His defeat would probably be considered a success by the National Right to Work Committee, ACA, National Associated Businessmen Inc. (NAB) and American Security Council (ASC), on the basis of vote performance.

Rep. E. Ross Adair (R Ind.), the ranking Republican on the Foreign Affairs Committee, was defeated. His opponent, J. Edward Roush (D), was endorsed by COPE, NCEC and Friends of the Earth. Adair was endorsed by ACA and opposed by Environmental Action.

The defeat of Rep. Philip J. Philbin (D Mass.), second-ranked Democrat on the Armed Services Committee and chairman of two of its subcommittees, marked a second victory against him by ADA, NCEC and SANE. Defeated in the primary, Philbin waged an independent write-in campaign but lost. Groups with whom he had rated highly on the basis of vote ratings included the NEA, IAM, COPE—which endorsed him—ASC, NFU, Leadership Conference on Civil Rights and Teamsters Union. Philbin rated low on vote charts of the American Farm Bureau Federation, ACA and NAB.

The United Federation of Postal Clerks, whose publication called defeated Sen. Yarborough "one of the staunchest supporters we ever had in the Senate," came back strong in the general elections. Yarborough was second-ranking Democrat on the Senate Post Office and Civil Service Committee.

The Federation's editors noted that more than half the Committee members were among Senators seeking re-election. Among winning members the union supported were Gale McGee (D Wyo.), chairman; Vance Hartke (D Ind.), chairman of the Retirement Subcommittee; Quentin N. Burdick (D N.D.), chairman of the Health Benefits and Life Insurance Subcommittee; Sen. Hiram Fong (R Hawaii), top-ranking Republican on the Committee, and Sen. Frank Moss (D Utah), a member of most of the subcommittees.

On the House side, the postal union endorsed winning Rep. Thaddeus J. Dulski (D N.Y.), chairman of the House Post Office and Civil Service Committee, and loser Rep. Arnold Olsen (D Mont.), third-ranking Democrat and chairman of the Postal Rates Subcommittee. The union unsuccessfully backed defeated Rep. Robert J. Corbett (R Pa.), top-ranking Republican on the Committee.

Americans for Constitutional Action endorsed 168 candidates, of whom 139 won. Americans for Democratic Action endorsed 58 candidates, of whom 37 won.

Among those whose earlier defeat in primary elections was significant among special interest groups was Rep. George H. Fallon (D Md.), chairman of the House Public Works Committee. Fallon rated well above 50 percent on the vote performance charts of the Leadership Conference on Civil Rights, NEA, IAM, Teamsters, COPE, ASC and NFU. He rated below on the Friends Committee on National Legislation, Farm Bureau, ACA, ADA and NAB.

Key

0 — Elections lost by group (In the case of EA, candidate's victory means defeat for group, since only opposition was registered by EA.)	* — Incumbent
	+ — Winning candidates
	√ — Elections won by group

---

1 **Americans for Constitutional Action.** *Endorsements by board of trustees released Oct. 22.*

2 **Americans for Democratic Action.** *Endorsements received by national headquarters from local chapters by Oct. 23. Minnesota and Southern California chapters declined to endorse candidates in the general election.*

3 **National Committee for an Effective Congress.** *Endorsements released Oct. 27 include only candidates receiving campaign contributions or considered by the committee to be in close races.*

4 **SANE.** *Formerly called Citizens' Committee for a Sane Nuclear Policy. Endorsements made over several months in newsletter SANE World with encouragement to readers to contribute to the candidates.*

5 **Friends of the Earth.** *The group's political arm, League of Conservation Voters, issued endorsements Oct. 15.*

6 **International Association of Machinists and Aerospace Workers.** *Endorsements for Senate by state councils or conference released Oct. 1.*

7 **United Mine Workers of America.** *Endorsements by national organization released Oct. 15.*

8 **Environmental Action.** *Listing consisted only of 10 House candidates opposed by the group, as announced before primary election.*

PRESSURE GROUPS AND SENATE

	ACA[1]	ADA[2]	NCEC[3]	SANE[4]	FOE[5]	IAM[6]	UMW[7]			ACA	ADA	NCEC	SANE	FOE	IAM	UMW			ACA	ADA	NCEC	SANE	FOE	IAM	UMW
ALASKA									**INDIANA**									**MONTANA**							
Kay (D)			0						*Hartke (D)	+		√	√		√	√		*Mansfield (D)	+		√			√	√
ARIZONA									Roudebush (R)	0								**NEBRASKA**							
Grossman (D)			0		0				**MAINE**									*Hruska (R)	+	√					
*Fannin (R)	+	√							*Muskie (D)	+		√			√			**NEW JERSEY**							
CALIFORNIA									**MARYLAND**									*Williams (D)	+		√	√	√	√	
Tunney (D)	+		√	√		√			*Tydings (D)			0			0	0		**NEW MEXICO**							
*Murphy (R)	0								**MASSACHUSETTS**									*Montoya (D)	+		√			√	√
CONNECTICUT									*Kennedy (D)	+		√			√			Carter (R)	0						
Duffey (D)			0	0	0	0			**MICHIGAN**									**NEW YORK**							
DELAWARE									*Hart (D)	+		√	√	√	√			Ottinger (D)			0			0	0
Zimmerman (D)						0			**MINNESOTA**									**NORTH DAKOTA**							
FLORIDA									Humphrey (D)	+					√			*Burdick (D)	+		√			√	√
Cramer (R)	0								**MISSISSIPPI**									Kleppe (R)	0						
ILLINOIS									*Stennis (D)	+	√							**OHIO**							
Stevenson (D)	+		√	√		√	√		**MISSOURI**									Metzenbaum (D)			0	0		0	0
*Smith (R)	0								*Symington (D)	+		√	√		√	√		Taft (R)	+	√					

	ACA[1]	ADA[2]	NCEC[3]	SANE[4]	FOE[5]	IAM[6]	UMW[7]
PENNSYLVANIA							
Sesler (D)			0			0	
*Scott (R)	+						√
RHODE ISLAND							
*Pastore (D)	+					√	
TENNESSEE							
*Gore (D)			0	0		0	0
Brock (R)	+	√					
TEXAS							
Bush (R)	0						
UTAH							
*Moss (D)	+		√		√	√	√
Burton (R)		0					
VERMONT							
Hoff (D)			0	0	0	0	
VIRGINIA							
Rawlings (D)				0		0	
*Byrd (Ind.)	+	√					
WASHINGTON							
*Jackson (D)	+					√	√
WEST VIRGINIA							
*Byrd (D)	+						√
WISCONSIN							
*Proxmire (D)	+		√		√		
WYOMING							
*McGee (D)	+				√		
Wold (R)	0						
Group Endorsements	15	9	20	6	3	27	13
Group Victories	6	5	13	2	1	17	10

PRESSURE GROUPS AND HOUSE

	ACA[1]	ADA[2]	NCEC[3]	SANE[4]	FOE[5]	EA[8]	UMW[7]
ALABAMA							
1*Edwards (R)	+	√					
2*Dickinson (R)	+	√					
3*Andrews (D)	+	√					
4*Nichols (D)	+	√					
5*Flowers (D)	+	√					
6*Buchanan (R)	+	√					
7*Bevill (D)	+						√
ALASKA							
AL Begich (D)	+		√				
ARIZONA							
1*Rhodes (R)	+	√					
3*Steiger (R)	+	√					
ARKANSAS							
3*Ham'rschm't (R)	+	√					
CALIFORNIA							
1 Kortum (D)			0				
*Clausen (R)	+	√					
5*Burton (D)	+		√				
6 Miller (D)			0				
7 Dellums (D)	+		√	√			
9*Edwards (D)	+		√	√			
10 McLean (D)			0				
*Gubser (R)	+	√					
11*McCloskey (R)	+		√	√	√		
14*Waldie (D)	+		√				
15 Van Dyken (R)	0						
18*Mathias (R)	+	√					
20*Smith (R)	+	√					
23*Clawson (R)	+	√					
24 Evers (D)			0				
*Rousselot (R)	+	√					
25*Wiggins (R)	+	√					
27*Goldwater (R)	+	√					
32*Hosmer (R)	+	√					
33*Pettis (R)	+	√					
34 Teague (R)	0						
35*Schmitz (R)	+	√					
36*Wilson (R)	+	√					
COLORADO							
1 Barnes (D)			0	0			
2 Gebhardt (D)			0	0			
3*Evans (D)	+			√			√
Mitchell (R)	0						
4*Aspinall (D)	+						√
CONNECTICUT							
6 Grasso (D)	+		√				
DELAWARE							
AL duPont (R)	+	√					
FLORIDA							
4*Chappell (D)	+	√					
5*Frey (R)	+	√					
6*Gibbons (D)	+		√				
Carter (R)		0					
7*Haley (D)	+	√					
8 Young (R)	+	√					
9*Rogers (D)	+	√					
10*Burke (R)	+	√					
GEORGIA							
3*Brinkley (D)	+	√					
4*Blackburn (R)	+	√					
5 Young (D)			0	0			
*Thompson (R)	+	√					
9 Cooper (R)	0						
HAWAII							
1 Cockey (R)	0						
IDAHO							
1 Brauner (D)			0				
*McClure (R)	+	√					
ILLINOIS							
2*Mikva (D)	+		√				
4*Derwinski (R)	+	√					
9*Yates (D)	+		√				
10*Collier (R)	+	√					
12 Cone (D)			0				
*McClory (R)	+	√					
13 Warman (D)			0				
*Crane (R)	+	√					
15*Reid (R)	+	√					
16*Anderson (R)	+	√					
17*Arends (R)	+	√					
18*Michel (R)	+	√					
20*Findley (R)	+	√					
21*Gray (D)	+						√
23*Shipley (D)	+						√
24*Price (D)	+						√
INDIANA							
2 Sprague (D)			0				
*Landgrebe (R)	+	√				0	
3*Brademas (D)	+		√				
4 Roush (D)	+		√	√			
*Adair (R)		0			√		
6*Bray (R)	+	√					
7*Myers (R)	+	√					
8 Huber (D)			0				
*Zion (R)	+	√			0		
10 Sharp (D)			0				
*Dennis (R)	+	√			0		
11*Jacobs (D)	+		√				
IOWA							
2*Culver (D)	+		√				
3*Gross (R)	+	√					
4 Blobaum (D)			0				
*Kyl (R)	+				0		
5*Smith (D)	+						√
6*Mayne (R)	+	√					
7*Scherle (R)	+	√					
KANSAS							
1*Sebelius (R)	+	√					
2*Mize (R)		0					
3 DeCoursey (D)			0				
*Winn (R)	+				0		
4*Shriver (R)	+	√					
5*Skubitz (R)	+	√					√
KENTUCKY							
1*Stubblefield (D)	+						√
2*Natcher (D)	+						√
3 Mazzoli (D)	+		√				
*Cowger (R)	+				√		
4*Snyder (R)	+	√					√
5*Carter (R)	+	√					√
6*Watts (D)	+						√
7*Perkins (D)	+						√
LOUISIANA							
5*Passman (D)	+	√					
MARYLAND							
1*Morton (R)	+	√					
4 Sarbanes (D)	+		√	√	√		
5 Hart (D)			0	0			
7 Mitchell (D)	+		√	√			
MASSACHUSETTS							
1*Conte (R)	+				√		
3 Drinan (D)	+		√	√	√		
6*Harrington (D)	+		√	√			
10 Yaffe (D)			0	0			
12 Studds (D)			0	0			
MICHIGAN							
1*Conyers (D)	+		√				
2*Esch (R)	+		√				
5*Ford (R)	+	√					
7*Riegle (R)	+						
8*Harvey (R)	+	√					
9*Vander Jagt (R)	+				√		
12*O'Hara (D)	+		√				
13*Diggs (D)	+		√				
15*Ford (D)	+		√				√
16*Dingell (D)	+					√	

Member	ACA	ADA	NCEC	SANE	FOE	EA	UMW
18 Scholle (D)		0					
19 Harris (D)		0					
MINNESOTA							
2*Nelsen (R)	+	√					
3 Rice (D)			0				
5*Fraser (D)	+		√				
6*Zwach (R)	+	√					
7 Bergland (D)	+		√				
*Langen (R)						√	
MISSISSIPPI							
1*Abernethy (D)	+	√					
2*Whitten (D)	+	√					
3*Griffin (D)	+	√					
4*Montgomery (D)	+	√					
5*Colmer (D)	+	√					
MISSOURI							
1*Clay (D)	+		√				
2*Symington (D)	+		√	√			
4*Randall (D)	+						√
7*Hall (R)	+	√					
9*Hungate (D)	+		√				
MONTANA							
1*Olsen (D)							0
2*Melcher (D)	+		√				√
NEBRASKA							
3*Martin (R)	+	√					
NEVADA							
AL*Baring (D)	+	√					
NEW HAMPSHIRE							
1*Wyman (R)	+	√					
NEW JERSEY							
1*Hunt (R)	+	√					
4*Thompson (D)	+		√				
7 Lesemann (D)		0					
9*Helstoski (D)	+		√	√			
NEW MEXICO							
1 Chavez (D)			0				0
2*Foreman (R)		0					
NEW YORK							
1 Smith (R-C)		0					
2*Grover (R-C)	+	√					
3*Wolff (D-L)	+		√	√			
4*Wydler (R)	+	√					
5*Lowenstein (D-L)			0	0	0		
Lent (R-C)	+	√					
6 Flynn (C)		0					
8*Rosenthal (D-L)	+		√				
12*Chisholm (D-L)	+		√				
14 Eikenberry (L)			0				
17*Koch (D-L)	+		√				
18 Rangel (D)	+		√	√			
19 Abzug (D)	+		√	√			
20*Ryan (D-L)	+		√				
21 Badillo (D-L)	+		√				
22*Scheuer (D-L)	+		√				
23*Bingham (D-L)	+		√				
26*Reid (R-L)	+			√			
27 Dow (D-L)	+			√			
28*Fish (R)	+					√	
29*Button (R-L)			0	0			
30*King (R-C)	+	√					
31*McEwen (R-C)	+	√					
40*Smith (R-C)	+	√					
NORTH CAROLINA							
1*Jones (D)	+	√					
2*Fountain (D)	+	√					
3 Howell (R)		0					
4 Hawke (R)		0					
5*Mizell (R)	+	√					
7*Lennon (D)	+	√					
8*Ruth (R)	+	√					
9*Jonas (R)	+	√					
10*Broyhill (R)	+	√					
OHIO							
1 Keating (R)	+	√					
2 Springer (D)			0				
*Clancy (R)	+	√					
4*McCulloch (R)	+	√					
5*Latta (R)	+	√					
6*Harsha (R)	+	√					
7*Brown (R)	+	√					
10 Arnett (D)			0				
*Miller (R)	+	√					
12 Goodrich (D)			√				
*Devine (R)	+	√					
14 Seiberling (D)	+		√				
Ayres (R)	0					√	
15*Wylie (R)	+	√					
16*Bow (R)	+	√					
17*Ashbrook (R)	+	√					
18*Hays (D)	+						√
19 Carney (D)	+						√
20 Stanton (D)	+		√				
22*Vanik (D)	+		√	√	√		
23 Mottl (D)			0				
*Minshall (R)	+	√					
OKLAHOMA							
1*Belcher (R)	+	√					
2*Edmondson (D)	+						√
3*Albert (D)	+						√
4 Wilkinson (R)		0					
*Steed (D)	+						√
5*Jarman (D)	+	√					
6*Camp (R)	+	√					
OREGON							
1*Wyatt (R)	+	√					
PENNSYLVANIA							
6*Yatron (D)	+						√
7*Williams (R)	+	√					
10*McDade (R)	+						√
11*Flood (D)	+						√
12*Whalley (R)	+	√					
14*Moorhead (D)	+		√				√
15*Rooney (D)	+						√
16*Eshleman (R)	+	√					
17*Schneebeli (R)	+	√					
18*Corbett (R)	+						√
19 Berger (D)			0				
*Goodling (R)	+	√					
20*Gaydos (D)	+						√
21*Dent (D)	+						√
22*Saylor (R)	+	√			√		√
23*Johnson (R)	+	√					
25*Clark (D)	+						√
26*Morgan (D)	+						√
27 Walgren (D)			0				
*Fulton (R)	+						√
SOUTH CAROLINA							
2 Spence (R)	+	√					
3*Dorn (D)	+	√					
4*Mann (D)	+	√					
5 Phillips (R)		0					
6*McMillan (D)	+	√					
SOUTH DAKOTA							
1 Gunderson (R)		0					
2 Abourezk (D)	+		√				
Brady (R)		√					
TENNESSEE							
3 Baker (R)	+	√					
4*Evins (D)	+						√
9*Kuykendall (R)	+	√					
TEXAS							
2*Dowdy (D)	+	√					
3*Collins (R)	+	√					
7 Archer (R)	+	√					
9*Brooks (D)	+		√				
18*Price (R)	+	√					
21*Fisher (D)	+	√					
22 Busch (R)				0			
UTAH							
1 Richards (R)		0					
2*Lloyd (R)	+	√					
VIRGINIA							
2 Fitzpatrick (D)			0				
3*Satterfield (D)	+	√					
4*Abbitt (D)	+	√					
Ragsdale (Ind.)			0				
5*Daniel (D)	+	√					
6*Poff (R)	+	√					
7 Robinson (R)	+	√					
8*Scott (R)	+	√					
9*Wampler (R)	+	√					√
10 Miller (D)			0				
*Broyhill (R)	+	√					
WASHINGTON							
1*Pelly (R)	+	√				√	
3*Hansen (D)	+						√
4*May (R)		0					
5*Foley (D)	+		√				
7*Adams (D)	+		√				
WEST VIRGINIA							
1*Mollohan (D)	+						√
2*Staggers (D)	+						√
3*Slack (D)	+						√
5*Kee (D)	+						√
WISCONSIN							
1 Aspin (D)	+		√				
*Schadeberg (R)	+					√	
3*Thomson (R)	+	√					
5*Reuss (D)	+		√				
7*Obey (D)	+		√				
8*Byrnes (R)	+	√					
9*Davis (R)	+	√					
10 Thoresen (D)			0				
WYOMING							
AL Roncalio (D)	+		√				
Roberts (R)		0					

	ACA	ADA	NCEC	SANE	FOE	EA	UMW
Group Endorsements	153	49	61	6	12	10	42
Group Victories	133	32	38	2	11	5	40

Congressional Endorsements by AFL-CIO's COPE

The Committee on Political Education (COPE), political action arm of the 13.5-million-member AFL-CIO and one of the most active pressure groups on the national scene, Nov. 2 released 361 endorsements by state AFL-CIO councils in the 1970 Congressional elections.

COPE endorsements included 31 Senate candidates and 330 aspirants for House seats. This was more than twice as many endorsements as were made by Americans for Constitutional Action, the next-highest group for whom pre-election lists were provided. Among COPE endorsements were Sen. Harrison A. Williams Jr. (D N.J.), who became chairman of the Senate Labor and Public Wel-

fare Committee in 1971, and Philip H. Hoff (D Vt.), opposing Sen. Winston L. Prouty (R Vt.), second-ranking Republican on the Committee. Prouty won re-election.

COPE's endorsements also included the first 19 Democratic members of the House Education and Labor Committee and opponents to five of the top nine Republican members.

In the following table, COPE endorsements are listed by state. A + preceding the name indicates winning candidates; a — indicates losing candidates. An * indicates incumbents.

SENATE

ALASKA
—Kay (D)
ARIZONA
—Grossman (D)
CALIFORNIA
+Tunney (D)
CONNECTICUT
—Duffey (D)
DELAWARE
—Zimmerman (D)
FLORIDA
+Chiles (D)

ILLINOIS
+Stevenson (D)
INDIANA
+Hartke (D)*
MAINE
+Muskie (D)*
MARYLAND
—Tydings (D)*
MASSACHUSETTS
+Kennedy (D)*
MICHIGAN
+Hart (D)*

MINNESOTA
+Humphrey (D)
MISSOURI
+Symington (D)*
MONTANA
+Mansfield (D)*
NEBRASKA
—Morrison (D)
NEVADA
+Cannon (D)*
NEW JERSEY
+Williams (D)*

NEW MEXICO
+Montoya (D)*
NEW YORK
—Ottinger (D)
NORTH DAKOTA
+Burdick (D)*
OHIO
—Metzenbaum (D)
PENNSYLVANIA
—Sesler (D)
RHODE ISLAND
+Pastore (D)*

TENNESSEE
—Gore (D)*
UTAH
+Moss (D)*
VERMONT
—Hoff (D)
VIRGINIA
—Rawlings (D)
WASHINGTON
+Jackson (D)*
WISCONSIN
+Proxmire (D)*
WYOMING
+McGee (D)*

HOUSE

ALABAMA
8+Jones (D)*
ALASKA
AL+Begich (D)
ARIZONA
1—Pollock (D)
2+Udall (D)*
3—Beaty (D)
ARKANSAS
3—Poe (D)
CALIFORNIA
1—Kortum (D)
2+Johnson (D)*
3+Moss (D)*
4+Leggett (D)*
5+Burton (D)*
6—Miller (D)
7+Dellums (D)
8+Miller (D)*
9+Edwards (D)*
10—McLean (D)
11+McCloskey (R)*
12—Riordan (D)
13—Hart (D)
14+Waldie (D)*
15+McFall (D)*
16+Sisk (D)*
17+Anderson (D)*
18—Miller (D)
19+Holifield (D)*
20—Stolzberg (D)
21+Hawkins (D)*
22+Corman (D)*
23—Chapman (D)
24—Evers (D)

25—Craven (D)
26+Rees (D)*
27—Kimmel (D)
28+Bell (R)*
29+Danielson (D)
30+Roybal (D)*
31+Wilson (D)*
33—Wright (D)
34+Hanna (D)*
35—Lenhart (D)
37+Van Deerlin (D)*
38—Tunno (D)
CONNECTICUT
1+Cotter (D)
2—Pickett (D)
3+Giaimo (D)*
4—Daly (D)
5+Monagan (D)*
6+Grasso (D)
DELAWARE
AL—Daniello (D)
FLORIDA
6+Gibbons (D)*
11+Pepper (D)*
12+Fascell (D)*
GEORGIA
4—Shumake (D)
5—Young (D)
HAWAII
1+Matsunaga (D)*
2+Mink (D)*
IDAHO
1—Brauner (D)
ILLINOIS
1+Metcalfe (D)

2+Mikva (D)*
3+Murphy (M. F.) (D)
4—Morgan (D)
5+Kluczynski (D)*
6—Collins (D)
7+Annunzio (D)*
8+Rostenkowski (D)*
9+Yates (D)*
11+Pucinski (D)*
13—Warman (D)
16—Devine (D)
20—Cox (D)
21+Gray (D)*
22—Miller (D)
23+Shipley (D)*
24+Price (D)*
INDIANA
1+Madden (D)*
2—Sprague (D)
3+Brademas (D)*
4+Roush (D)
5—Williams (D)
6—Straub (D)
7—Roach (D)
8—Huber (D)
9+Hamilton (D)*
10—Sharp (D)
11+Jacobs (D)*
IOWA
1—Mezvinsky (D)
2+Culver (D)*
3—Taylor (D)
4—Blobaum (D)
5+Smith (D)*
6—Moore (D)

7—Galetich (D)
KANSAS
1—Jellison (D)
2+Roy (D)
3—DeCoursey (D)
4—Juhnke (D)
5—Saar (D)
KENTUCKY
2+Natcher (D)*
4—Webster (D)
7+Perkins (D)*
LOUISIANA
2+Boggs (D)*
7+Edwards (D)*
MAINE
1+Kyros (D)*
2+Hathaway (D)*
MARYLAND
1—Aland (D)
2+Long (D)*
3+Garmatz (D)*
4+Sarbanes (D)
5—Hart (D)
6—Hughes (R)
7+Mitchell (D)
8+Gude (R)*
MASSACHUSETTS
2+Boland (D)*
3—Philbin (Ind.)*
4+Donohue (D)*
5+Morse (R)*
6+Harrington (D)*
7+Macdonald (D)*
8+O'Neill (D)*
10+Heckler (R)*

11+Burke (D)*
12—Studds (D)
MICHIGAN
1+Conyers (D)*
2—Stillwagon (D)
3—Enslen (D)
4—McCormack (D)
5—McKee (D)
6—Cihon (D)
7+Riegle (R)*
8—Davies (D)
9—Rogers (D)
10—Parent (D)
11—Green (D)
12+O'Hara (D)*
13+Diggs (D)*
14+Nedzi (D)*
15+Ford (D)*
16+Dingell (D)*
17+Griffiths (D)*
18—Scholle (D)
19—Harris (D)
MINNESOTA
2—Adams (D)
3—Rice (D)
4+Karth (D)*
5+Fraser (D)*
6—Montgomery (D)
7+Bergland (D)
8+Blatnik (D)*
MISSOURI
1+Clay (D)*
2+Symington (D)*
3+Sullivan (D)*
4+Randall (D)*

5+Bolling (D)*
8+Ichord (D)*
9+Hungate (D)*
10+Burlison (D)*
MONTANA
1—Olsen (D)*
2+Melcher (D)*
NEBRASKA
1—Burrows (D)
2—Hlavacek (D)
3—Searcy (D)
NEW HAMPSHIRE
1—Merrow (D)
2—Daniell (D)
NEW JERSEY
1—Mansi (D)
2—Hughes (D)
3+Howard (D)*
4+Thompson (D)*
5—Eisele (D)
7—Lesemann (D)
8+Roe (D)*
9+Helstoski (D)*
10+Rodino (D)*
11+Minish (D)*
12+Dwyer (R)*
13+Gallagher (D)*
14+Daniels (D)*
15+Patten (D)*
NEW MEXICO
1—Chavez (D)
NEW YORK
1+Pike (DL)*
2—Sherman (DL)
3+Wolff (DL)*
5—Lowenstein (DL)*
6+Halpern (RL)*
7+Addabbo (DLR)*
8+Rosenthal (DL)*
9+Delaney (DRC)*
10+Celler (DL)*

11+Brasco (D)*
12+Chisholm (DL)*
13+Podell (D)*
14+Rooney (D)*
15+Carey (D)*
16+Murphy (D)*
17+Koch (DL)*
18+Rangel (DR)
19—Farber (RL)
20+Ryan (DL)*
21+Badillo (DL)
22+Scheuer (DL)*
23+Bingham (DL)*
24+Biaggi (DC)*
25—Dretzin (D)
26+Reid (RL)*
27+Dow (DL)
28—Greaney (D)
30—Pattison (DL)
31—Bornstein (DL)
32—Simmons (D)
33—Bernstein (DL)
34—McCurn (D)
35+Hanley (D)*
36+Horton (R)*
37—Anderson (DL)
38—Cretekos (D)
39—Flaherty (DL)
40—Cuddy (DL)
41+Dulski (DL)*
NORTH CAROLINA
4+Galifianakis (D)*
6+Preyer (D)*
8—Blue (D)
11+Taylor (D)*
NORTH DAKOTA
1—Brooks (D)
2+Link (D)
OHIO
1+Keating (R)

2—Springer (D)
3+Whalen (R)*
5—Sherer (D)
6—Stevens (D)
9+Ashley (D)*
10—Arnett (D)
11—Rudd (D)
12—Goodrich (D)
13—Bartolomeo (D)
14+Seiberling (D)
15—McGee (D)
16—Musser (D)
17—Hood (D)
18+Hays (D)*
19—Carney (D)
20+Stanton (D)
21+Stokes (D)*
22—Vanik (D)
23—Mottl (D)
24—Ruppert (D)
OKLAHOMA
1—Jones (D)
2+Edmondson (D)*
3+Albert (D)*
4+Steed (D)*
OREGON
2+Ullman (D)*
3+Green (D)*
4—Weaver (D)
PENNSYLVANIA
1+Barrett (D)*
2+Nix (D)*
3+Byrne (D)*
4+Eilberg (D)*
5+Green (D)*
6+Yatron (D)*
7—Breslin (D)
9—Waldmann (D)
10+McDade (R)*
11+Flood (D)*

12—Karycki (D)
14+Moorhead (D)*
15+Rooney (D)*
16—Pflum (D)
17—Zurick (D)
19—Berger (D)
20+Gaydos (D)*
21+Dent (D)*
22—O'Kicki (D)
23—Harrington (D)
24+Vigorito (D)*
25+Clark (D)*
26+Morgan (D)*
27+Fulton (R)*
RHODE ISLAND
1+St. Germain (D)*
2+Tiernan (D)*
SOUTH CAROLINA
2—McDonald (D)
SOUTH DAKOTA
2+Abourezk (D)
TENNESSEE
1—Shine (D)
2—Cowan (D)
3—Winningham (D)
4+Evins (D)*
5+Fulton (D)*
6 | Anderson (D)*
7+Blanton (D)*
8+Jones (D)*
9—Osborn (D)
TEXAS
1+Patman (D)*
3—Mead (D)
8+Eckhardt (D)*
9+Brooks (D)*
10+Pickle (D)*
12+Wright (D)*
14+Young (D)*
16+White (D)*

20+Gonzalez (D)*
23+Kazen (D)*
UTAH
1+McKay (D)
2—Nance (D)
VIRGINIA
2—Fitzpatrick (D)
3—Wilkinson (R)
4—Ragsdale (Ind.)
6—White (D)
8—Stearns (D)
9—Buchanan (D)
10—Miller (D)
WASHINGTON
1—Hughes (D)
1+Pelly (R)*
2+Meeds (D)*
3+Hansen (D)*
4+McCormack (D)
5+Foley (D)*
6+Hicks (D)*
7+Adams (D)*
WEST VIRGINIA
1+Mollohan (D)*
2+Staggers (D)*
3+Slack (D)*
4+Hechler (D)*
5+Kee (D)*
WISCONSIN
1+Aspin (D)
2+Kastenmeier (D)*
3—Short (D)
4+Zablocki (D)*
5+Reuss (D)*
7+Obey (D)*
8—Cornell (D)
9—Tabak (D)
10+O'Konski (R)*
WYOMING
AL+Roncalio (D)

ENDORSEMENT REASONS

Some of the pressure groups which were most active in the 1970 Congressional elections had a vested interest in retaining the status quo in selected areas of Congress. Purposes ranged from an interest in retaining Democratic control of both houses of Congress, on the part of some, to a limited interest in a few important committee posts.

Many groups, nevertheless, tended to straddle the political parties and attempt to keep sympathetic Members of both major parties climbing the rungs to upper levels on committees dealing with their specialties.

Members who return for repeated terms in Congress with the backing of certain groups in their states or districts eventually rise through the seniority system to powerful posts on committees or in the leadership. A mutual dependence often develops between officeholders and the factions on whom they rely for election support.

It is not uncommon to find interest groups supporting both Republican and Democratic committee leaders. In the Nov. 3 elections, among key majority Members who won re-election to the Senate with varying degrees of group support were:

Sen. Edmund S. Muskie (D Maine), who became second-ranking Democrat on the Public Works Committee. Based on vote ratings and endorsements, groups with reason to favor his re-election included NCEC, IAM, LCCR, FCNL, NEA, Teamsters, COPE, ADA and NFU. Groups with reason on those grounds to oppose his re-election included NRWC, ACA, NAB and ASC. (Group names, p. 45-46)

Sen. Philip A. Hart (D Mich.), chairman of Judiciary Antitrust and Monopoly Subcommittee and chairman of Commerce Energy, Natural Resources and Environment Subcommittee. With reason to favor were ADA, NCEC, FOE, IAM, LCCR, FCNL, NEA, Teamsters, COPE and NFU. Having reason to oppose him were NRWC, ACA, NAB and ASC.

Sen. Stuart Symington (D Mo.), third-ranked Democrat on the Armed Services Committee and only Senator on both that and the Foreign Relations Committee. Having reason to favor included ADA, NCEC, IAM, UMW, LCCR, FCNL, NEA, Teamsters, COPE and NFU. Having grounds to oppose were ACA, NAB and ASC.

Sen. Mike Mansfield (D Mont.), Majority Leader. Having reason to favor were NCEC, IAM, UMW, LCCR, FCNL, NEA, Teamsters, COPE, NFU and ADA. With reason to oppose were ACA, NAB and ASC.

LOBBY COALITIONS

Alliance-Building a Major

Strategy in Groups' Pursuit of Power

The ultimate objective of attempts to influence government is power. The Washington lobby knows that while others may talk, only those in official positions can act.

But it also knows its own strength, regardless of who holds the reins of government. This strength reaches its peak when a number of organizations combine forces. A successful coalition, with its impact on public opinion, can force even the President to take it into account.

With the assurance of sufficient coalition support, a legislator or executive can act even on unpopular matters largely with impunity; without it he may find his power fleeting and perhaps more theory than fact.

The prospect of election backing or opposition by powerful organizations—their ultimate weapon—can force any vulnerable Senator, Representative or elective official to weigh the costs of his stand.

Insiders' recognition of the potential for group influence has been demonstrated many times. It is particularly evident when a change of administrations transposes the "ins" and "outs" in Washington. After the Republican Administration took over in 1969, many former high officials of the Democratic Kennedy-Johnson Administrations became active in pressure groups which sought to influence national policy they once helped to execute. For example:

• A group called the National Council for an Indochina Deadline formed in 1971 to urge U.S. withdrawal from Indochina by the end of 1971 included among its 56 sponsors Nicholas deB. Katzenbach, Attorney General (1964-66) and Under Secretary of State; Ramsey Clark, Attorney General (1966-69), who also became a leader of the American Civil Liberties Union; Clark M. Clifford, Secretary of Defense (1968-69), and his law partner, Paul C. Warnke, former general counsel and Assistant Secre-

tary of Defense; Alfred B. Fitt, Roswell L. Gilpatric, Richard C. Steadman, Adam Yarmolinsky and Herbert York, all former top Defense Department officials; Walter Heller, former chairman of the Council of Economic Advisers in the Johnson Administration; Stewart L. Udall, Secretary of the Interior (1961-69), and Arthur J. Goldberg, Secretary of Labor (1961-62), Supreme Court Justice and Ambassador to the United Nations.

• James J. Reynolds, former second-ranking Labor Department official, became head of the American Institute of Merchant Shipping, an influential shipping organization.

• James L. Goddard, Commissioner of the Food and Drug Administration in the Johnson Administration, helped the American Public Health Association to oppose drug law proposals of the Nixon Administration.

• John W. Gardner, Secretary of Health, Education and Welfare (1965-68), headed a new pressure group called Common Cause which made ending the war its top priority and pushed an alternative national budget pegged to domestic issues. He was later joined by Jack T. Conway, the number two official in housing and antipoverty programs in preceding Democratic administrations. (Common Cause p. 53)

• Peter Libassi, Gardner's director of civil rights, shared leadership of the National Urban Coalition with Gardner while it founded the broader-based Common Cause. Jack Hood Vaughn, former Peace Corps director and U.S. Ambassador, and Sol M. Linowitz, an Ambassador, became leaders of the National Urban Coalition, which pressured for cuts in defense spending and troop withdrawals from Europe.

A similar exodus from government to pressure groups, or vice versa, occurs regardless of which political party moves into power. Specialized interests as a matter of course have their sights set on having sympathetic individuals in seats of power.

Among their targets are Congressional committees and subcommittees dealing with their field and committee staffs in Congress; the Presidency, Cabinet officers and top assistants, regulatory agencies and a long string of career posts at secondary levels in the Executive Branch, and key judgeships including the Supreme Court. When incumbents are ousted, many naturally try to put their expertise to work.

Power Bases. Masses of unorganized individuals ordinarily exert little direct influence on the major activities of the Federal Government. As they organize in groups geared to specialized interests and goals, they build power bases from which their leaders and spokesmen can promote those interests.

Hence the formation of trade associations, labor and professional political action committees, self-styled citizens' groups and other organizations of many kinds that together make up the Washington lobby.

As the nation has grown, and with it the crush of competing interests, individual interest groups even as large as the American Farm Bureau Federation, AFL-CIO or the Chamber of Commerce of the United States have found they sometimes lack sufficient impact to achieve their legislative purposes unassisted.

A major trend in the mid-twentieth century has been the pyramiding of pressure group on pressure group into combinations aimed at accumulating enough collective strength to compel power holders to heed them.

While this movement toward coalitions has accelerated since World War II, it is far from new. For example, Secretary-Treasurer Roger Fleming of the American Farm Bureau Federation in 1971 noted the emergence of an opposition farm coalition and said: "But the greatest farm coalition ever assembled was when the American Farm Bureau Federation was founded in 1919." He explained its basis as follows:

"Farm Bureau offered a means whereby producers of every commodity in every area of the country could get together, regardless of their political affiliation, to reconcile their differences, and thereby develop honest-to-goodness farm unity." As for intergroup alliances on the legislative front, Fleming said: "We, in fact, have allies on practically every issue in which we are involved."

Education is another of the many fields in which interest groups have formed alliances to pressure national policy. John Lumley, director of the National Education Association's office of legislation, told Congressional Quarterly in 1970 while discussing proposals to merge the NEA and the AFL-CIO's American Federation of Teachers: "Legislatively, we've worked together through the years through the AFL-CIO."

By 1950 the House Select Committee on Lobbying Activities said in a report: "The lone-wolf pressure group, wanting nothing more from other groups than to be left unmolested, is largely a thing of the past."

Prof. Stephen K. Bailey went so far as to tell the House Committee his conclusion was "that lobbying can be understood only as the reflection of interests shared by shifting coalitions made up by Members of Congress, outside pressures, and executive agencies." He added: "If this is a correct assumption, then it seems to me that your problem is the enormously complicated one of ana-

lyzing the interrelationships among private group interests, Members of Congress, and agency personnel."

Ways of Coalition. In the pursuit of power, the ways of coalition are many. Their workings are sometimes open, easily traced and readily acknowledged by all. At other times, the cooperation is concealed, perhaps detectable mainly through after-the-fact disclosure that participants with seemingly variant interests arrive at the same legislative or executive result by divergent routes or that the same individuals show up in different places wearing different hats.

Some coalitions may be more apparent than real. Rather than indicating strength, they can at times suggest weakness among the separate entities and a lack of unity within the organizations. A frequent practice is the selection of certain top officers of various organizations to head a cluster of groups under a separate name.

Such a coalition may in fact be composed of a comparative handful of individuals and may operate under its own internal governing structure and bylaws which may or may not conform with those of the cooperating groups. Their responsible posts put coalition leaders in a position to draw upon the financial and educational resources, prestige and pressures mechanisms of individual groups to exert pressure on public officials.

In the case of organizations with millions of members, real internal unity would suggest the strong possibility of remedies at the polls and less necessity for combined pressure activities. This aspect sometimes prompts opponents in Congress to refer to coalitions of leaders as "generals without troops." This naturally draws stout rebuttals, and there are strong incentives for alliances from group leaders' viewpoint.

Two fairly lasting coalitions which have operated from time to time since the 1930s have been a coalition of northern liberals, civil rights and labor organizations opposed on some issues by a coalition of Republicans and southern conservatives. This has been demonstrated in pressure groups as in Congress. The clash between the two forces came into evidence in the battles over Senate confirmation of Supreme Court nominees Clement F. Haynsworth Jr. and G. Harrold Carswell, both rejected. *(Labor-civil rights coalition, p. 57)*

A leading advocate of coalition action is Bayard Rustin, an anti-war activist since World War II and a leading strategist of the civil rights and anti-poverty movements. Rustin told the AFL-CIO 1969 convention that alliances of the kind formed in the Haynsworth battle "are not made in the way in which one marries his wife. Alliances are not made out of affection. Alliances are made out of mutual interest, and although there will be difficult times for us, we must remember that this mutual interest does in fact exist and we must hold on to it.... Let us build upon that which unites us."

Cooperative efforts to influence American government are by no means limited to combinations among domestic interest groups. Nelson A. Stitt, director of the United States-Japan Trade Council financed primarily by the Japanese government, told Congressional Quarterly in 1971 when U.S. trade policy was at issue:

"One of the glories of this country is that it is an open society, affording a hearing to all interests, domestic and foreign. Where their interests coincide, domestic and foreign groups naturally make common cause."

COMMON CAUSE

National Urban Coalition Expands Political Base

"At the heart of everything we are trying to do is the principle of coalition.... We are not just another organization. We're unique, and our uniqueness lies in the fact that we bring together elements of American life that do not normally collaborate in the solution of public problems."
— *John W. Gardner*

Leaders of the National Urban Coalition and its lobby arm began a drive in August 1970 to build a broad-based political and lobbying organization across political party lines. The move followed by less than four months a merger of the original Urban Coalition and Urban America Inc. to form what then became the National Urban Coalition.

Backers hailed the muscle-building campaign as more successful than expected. From the beginning, success indicated the probability of further controversy on the national scene. The Urban Coalition, through its related Urban Coalition Action Council, had been in the thick of some of the most heated Congressional pressure battles of 1969-70. Some participants were prominent in civil rights and anti-poverty struggles throughout the 1960s.

Statements by the coalition's chief spokesman took on an increasingly critical tone in 1970 and, along with the organization's goals, presaged other conflicts on varied fronts across the nation. Counter-attacks were not long in coming.

In March 1971 Jack T. Conway, administrative assistant from 1946-61 to the late Walter P. Reuther, president of the United Auto Workers, was named president and chief operating officer.

There was published speculation, expectable under the circumstances, that the coalition's buildup action could develop into a third party or candidate-promoting movement. Such speculation drew only partial denials at first, and the speculation persisted.

New Organization

While a separate entity named Common Cause was incorporated for the operation to raise membership and funds, a coalition spokesman told Congressional Quarterly at the time that "it really isn't a new organization. It is an extension of the one that exists." And John W. Gardner, chairman and "chief executive" of Common Cause, said in 1971 it was "a direct outgrowth of an earlier group known as the Urban Coalition Action Council."

The new group operated initially under the same executive committee that governed both the National Urban Coalition and the Urban Coalition Action Council. A few changes were made subsequently. *(See below.)*

That executive committee, which listed 21 members and was part of a 75-member steering committee, included the presidents of the AFL-CIO, United Auto Workers and National Council of Churches and executives of the National Urban League and the Leadership Conference on Civil Rights—itself a coalition of more than 100 groups.

Urban Coalition Leaders

Following is a list of Urban Coalition leaders as of August 1970:

Chairman: John W. Gardner, former president of Carnegie Corporation of New York; Secretary of Health, Education and Welfare (1965-68).

Cochairmen: Andrew Heiskell, chairman of the board, Time Inc., New York City; A. Philip Randolph, international president emeritus, Brotherhood of Sleeping Car Porters (AFL-CIO), New York City; Whitney M. Young Jr., executive director, National Urban League, New York City; William D. Eberle, president, American Standard Inc., New York City.

Executive Committee: Joseph H. Allen, president, McGraw-Hill Publications, New York City; Arnold Aronson, secretary, Leadership Conference on Civil Rights, New York City; Jordan C. Band, chairman, National Jewish Community Relations Advisory Council, Cleveland, Ohio; Joseph J. Bernal, state senator, San Antonio, Texas.

Frederick J. Close, chairman of the board, Aluminum Company of America, Pittsburgh; Eberle; the Rev. George H. Guilfoyle, bishop of Camden, N.J.; Mrs. Patricia R. Harris, firm of Strasser, Spiegelberg, Fried, Frank, and Kampelman, Washington, D.C.; Richard G. Hatcher, mayor of Gary, Ind.; Heiskell; Vivian W. Henderson, president, Clark College, Atlanta, Ga.

Vernon Jordan, executive director, United Negro College Fund; John V. Lindsay, mayor, New York City; George Meany, president, AFL-CIO, Washington, D.C.; Martin Meyerson, president, University of Pennsylvania; J. Irwin Miller, chairman of the board, Cummins Engine Company, Columbus, Ind.

Randolph; James H. J. Tate, mayor, Philadelphia; Mrs. Theodore O. Wedel, president, National Council of Churches, New York City; Leonard Woodcock, president, United Auto Workers, Detroit, Mich.; and Young.

Others listed by the coalition as on the executive committee included the mayors of New York City, Philadelphia and Gary, Ind., and several business figures, among them the board chairman of the Aluminum Company of America. The larger steering committee included the board chairmen of American Telephone and Telegraph Company, General Motors Corporation and Ford Motor Company and the presidents of Pepsico Inc. and Prudential Insurance Company of America.

The coalition's steering committee included leaders of more than half of the 10 organizations which sponsored the 1963 "March on Washington for Jobs and

Freedom," the largest public demonstration ever held to that time in the nation's capital and a major stepping stone toward the buildup of massive pressure which overcame a Senate filibuster and produced the eventual enactment of the Civil Rights Act of 1964. Among those on the steering committee were the executive directors of the Southern Christian Leadership Conference and the National Association for the Advancement of Colored People.

A. Philip Randolph, director of the 1963 march and honorary chairman of the White House Conference "To Fulfill These Rights" held June 1-2, 1966, was a founder and cochairman of the coalition. Also active was socialist Bayard Rustin who served as Randolph's deputy in organizing the 1963 demonstration. Rustin is executive director of the A. Philip Randolph Institute, which in 1966 published a "Freedom Budget" recommending a guaranteed annual income and greatly increased spending for domestic purposes in the decade ahead.

The leadership of the coalition included a number of former officials in the Executive Branch of the Government. The top official (John W. Gardner) and the chief executive officer (Peter Libassi) were the Secretary of Health, Education and Welfare (HEW) under President Johnson and his assistant in charge of civil rights, respectively, at the time the original Urban Coalition was founded.

Goals and Controversy

Gardner, chairman of the National Urban Coalition and of the Urban Coalition Action Council, announced in July 1970 a recruiting drive to develop what some supporters thereafter called a national citizens' lobby. The expressed aim: to recruit 100,000 dues-paying members at first, perhaps as many as 400,000 eventually. Organizations represented by their presidents on the coalition's executive committee alone claimed memberships of more than 50 million.

An official said the new organization would be established, as was the Action Council, on a tax exempt basis but with contributions not tax deductible. The National Urban Coalition itself is tax exempt with contributions deductible for Federal income purposes.

Gardner set out to raise $500,000 from private sources, the names of which were not made public.

Common Cause had two main goals, its proponents said: to change political structures so they would be more responsive to social needs and to produce a major reordering of national priorities. The former occupied the attention of Urban America Inc.; the latter was a primary goal of the Urban Coalition from the beginning.

"Our political and governmental processes have grown so unresponsive, so ill-designed for contemporary purposes, that they waste the taxpayers' money, mangle good programs and smother every good man who gets into the system," Gardner said.

Both major goals meant controversy. While plans were described as still evolving, energetic attempts to achieve the avowed purposes would inevitably involve collisions not only with the status quo but with defenders of established institutions and vested interests.

The coalition threw its weight behind the recommendations of two Presidential commissions which

studied the background of violent outbreaks in the United States and proposed costly changes and revamping of national priorities. Gardner held a press conference Feb. 4, 1970, with Chairman Milton S. Eisenhower of the National Commission on the Causes and Prevention of Violence to announce that the Urban Coalition Action Council would work to get the commission's proposals carried out.

Gardner proposed further reduction in defense spending, retention of the remaining 5-percent surtax (which subsequently expired on schedule) and action to increase Federal revenues, among other things. The coalition was among organizations which published and distributed copies of the violence commission's final report which was originally issued Dec. 12, 1969. The commission's report recommended that at least $20-billion a year be committed to solving social problems.

In cooperation with Urban America Inc., the coalition on Feb. 27, 1969, issued an updated version of the report a year earlier of the National Advisory Commission on Civil Disorders, headed by former Illinois Gov. Otto Kerner (D). The Kerner commission's report said, "Our nation is moving toward two societies, one black, one white—separate and unequal." The coalition's report, prepared by some of the same individuals, said the nation was "a year closer to two societies—black and white, increasingly separate and scarcely less unequal."

Nicholas deB. Katzenbach, former Attorney General who was chairman of the President's Commission on Law Enforcement and Administration of Justice, was named in 1969 to head the Urban Coalition's task force on law and government. The commission, commonly known as the President's Crime Commission, made broad recommendations in 1967 for changes in the nation's criminal justice and law enforcement systems, some of which have been implemented.

All told, the findings of the various study commissions may be cited to support the view expressed by Gardner to the National Governors Conference July 22, 1968, that "a great deal more" Federal spending was needed to cure city problems. Gardner asked the Governors to reject what he called "the rhetoric of public men who offer big ideas with small price tags...or no price tags at all." Many of the Governors present disputed some of his statements. Nor were the commissions' proposals universally accepted.

Controversy was new neither to Gardner nor to the coalition which came into existence amid serious city rioting in 1967 and was immersed in political issues thereafter. Nor was it new to Mayor John V. Lindsay of New York City, a key figure in forming the original Urban Coalition and described in a 1970 Urban America publication as one of the "key architects" of the movement toward a new political coalition.

After failing in a bid for the Republican nomination for re-election in 1969, Lindsay won another term as mayor as the candidate of the established state Liberal party in New York and his new Independent party. Lindsay, a former U.S. Representative (R N.Y. 1959-65), generally aligned himself with the liberal wing of the Republican membership in Congress. Americans for Democratic Action rated him above 70 percent over-all.

Gardner, a Republican who served in the Cabinet of a Democratic President, said solutions to the nation's problems require "money, guts and leadership."

His many public statements as spokesman for the coalition made clear that he favored an ousting of what he might call the "old guard" from leadership in political offices and in major pressure groups as well.

In 1970, Gardner tangled increasingly with the Nixon Administration. He advocated sweeping changes in Congressional procedures which, if adopted, would dislodge many Members from long-held sources of power. Gardner rapped members of at least two professions —health and his own field of education—as frequently serving as "obstacles to change rather than promoters of it."

Expansion and Dissension

The expansion drive was the latest move in a brief but turbulent career for a potent pressure group which had become the principal national nonprofit coalition dedicated to coping with urban problems.

Internal dissension hit the coalition in 1969-70, resulting in some departures and new faces. Troubles plagued its local coalitions, including the largest in New York City, and those in Washington, D.C., Boston and Newark, N.J. The weakening effects of the internal difficulties were attributed by some as a major factor behind both the merger earlier in 1970 and the decision to seek a wider power base.

Meanwhile, the Action Council—the coalition's lobbying branch—had participated separately or within larger coalitions such as the Emergency Committee for Full Funding of Education Programs in some of the major lobby confrontations during the Nixon Administration.

Gardner announced formation of the National Urban Coalition March 22, 1970, through the merger of the Urban Coalition and Urban America Inc. Urban America was formed in January 1965 by the late Stephen Currier as a continuation of the American Planning and Civic Association. A few months later, it merged with a group called Action Inc. Urban America's main programs thereafter were in the areas of urban information, technical assistance in housing, and urban design and planning, the National Urban Coalition says. William K. Slayton resigned in 1969 as president of Urban America, becoming president of the American Institute of Architects Dec. 1, 1969. His successor, William D. Eberle, president of American Standard Inc., New York City, was formerly active in Republican politics in Idaho.

The Urban Coalition came into existence July 31, 1967, when riots rocked some U.S. cities. An "emergency convocation" of 22 persons was sponsored by New York's Mayor Lindsay and Pittsburgh's Mayor Joseph M. Barr, then president of the United States Conference of Mayors. Lindsay had been appointed a few days earlier by President Johnson as vice chairman of the Special Advisory Commission on Civil Disorders to investigate the causes of urban riots.

Lindsay said in a keynote speech that the nation's foreign commitments "should not be allowed to weaken our resolve at home." He said if any commitments abroad were "blocking a vigorous effort" to solve city problems, "those commitments should be reassessed." The United States was deeply involved in the Vietnam War.

Original leaders in addition to Mayors Lindsay and Barr included Andrew Heiskell, chairman of the board at Time Inc., and A. Philip Randolph, president of the

Brotherhood of Sleeping Car Porters (AFL-CIO). Ten of the original 22 founders of the Urban Coalition were still on the steering committee in 1970.

Gardner joined the Carnegie Corporation of New York in 1946 and held various posts with it the next 19 years. He was president of the corporation and the Carnegie Foundation for the Advancement of Teaching from 1955 to July 27, 1965, when he was appointed Secretary of Health, Education and Welfare by President Johnson. Gardner was in the Cabinet when the Urban Coalition was formed in 1967. Libassi was his special assistant and Director of the Office of Civil Rights in the HEW Department.

After leaving the Administration in January 1968, Gardner became chairman of the Urban Coalition. Libassi served a year as vice president in charge of the coalition's field staff, then in 1969 was named by Gardner as executive vice president for the coalition, and subsequently for the National Urban Coalition.

Personnel Changes. Despite earlier denials that Gardner would resign as chairman of the National Urban Coalition, he stepped out in September 1970 and was described as confining his activities thereafter to the chairmanship of Common Cause. Sol M. Linowitz, former U.S. ambassador to the Organization of American States (1966-69), was announced Sept. 29, 1970, as the new chairman of the coalition in Gardner's place.

Linowitz, a senior partner in the law firm of Coudert-Brothers, was chairman and general counsel of the Xerox Corporation (1955-66). In 1970 he was chairman of the national council of the Foreign Policy Association.

Libassi left at the same time. His place was taken on Oct. 8, 1970, by Jack Hood Vaughn, former director of the Peace Corps who had resigned June 10, 1970, as U.S. ambassador to Colombia. Vaughn became president and chief executive officer of the National Urban Coalition.

With the success of its initial membership drive, Common Cause also made changes. Gardner said the group topped the 100,000-member mark on Feb. 19, 1971, six months ahead of schedule. Gardner announced Conway's appointment as president and chief of day-to-day operations on March 2, 1971. Gardner himself continued as chairman and chief executive.

Like Gardner, Conway had served in Federal office. In the 1960s after leaving the United Auto Workers, he was deputy administrator of the Housing and Home Finance Agency and deputy director of the Office of Economic Opportunity. He also served as executive director of the AFL-CIO's Industrial Union Department.

From December 1968 until his appointment to Common Cause he was president of the Center for Community Change, a nonprofit anti-poverty organization formed with a $3.5-million Ford Foundation grant through merger of the former Citizens Crusade Against Poverty (headed by Reuther), the Citizens Advocate Center and the Social Development Corporation—headed by Conway.

Harold Willens, Los Angeles businessman and co-founder and national co-chairman of Business Executives Move for Vietnam Peace, was appointed a special adviser to Gardner in spring 1971.

"There is nothing altruistic about working for nonviolent change of revolutionary proportion; upon such change depends survival of those I care about most, as well as survival of free enterprise democracy," Willens

Common Cause Leaders

Chairman: John W. Gardner.

President: Jack T. Conway, former administrative assistant to Walter P. Reuther, president of United Auto Workers (1946-61).

Executive Director: Lowell R. Beck.

Executive Committee: Joseph H. Allen, president, McGraw-Hill Publications, New York City; Albert E. Arent, member of the law firm Arent, Fox, Kintner, Plotkin & Kahn; Arnold Aronson, secretary, Leadership Conference on Civil Rights, New York City; Mrs. Bruce B. Benson, president, League of Women Voters of the United States; Joseph J. Bernal, state senator, San Antonio, Texas.

William D. Eberle, president, American Standard Inc., New York City; Gardner; the Rev. George H. Guilfoyle, bishop of Camden, N.J.; Richard G. Hatcher, mayor of Gary, Ind.; Andrew Heiskell, chairman of the board, Time Inc., New York City; Vivian W. Henderson, president, Clark College, Atlanta, Ga.; Mrs. Aileen C. Hernandez, western regional director, National Committee Against Discrimination in Housing.

Vernon E. Jordan Jr., executive director, United Negro College Fund Inc.; John V. Lindsay, mayor, New York City; Martin Meyerson, president, University of Pennsylvania; Bayard Rustin, executive director, A. Philip Randolph Institute; James H. J. Tate, mayor, Philadelphia; Mrs. Theodore O. Wedel, president, National Council of Churches, New York City; Leonard Woodcock, president, United Auto Workers, Detroit, Mich.

Policy Council (in addition to those above): Julian Bond, state representative, Georgia; James E. Cheek, president, Howard University; Kenneth B. Clark, president, Metropolitan Applied Research Center; Edwin D. Etherington, Old Lyme, Conn.

Arthur S. Flemming, president, Macalester College, Minnesota (former Secretary of HEW Department); Hector P. Garcia, Corpus Christi, Texas; Ernest Green, director, Joint Apprenticeship Program; Mrs. Fred (Patricia) R. Harris, president, Americans for Indian Opportunity, and wife of the Senator; Miss Dorothy I. Height, president, National Council of Negro Women Inc.

Howard W. Johnson, president, Massachusetts Institute of Technology; Joseph D. Keenan, international secretary, International Brotherhood of Electrical Workers; Donald S. MacNaughton, chairman and chief executive officer, Prudential Insurance Company of America; James W. Rouse, president, The Rouse Company; Henry Santiestevan, Phoenix, husband of *ADA World* editor.

Rabbi Solomon J. Sharfman, president, Synagogue Council of America; Mark R. Shedd, superintendent of schools, Philadelphia; Asa T. Spaulding, Durham, N.C.; Carl B. Stokes, mayor, Cleveland; Martin Stone, president, Monogram Industries Inc.; John Wheeler, president, Southern Regional Council, and Andrew J. Young Jr., executive director, Community Relations Commission, Atlanta, Ga. *(List announced by Common Cause in March 1971.)*

said in a statement published by Common Cause in March 1971.

Policymakers. "Common Cause is governed by a Policy Council of 40 men and women and an Executive Committee of 19," Gardner said in March 1971. Of the 19 members of the executive committee, 15 had been on the executive committee of the National Urban Coalition and its Action Council seven months earlier. Among those who had since resigned were the AFL-CIO's George Meany and Frederick J. Close of the Aluminum Company of America. A. Philip Randolph had resigned for health reasons, but Bayard Rustin of the A. Philip Randolph Institute was added to the committee. The larger Policy Council, Gardner said, was inherited from the Urban Coalition Action Council and was to be expanded further.

Common Cause lobbyists included Peter Edelman, legislative assistant to the late Sen. Robert F. Kennedy (D N.Y. 1965-68) and Morton H. Halperin, senior fellow with Brookings Institution.

Activities

Seniority. Common Cause's first major battle was an attempt to change the Congressional seniority system. Gardner was leadoff witness at independent hearings in January 1971 by Senators Fred R. Harris (D Okla.) and Charles McC. Mathias Jr. (R Md.) on their proposals to change the system.

Campaign Spending. The organization filed suit in January 1971 in U.S. District Court against the Republican and Democratic National Committees and the Conservative Party, New York, on grounds of bringing campaign spending practices in line with existing law.

Voting Restrictions. Gardner announced a campaign in February 1971 to eliminate or reduce state and local restrictions on voter registration and voting participation. It was directed by Mrs. Anne Wexler of Connecticut and focused on residency and registration requirements.

End the War. Common Cause announced a national lobbying campaign on Feb. 23, 1971, to persuade Congress to "legislate an end to the war." Gardner said Congress should "reassert its role" and fix a date for complete withdrawal from Indochina.

Other issues in which the lobby was involved included ratification of the 18-year-old vote, environmental and lobbying law matters.

Republican Criticism

The Republican National Committee's publication *Monday* in April 1971 ran two articles saying Common Cause and Gardner were "purveyors of the radical Democrat line." The publication challenged the group's claim to nonpartisanship. It said it had asked Common Cause and Americans for Democratic Action about statements there were no differences between them. "Neither could think of one major issue on which the other differed substantially," it said.

Gardner called the account "shamelessly selective in its presentation of evidence," naming Democrats on the staff but not Republicans. He said it ignored Common Cause's support of President Nixon's family assistance plan, minority employment plan and Federal reorganization program.

LABOR-CIVIL RIGHTS

Longstanding Coalition Strained by Demand for Jobs

The long established and politically effective labor-civil rights coalition is being strained by increasing Negro demands for union jobs.

Antagonism grew in 1969 as organized labor supported a Congressional attempt to defeat the Administration's "Philadelphia Plan," a proposal to provide jobs for Negroes on Federal construction projects. *(Box p. 58)*

Labor has worked to weaken legislation that would give the Equal Employment Opportunity Commission enforcement powers.

Much of the pressure on union leaders comes from rank-and-file white workers who fear that such moves as the Philadelphia Plan will cost them jobs.

Charges of race bias have prompted black workers in some industries to organize militant labor groups, such as in the automobile industry. Tactics of these groups have included disruption of production for short periods and isolated reports of sabotage.

Rising unemployment and bitter fights over new contracts have exacerbated the situation for white workers who see themselves paying for social change at the cost of personal and family security.

Clarence Mitchell, Washington lobbyist and director of the National Association for the Advancement of Colored People (NAACP), complained of stories that came from the White House after the Senate's attempt to kill the Philadelphia Plan.

Mitchell said the Administration intimated that civil rights leaders were sitting on the sidelines while labor lobbyists tried to kill the plan. On Dec. 23, 1969, Mitchell said it was a "calculated attempt coming right from the President's desk to break up the coalition between Negroes and labor unions. Most of the social progress in this country has resulted from this alliance."

Another NAACP official, labor specialist Herbert Hill, also criticized the Administration for a "reversal of policy" aimed at destroying the Philadelphia Plan. "The Nixon Administration has again and again demonstrated that it clearly has no intention of fulfilling its legal obligations," Hill said in June, 1970. "In fact, it is a party to the continued violation of the law."

Background

When the American Federation of Labor was founded in 1886, it held to a policy of nondiscrimination against Negro workers. But it believed that the growth of independent trade unionism should be based on craft autonomy rather than centralized control. Each of the federation's constituent unions had its own governing body and determined its own policies.

Many locals began to back away from the federation's nondiscrimination policy in the mid-1890s, a period when racial segregation was becoming institutionalized in many sectors of American life. At the same time, the federation decided it would grant charters to all-Negro unions, partly to minimize the possibility that Negroes would be used as strikebreakers.

Restrictive membership practices and strict union control over certain skilled jobs worked to exclude Negroes from the ranks of organized labor beyond the end of World War I. A. Philip Randolph, the Negro organizer and leader of the Sleeping Car Porters, argued as early as 1919 that the structure of craft unionism was discriminatory. "The present American Federation of Labor is the most wicked machine for propagation of race prejudice in the country," he said.

With the Depression and the coming of the Roosevelt era in the 1930s, political influence of black workers began to increase. Trade unionists determined to unionize the mass-production industries realized that they could not succeed without winning the support of black workers. The Congress of Industrial Organizations, formed in 1938, made overt attempts, with some success, to win black support during World War II.

President Franklin D. Roosevelt realized the political benefits that would accrue to the Democratic party with an amalgamation of black and white workers. He conveyed a sense of commitment to the cause of Negroes, who had been largely apolitical or Republican after the end of the Civil War.

The Roosevelt coalition of Negroes, blue collar workers, urban residents and the South was cemented by common economic and social goals. It survived through 1955, when the American Federation of Labor merged with the Congress of Industrial Organizations (AFL-CIO). At that time, out of 15 million organized workers, 1.5 million were black.

During the terms of Presidents Kennedy and Johnson in the 1960s, new forces developed in the civil rights movement. Black consciousness and militancy began to emerge within labor organizations, and labor responded by giving political support to such legislation as the Civil Rights Acts of 1964 and 1968 and the Voting Rights Act of 1965.

Charges of racial discrimination in organized labor in recent years have been aimed primarily at craft unions—those consisting of workers possessing a specific skill or a closely related set of skills. Construction trades have come in for particularly harsh criticism. Industrial unions, which attempt to organize all workers in a given industry regardless of their particular skills, generally have escaped charges of racial discrimination.

Erbin Crowell Jr., an editor of *Civil Rights Digest*, wrote in 1969: "The dilemma of labor unions is in many ways the dilemma of the nation: Words don't match deeds; pronouncements by leaders are ignored or even opposed by large numbers of the citizenry; the sham of tokenism is revealed by continuing injustice and prejudice."

(Continued on p. 59)

The Philadelphia Plan: Forcing Organized Labor's Hand

The Nixon Administration instituted in 1969 a program that could provide jobs for thousands of black construction workers on Federal building projects.

Called the "Philadelphia Plan" for the city in which it first went into effect, it set "goals" for the numbers of nonwhite employees to be hired on construction projects financed by Federal funds. The construction trades industry is dominated by largely white unions.

Announcement of the plan seemed to underscore the Administration's movement toward concentrating its civil rights activity in the field of equal job opportunities.

But labor was generally critical of the proposal. AFL-CIO President George Meany, speaking in January 1970—several months after the plan took effect—termed the plan "a concoction and contrivance of a bureaucrat's imagination" to offset criticism of the Administration's civil rights record.

Meany said the plan would not bring a single added black worker into the Philadelphia work force. Contractors would merely switch existing Negro workers from private to Government projects, he said.

Background. The plan was announced June 27, 1969, by former Labor Secretary George P. Shultz and was implemented Sept. 23, 1970, in Philadelphia. Under the plan, contractors working on Federally assisted projects would be required to set specific, contractual goals within the Federal guidelines for hiring members of minority groups. The Labor Department intended to make the plan a model for Federal construction projects throughout the country.

Affected were six skilled construction crafts—ironworkers, steamfitters, sheetmetal workers, electrical workers, elevator construction workers and plumbers and pipefitters. Employers would be expected to demonstrate "good faith efforts" at meeting minority levels ranging from 4 percent in 1969 to 26 percent in 1973.

Mandatory guidelines were attacked by both labor and Congressional spokesmen as a "non-negotiable quota system" that would violate the Civil Rights Act of 1964 by setting racial proportions. An opinion to that effect was given Aug. 5, 1969, by Comptroller General Elmer B. Staats, who worked for Congress, not the Executive Branch. But Attorney General John N. Mitchell issued a Justice Department ruling Sept. 22, 1969, which said that nothing in the plan violated the 1964 Act.

G. C. Haggerty, president of the construction and building trades department of the AFL-CIO, speaking Sept. 23, 1969, for the federation, said, "We are 100 percent opposed to a quota system, whether it be called the Philadelphia Plan or whatever."

Congressional Resistance. An attempt was made in the Senate in December 1969 by the Senate Appropriations Committee to render the Philadelphia Plan ineffective. An amendment to the 1970 supplemental appropriations bill supported the Comptroller General's ruling against the plan, and would have forbade use of any Federal funds as direct aid or through contracts or agreements which the Comptroller General "holds to be in contravention of any Federal statute." Leaders in the fight for the amendment were Senators Paul J. Fannin (R Ariz.), Roman L. Hruska (R Neb.) and Sam J. Ervin Jr. (D N.C.). The Senate approved the measure Dec. 18, 1969. However, the House deleted the Philadelphia Plan amendment Dec. 22, 1969, when it accepted the conference report. The Senate agreed to the House action.

Extension of Plan. The Department of Labor announced Feb. 9, 1970, that the Philadelphia Plan concept would be extended to 18 other cities across the nation. A "Washington Plan" for the District of Columbia and Maryland and Virginia suburban areas was announced June 1, 1970.

Labor Secretary James D. Hodgson July 9, 1970, warned that Federal quotas could be extended to 73 additional cities if more jobs for Negroes were not opened in the construction trades. Hodgson said "There has been too much of a lag in this work and the big push is on."

"Hometown Solutions." Hodgson has attempted to put "good faith effort" on the part of contractors, unions and minority groups to use in finding "hometown solutions"—voluntary, area-wide agreements on labor disputes. He emphasized that the "hometown" program was developed in response to requests for assistance from numerous cities.

"The Labor Department intends to give metropolitan areas every opportunity and assistance to work out agreements because experience shows that they provide broader employment opportunities than imposed solutions which are limited to Federal Government contractors," Hodgson said July 9, 1970.

"Where an area-wide agreement is not possible, the Labor Department will continue its policy of imposing solutions," he said.

Of the 93 target cities, however, only 13 had produced voluntary plans by December, 1970, and even in those cities results were doubtful. Implementation of hiring plans in Pittsburgh and St. Louis had been repeatedly delayed. In Chicago, where the plan called for the immediate entry of 1,000 blacks into craft unions, only 75 were admitted after eight months, the U.S. Civil Rights Commission reported.

Future of Plan. Many civil rights activists saw the Philadelphia Plan and similar projects in other cities as the chief hope for civil rights progress under the Nixon Administration.

But *The Wall Street Journal* Dec. 3, 1970, cited criticism of labor union tactics allegedly used to subvert the plan. A typical ploy, said critics, was to shuffle Negro workers on privately financed projects to Federal ones, without actually hiring any new blacks.

Even Administration spokesmen expressed dissatisfaction with progress under the plan. Arthur Fletcher, Assistant Secretary of Labor, said, "The parties involved haven't been putting out a 100 percent effort to make it work." But other officials, including John Wilks, director of the Office of Federal Contract Compliance, said more time was needed to allow the plan to take effect.

EEOC: A Legislative Profile

Title VII of the Civil Rights Act of 1964 set up a five-member Equal Employment Opportunity Commission (EEOC) to investigate charges of employment discrimination based on race, color, religion or national origin. However, the Act gave the EEOC no enforcement powers; it vested the agency only with authority to conciliate disputes arising under Title VII and EEOC guidelines.

Each year since the EEOC was set up, bills have been introduced in Congress to provide it with enforcement powers, to allow it to initiate lawsuits, to permit it to issue cease-and-desist orders to recalcitrant employers and to order the hiring or reinstatement of aggrieved workers. These measures were backed by President Johnson in 1966, 1967 and 1968 but were not enacted. One such bill passed the House but died in the Senate in 1966; another was reported in the Senate in 1968, but received no further action.

In April 1969, Clifford L. Alexander Jr., the commission's chairman, resigned, charging that lack of support by the Nixon Administration crippled the EEOC. The late Sen. Everett McKinley Dirksen (R Ill. 1951-69) said April 29, 1969, that President Nixon planned to expand the powers of the EEOC to make it a quasi-judicial agency similar to the National Labor Relations Board.

S 2453 was introduced June 19, 1969, by Harrison A. Williams Jr. (D N.J.), chairman of the Labor Subcommittee of the Senate Labor and Public Welfare Committee, and 34 other Senators. S 2453 would expand the coverage of Title VII of the 1964 Act, authorize the EEOC to issue cease-and-desist orders, and transfer to the EEOC—from the Civil Service Commission—the responsibility for supervising the Federal equal employment program.

The Nixon Administration opposed S 2453, and proposed an alternative bill (S 2806) which would authorize the EEOC to bring charges against recalcitrant employers in Federal district courts. William H. Brown III, EEOC chairman, and other proponents of the Administration bill, said it would provide for swifter settlement of disputes than would the cease-and-desist proposal.

The AFL-CIO gave mild support to S 2453 in hearings on the bill in 1969. However, in September 1970, passage of the measure was jeopardized when organized labor threatened to withdraw its support. A spokesman for the AFL-CIO described labor's two objections to the bill on Sept. 23, 1970.

• Unions opposed a provision that would allow payment of legal fees for indigent persons filing complaints to the EEOC and would grant a complainant the right to file a court suit with such legal help, even though the commission had found that his case had no merit.

• Labor wanted the final bill to include a provision transferring the Office of Federal Contract Compliance from the Department of Labor to the EEOC, on the ground that such authority should come under a single agency responsible for civil rights enforcement.

Labor leaders argued that consolidation of all anti-discrimination programs in one agency would result in more efficient administration. Civil rights spokesmen suspected that organized labor—particularly the building trades—was intent on weakening the Labor Department's Philadelphia Plan. In the end, the AFL-CIO could find no pro-labor Senator willing to offer its amendments.

The Senate passed S 2453 Oct. 1, 1970, by a 47-24 vote, with most of the opposition coming from southern Senators. Approval of the bill marked the first time in three attempts that the Senate had acted favorably on a bill to strengthen the EEOC.

The House, which had approved a similar bill in 1966, was hampered by the Rules Committee's reluctance to report the House measure (HR 17555) to the floor. Augustus F. Hawkins (D Calif.), who introduced the bill, said Nov. 19, 1970, he would get up a discharge petition to force the Committee to release the bill.

Although labor's position on the bill appeared to put a crack in the labor-black alliance, both the NAACP's Mitchell and the AFL-CIO's chief lobbyist, Andrew J. Biemiller, said the disagreement was not a split, but a misunderstanding. Nevertheless, a law to strengthen the EEOC did not pass the 91st Congress.

Negroes, Labor and the Administration

Since it came into office, the Nixon Administration has been accused of fomenting a breakup of the political bond between white and black workers.

Herbert Hill, a civil rights labor specialist with the NAACP, June 29, 1970, accused the Nixon Administration of destroying the Philadelphia Plan for curbing job discrimination as a "payoff to the building trades' unions for their support of the war in Indochina." He said the Federal Government had abandoned "any pretense of enforcing the Federal guidelines" against job discrimination on Government construction contracts.

NAACP spokesman Mitchell Nov. 19, 1970, charged that "various emissaries from the White House went out during the campaign and tried to blame unions for black unemployment." Mitchell said the Administration placed the blame of job discrimination on labor organizations "when in fact unions control very few jobs. The heat also should be put on management, on the employer."

Rep. Hawkins told Congressional Quarterly the Administration's economic policies were pitting black workers against whites. "The same Administration that promises jobs for Negroes is cutting back on jobs for everybody," he said.

"Nixon's people are forcing employers to lay off workers and then telling them to put a certain quota of blacks into those vacancies. It is a strategy designed to increase friction between labor and Negroes," Hawkins said.

A central figure in the Administration's dealing with blacks and labor is Arthur A. Fletcher, Assistant Secretary for wage and labor standards in the Department of Labor. Fletcher, 45, a Negro and former professional football player, July 30 criticized both unions and civil rights groups for failing to pressure Congress to provide funds for enforcement of equal job opportunity legislation.

"Unions don't want equal employment enforced," he said, "and civil rights groups often fail to follow up their programs in Congress." Fletcher was an active campaigner for Republican candidates in the 1970 Congressional elections.

On Sept. 24, 1970, Fletcher made his strongest attacks on labor unions in testimony before the House

Armed Services Subcommittee on Defense Aspects of Equal Opportunity Programs. He accused unions of using Congressional influence to perpetuate segregation in organized labor.

"I have found that the labor unions have been able to jawbone on civil rights for so long and have been able to come to the Congress and line up with the civil rights organizations and promote the package of civil rights legislation that they have felt they were above and beyond actually getting busy and complying themselves," Fletcher told the Subcommittee. "The moment of truth has finally arrived for the labor unions and especially the construction unions."

Fletcher said unions had been uncooperative in bringing nonwhites into locals and in dealing with Negro problems in collective bargaining agreements.

"Unions feel they have a lot of friends on the hill," he said. "They put a lot of money into Congressional campaigns, and consequently they have the ability at least to get into the door and persuade. Labor is playing all these cards before they start complying."

Mitchell believes that Fletcher placed too much blame on the unions and not enough on the employers. "An employer—if he has guts enough and sufficient respect for the law—can end job discrimination at the hiring gate," Mitchell said.

The NAACP lobbyist believes that the strife between labor and blacks is concentrated at the local level. "We're as close as ever as far as work on the national level is concerned. We've never had a disagreement that prevented joint action on a bill."

Political Implications

Political analysts have predicted that rising Negro militancy eventually will work to the disadvantage of the Democratic party. Samuel Lubell, a political scientist, wrote more than a decade ago, "All the elements of the coalition will find themselves caught between rising Negro pressures for more vigorous action and the instinct of many white Democratic voters to go slow...."

Lubell argued that economic self-interest had held Negroes and white workers together in the Democratic coalition, but that prosperity would weaken the ties. This has not happened to any great extent in recent elections. Negroes and white labor voted overwhelmingly for Democratic candidates in 1968 and 1970. Of 23 black candidates for the House in 1970, the AFL-CIO endorsed 15 of which only two were unsuccessful.

Conflicting Negro Viewpoints

Julius Jacobson, writing in *The Negro and the American Labor Movement,* published in 1968, said, "The (Negro-labor) alliance can be protected in one of two contradictory ways: Either pressure can be put on the labor movement to clean its house, to break down its discriminatory policies, and, generally, to make itself worthy of a continuing alliance, or, moving in the opposite direction, one can exert pressure on civil rights militants to cool it for the sake of preserving allies in the labor movement...."

An example of the first alternative is evident in the automobile industry, where militant black auto workers have organized to demand concessions from both unions and management. Marcellius Ivory, a Negro member of the United Automobile Workers' executive board, has acknowledged "a polarization of extremist black and white positions" in the automobile union. "I'm scared of it," he said. "I don't know where the hell it will lead us."

Groups formed in the automobile industry include DRUM (Dodge Revolutionary Union Movement), General Motors' "GRUM," and Chrysler's "ELDRUM." The purpose of the groups is "to break the bonds of white racist control over the lives and destiny of black workers," say leaders. To do this, the radical workers say it will be necessary to "get rid of the racist, tyrannical and unrepresentative UAW as representation for black workers, so that we can deal directly with our main adversary, the white racists, owners of the means of production" and "bring down this exploitative system."

A second method is advocated by Bayard Rustin, a Negro organizer and director of the A. Philip Randolph Institute. He wrote in January 1970 that Negroes should form "interracial alliances" on the basis of class. If a black worker defines the problem as one of poverty, Rustin says, he will be aligned with the white worker against management.

"It is the trade union movement and the Democratic party which offer the greatest leverage to the black struggle," Rustin said. "The trade union movement is essential to the black struggle because it is the only institution in the society capable of organizing the working poor, so many of whom are Negroes. It is only through an organized movement that these workers, who are now condemned to the margin of the economy, can achieve a measure of dignity and economic security."

Rustin and others contend that unions organize workers on the basis of common economic interests, not by virtue of racial affinity. Mitchell believes that labor's legislative program for full employment, housing, urban reconstruction, tax reform, improved health care and expanded educational opportunities is designed specifically to aid whites and blacks in the lower-income and lower-middle-income classes where the potential for racial polarization is most severe.

Outlook

The schism that has appeared in the Negro-labor alliance is small, but the potential for it to become an irreconcilable division remains large. Statements of commitment to the principle of equality in employment, issued often in recent years by officials of the Federal Government and of organized labor, have done relatively little to break down the barriers that keep minority-group members from obtaining their share of skilled, higher-paying union jobs, some critics say.

The primary reason for the gap between principle and performance is that autonomous local craft unions instinctively resist any outside pressure to reform their membership policies. And any effort in Congress to restrict union authority in that field would be opposed by organized labor as a form of "union busting."

The prospect is that conflict between Negroes and unions over membership and jobs will continue. The alliance for larger economic goals and social reform is jeopardized by the situation at the local level.

THE PRESIDENTIAL LOBBY

The Executive Branch: Strongest of

the Many Pressures Focused on Congress

The Executive Branch of the Federal Government has become the most dominant and formidable of the lobby forces affecting Congress, particularly since the advent of the New Deal.

In the face of repeated crises, in overcoming a crippling depression, waging a world war and managing a precarious and complicated postwar peace, the role of the Chief Executive has changed and expanded.

No longer the position of passive leadership typified by the Coolidge, Harding and Hoover administrations, the Presidency since 1933 has demanded forceful leadership. And any President wishing to move the nation has required the cooperation of Congress.

In the opening days of the first session of the 73rd Congress in 1933, Rep. Clinton A. Woodrum (D Va. 1923-45) reminded his Democratic colleagues "that when the *Congressional Record* lies on the desk of Mr. Roosevelt in the morning, he will look over the roll call and from that he will know whether or not the members of his own party were willing to go along with him in his great fight to save the country."

President Roosevelt's mandate from a frightened nation was unprecedented. The swollen Democratic ranks in Congress—there were 150 Democratic freshmen in the House—had created the conditions whereby the Speaker of the House, Henry Thomas Rainey (D Ill. 1903-21, 1923-34), could announce to his troops, much in the manner of a basic training drill sergeant: "We *will* put over Mr. Roosevelt's program!" Few argued.

Thirty-two years later, President Lyndon B. Johnson enjoyed similar circumstances. Only an unusual degree of ticket-splitting in the 1964 Presidential election had saved the Republican Party from near annihilation in races for Congressional and state posts. As it was, Re-

publicans were reduced to their lowest Congressional levels since the first days of the depression.

The result was one of the most productive Congresses in history—the 89th. The scope of the legislation it passed was even more imposing than the number of major new laws. Measures which individually would have crowned the achievements of any Congress were enacted in a seemingly endless stream.

But the 73rd and 89th Congresses were the exceptions. The New Deal soon ran into opposition from powerful interest groups, while the huge Democratic majority in Congress became unwieldy. The formation of the coalition of Republicans and southern Democrats toward the end of the Roosevelt Presidency marked the beginning of organized opposition in Congress to much of the social legislation offered in the subsequent Administrations.

And President Johnson lost ground amid emotional and often ugly debate in the House and Senate over American involvement in Southeast Asia.

Powers of the Presidency

White House staff aides, past and present, charged with maintaining friendly relations between the White House and Capitol Hill, would have it believed that a President's powers in dealing with Congress are limited to presenting the arguments for and against a piece of legislation to the proper Members of the House and Senate, then hoping for the best. The merits eventually will determine the fate of the legislation, they contend, because of public pressure for or against it and the ultimate good sense of Congress. Nevertheless, a President has a number of useful tools at hand other than convincing arguments.

The powers of the President and Congress are inexorably intertwined; each branch needs the other. Congress can appropriate funds, authorize and then audit programs, exert the legislative veto and conduct investigations.

The President's leverage stems from his control of patronage, the national budget (vested in him by Congress in the Budget and Accounting Act of 1921), and the location of Federal grants-in-aid and public works projects; the executive veto and his control of events in formulating and proposing both domestic and foreign policy.

When the Defense Department, for example, must cut back military bases in an economy move, the votes of Senators and Representatives on various issues well may have some bearing on which installations in which states and Congressional districts the Pentagon selects to phase out.

In influencing public opinion, a President's strongest weapons are the prestige of his office, his independent and co-equal status with its own powers and responsibilities and his position in the eyes of the public as the head of government and embodiment of the dignity, majesty and might of the United States. He is the single most important opinion-maker in the country.

Especially in the last decade, the apparatus of "legislative liaison" in the Executive Branch has grown enormously. Aside from the President's personal Congressional relations staff, each agency and department in the Federal Government employs personnel whose sole responsibilities are in dealing with Congress.

The President's political power in his own party, his over-all control of Federal operations and patronage, his power to engage in legislative "logrolling" and even his social contacts with individual Senators and Representatives all are used as pressure tactics.

Executive Lobbying: 1933-71

Of the last six Presidents, four—Truman, Kennedy, Johnson and Nixon—had served in Congress. Roosevelt had been Governor of New York. Eisenhower never held an elected public office.

Throughout the post-World War II period, it was usually the Executive Branch which proposed major new programs in education, welfare and domestic aid—programs which Congress accepted slowly if at all.

Congress' hesitance in initiating new programs was based largely on the committee seniority system and restrictive legislative rules. Committee leaders often were southern Democrats or midwestern Republicans, representing the most rigidly held districts and states. Members of Congress least able to accrue seniority, and thus the least likely to head committees with their great power over legislation, were those from the politically volatile suburbs and city fringe areas where the major new population movements—and many major problems—of the postwar era occurred.

The New Deal. As Members of the House applauded, Rep. John Young Brown (D Ky. 1933-35) set the tenor of President Roosevelt's "100 Days" in an early debate of the first session of the 73rd Congress in 1933.

"Not a solitary one of you on the Democratic side of this House came here on any platform other than the platform of the New Deal," Brown said. "You did not think of that yourself. The President of the United States thought of that. He pledged you to support his program.... I had as soon start a mutiny in the face of a foreign foe as start a mutiny against the program of the President of the United States."

Thus it began. Bills were considered overnight by committees and passed as fast as they could be printed. Floor debate on sweeping measures rarely lasted more than a few hours. Republicans offered minimal opposition, if any, and the President usually ignored them in planning strategy, concentrating instead on tight control of his own party.

Roosevelt was, in effect, the supreme lobbyist with an acute sense of timing. He carefully controlled the plentiful patronage positions an expanding government offered, doling them out on the strict basis of "*quid pro quo.*"

Constantly on the telephone and in meetings with key Members, he generally treated Congress with courtesy and respect. Requests for legislative action were accompanied by well-drafted messages and prototype bills. If the President reached an impasse with Congress over some legislative request, he would seek support from the nation on the radio and Congress soon would feel the heat through the mail.

In time the pace slackened, and the Democratic majority grew increasingly unwieldy. Under the pressure of unmitigating economic trouble, the maze of competing interest groups in the House and Senate stymied much of the Administration's program for reorganization and reform.

After Pearl Harbor, the nation turned its attention away from domestic problems and by the 12th year of Roosevelt's Presidency, the powerful coalition of conservative Republicans and southern Democrats had taken hold.

The Fair Deal. Harry S Truman entered the Presidency enjoying mass popularity and support; polls showed his popularity higher than that of Roosevelt. But in only a matter of months, the conservative coalition—now even meeting in its own caucus—showed its strength in Congress.

Despite the fact that he had been personally popular as a Senator, President Truman lacked Roosevelt's sixth political sense in dealing with Congress.

The House and Senate leaders were not consulted before the President made his strategic moves. Truman sent piles of poorly-prepared proposals to Capitol Hill with little direction as to what should be considered first and last. To the delight of his Congressional opponents, the President's friends in Congress rarely even were asked for assistance. In one year, Mr. Truman's popularity with the electorate cascaded 44 points.

During the 80th Congress, called the "do-nothing" Congress by Truman, the President and the Republican majority usually were at loggerheads over domestic affairs. The most significant piece of domestic legislation, passed over President Truman's veto, was the 1947 Taft-Hartley Act, which outlawed the closed shop, jurisdictional strikes and secondary boycotts.

But in the area of foreign affairs, the President was successful in securing Congressional unanimity, with Sen. Arthur H. Vandenburg (R Mich. 1928-51) leading his once

Nixon Aide MacGregor: "I care about Congress."

Clark MacGregor, President Nixon's counsel for Congressional relations, came to his job in 1971 with 10 years of experience in Congress.

From 1961, when he was elected to represent Minnesota's 3rd Congressional District until 1971, when he retired from the House after being defeated by Hubert H. Humphrey (D Minn.) for the Senate, MacGregor was known as a popular, moderate Republican.

A long-time friend of Richard Nixon, MacGregor was one of his early supporters for the Presidency. In 1968, MacGregor served as Mr. Nixon's Midwest campaign manager.

MacGregor made it clear after he had accepted the job that the Congressional relations staff he had inherited was not to blame for the past frigidity between the White House and Capitol Hill. Instead, he said candidly, the fault lay with some of the President's top aides who never had served in the House or Senate themselves.

Nixon Statement. But only one day after MacGregor had moved into his new quarters in the west wing of the White House near the President's office, Mr. Nixon himself provided an example of the rhetoric that typified Executive-Congressional relations for the first two years of the Nixon Presidency. On that day, Jan. 5, 1971, the President issued a blistering statement criticizing the 91st Congress.

Asked two weeks later what the statement had accomplished, MacGregor replied that it had achieved nothing and that he intended to see that it was not repeated.

Buttons. Shortly thereafter, MacGregor ordered red-white-and-blue buttons saying "I Care About Congress" for White House staffers. Although no aides actually were seen wearing the buttons, the point was made.

"The agonies of late 1969 and 1970" in Executive Branch relations with Congress "are a thing of the past," he told reporters not long after taking office. "My philosophy, which I expressed to the President before I took this job, is that bloody defeats in Congress are not helpful to him or the country. My view is that the best politics for Richard Nixon is success for the legislative program."

MacGregor said he told Mr. Nixon "that I believed I could play a role in increasing the receptivity of Congress to his programs by virtue of my personal friendships with Senators and Representatives of both parties."

Noticeable Impact. MacGregor's impact was quickly noticeable. Senators and Representatives of both parties soon found themselves trooping in and out of the White House in unprecedented numbers for briefings on the President's legislative program. Occasionally, Mr. Nixon would drop in unannounced on meetings MacGregor had scheduled and offer his own comments.

In line with his policy of stressing conciliation rather than confrontation, especially in dealing with fellow Republicans, MacGregor moved to reassure jittery liberal GOP Senators that the Administration had no intention of making Vice President Spiro T. Agnew's purge of Sen. Charles E. Goodell (N.Y.) during the 1970 election a general policy.

For the liberal GOP Senators, MacGregor's reassurances were all the more credible because during his own 1970 campaign for the Senate against Humphrey, MacGregor called for an end to Agnew's attacks on Goodell.

Preparation and Presentation. In an interview with Congressional Quarterly May 17, 1971, MacGregor described his job:

"The old days of Presidential power to offer or withhold from a Congressman some particular project in exchange for his vote are virtually gone," he said.

"My job is legislation, I spend my day—day after day—in the preparation of legislation which includes the President's ideas.... I help to supervise plans whereby key Members of Congress are consulted about the program before it's submitted to Congress."

"I help organize and draft the President's message accompanying the legislation that goes to Congress. I help to plan and organize the presentation of the Administration's position in hearings before Congressional committees by members of the Cabinet and subcabinet."

MacGregor concluded that "my work is related to the presentation, in the best possible form, of the President's legislative program, as opposed to 'back-scratching' or lobbying for votes as such. It's my job to marshal arguments based upon reason and logic."

isolationist party colleagues into a new bipartisan foreign policy with the Democratic Administration. Congress approved both the President's plan for U.S. aid to Greece and Turkey (the Truman Doctrine) and the concept of massive assistance to European nations to assist them in their postwar recovery (the Marshall Plan, named after its author, Secretary of State George C. Marshall).

Although Truman's surprise re-election victory in 1948 returned control of Congress back to the Democrats, the conservative coalition succeeded in frustrating most of the President's domestic proposals.

Eisenhower's Years. During Dwight D. Eisenhower's first Congress, the 83rd, there was a more harmonious relationship between the President and Congress than at any time since World War II. Congress produced few innovations in domestic or foreign policy, nor did it reverse any of the New Deal social measures.

The President's lack of political experience hindered his performance both as a party leader and as chief proponent of his own legislative program. The Democratic leadership cooperated substantially with the President especially in foreign affairs. But in spite of his enormous prestige, Eisenhower was almost unaggressive in pushing his domestic program.

Only in the last two years of his Presidency, after his trusted aide, Sherman Adams, had been forced to leave the White House, did the President exert any leadership on his own.

The New Frontier. Although President John F. Kennedy had himself served in the House for six years and the Senate for eight, relations between his Administration and Congress were far from ideal. The changes in Democratic leadership in both houses, some Congressional apprehension about the use of political power by the "New Frontiersmen" and the enduring power of the conservative coalition all worked to slow down if not wreck large portions of the Kennedy legislative program.

The elevation of Lyndon B. Johnson to the Vice Presidency removed one of the strongest Majority Leaders in Senate history. The same was true in the House with the death of Speaker Sam Rayburn (D Texas 1913-1961). Their successors, Sen. Mike Mansfield (D Mont.) and Rep. John W. McCormack (D Mass. 1928-71), did not exercise as much strong leadership.

Critics of the President complained that although he attempted to keep his relations with Congress smooth and amicable, there was far too much of an "Are you with us or against us?" attitude displayed by his aides on Capitol Hill. Typically, the Congressional setbacks for Mr. Kennedy involved measures which would have transferred greater amounts of authority to the Executive Branch. Of nine executive reorganization plans submitted in 1961 and 1962, for instance, four were rejected.

Compounding Kennedy's problems with a recalcitrant Congress was a long-time feud between the House and Senate which came to a head at the end of the 87th Congress. The disagreement centered on such issues as the House's long-asserted right to be the sole originator of appropriations bills, frequent Senate restoration of funds clipped by the more frugal House Appropriations Committee, the chairmanship of the House-Senate conferences on appropriations bills and even the physical locations of conference meetings. The dispute held up a number of funds bills for months, well beyond the start of the new fiscal year.

The Great Society. Few men have occupied the White House who have understood Congress and its relationship with the Executive Branch better than Lyndon Johnson.

He had skillfully served as his party's Minority Leader (1953-54) and Majority Leader (1955-61) in the Senate and generally was credited with rewriting the rulebook for pushing through legislation. He was appreciated by Republicans for his efforts to secure Democratic votes for the Eisenhower program and by Democrats for his firm leadership of the party in the Senate while the White House was in the hands of the opposition.

As President, Johnson took full advantage of the fresh feeling of cooperation abundant in Congress in the wake of President Kennedy's death and was almost totally successful in clearing the New Frontier legislative program through Congress.

In addition to this break in attitude in Congress, President Johnson seemed to have an unusual sensitivity in dealing with Congress which his predecessor had sometimes lacked. This was largely a matter of knowing when the President's role should be muted, so as not to offend, and sensing when a specially strong Presidential voice and strategy was called for.

In the end, Lyndon Johnson's relations with the Legislative Branch were near the breaking point. The war in Vietnam, which had crept into Congressional debate by

1965, subsequently spoiled the President's plan for his Great Society.

Nixon Years. Richard M. Nixon went into the Presidency with a background of three years as a U.S. Representative (R Calif. 1947-50) and three years as a U.S. Senator (R Calif. 1950-53). Besides that he presided over the Senate for eight years (1953-61) as Vice President.

Mr. Nixon was the first President in more than a century to face throughout his first term a Congress dominated by the opposition party. His Senate spokesman, Minority Leader Hugh Scott (R Pa.), said midway through the term that Congress had "dawdled, postured, delayed" for two years, leading to "confusion and loss of confidence in government" and to "embarrassment" of the Congress. Mr. Nixon himself criticized the 91st Congress for failing to enact some of his major proposals.

Presidential vetoes had contributed to the slow legislative pace. Four of the President's six vetoes were sustained. Two of the four were appropriation bills which had to be rewritten. Congressional Quarterly's annual Boxscore showed Congress approved 32 percent and 46 percent of Mr. Nixon's specific requests in 1969 and 1970.

As time passed, the President's task in dealing with a House and Senate controlled by the other major party was further complicated by the fact that almost all of the half-dozen seriously considered prospects for the Democratic Presidential nomination in 1972 were in Congress. All but one were in the Senate, the springboard into national prominence for Presidents Truman, Kennedy, Johnson and Nixon.

The difficulties this presented became increasingly apparent in clashes between the Republican Administration and Democratic Congress over the two major issues: the Vietnam War and the domestic economy. The gulf also was demonstrated in the Senate's refusal to confirm two of Mr. Nixon's first three Supreme Court nominations.

The Administration's legislative staff was criticized the first two years for alleged failure to perform such basic legislative techniques as keeping accurate head counts and contacting the proper people at the right time. The President's appointment of former Rep. Clark MacGregor (R Minn.) to head his Congressional liaison was taken by some as indicating the importance which Mr. Nixon attached to upgrading the position. *(Box p. 63)*

Outlook

In the late 1960s and early 1970s, officials in the Executive Branch responsible for Congressional liaison had to contend with a feeling prevalent among many Members of Congress that the traditional system of checks and balances between the White House and Capitol Hill had somehow come out of kilter.

Spawned by the debate over U.S. involvement in Indochina and obligations in other areas of the world, and exacerbated by such revelations as the degree to which civilian and military agencies were spying on private citizens, the new attitude provided an additional strain on relations between the Executive Branch and Congress.

Whether or not a resurgence of Congressional authority would ensue remained to be seen, but it was significant that the Presidency, the most formidable lobby in Congress, was being questioned at all.

CASE STUDIES IN LOBBYING

Washington Lobby Employs Many

Methods to Attain Objectives

When the Washington lobby is studied in action, certain patterns frequently recur.

The organizations that make it up and their representatives, often operating at cross-purposes, work toward these goals:

- To enact new laws or to block their passage.
- To change existing laws or to block their change.
- To affect the way laws are administered.
- To replace the Members of Congress who pass the laws—or to maintain them in office.
- To unseat the President and with him the entire hierarchy of the Executive Branch which interprets and enforces the laws—or to support his re-election or the election of a likeminded candidate, by interest group standards.

The members of the Washington lobby well know that on the election of a President, moreover, depends the appointments of scores of Federal judges from the Supreme Court down—all with lifetime tenure and together supplying the decisive factor in determining the validity of actions by the Legislative and Executive Branches.

To achieve these goals, which vary with the groups involved, organized interests resort to the whole range of strategems found in the world of politics.

Pressure Tactics

The methods used to influence the policies of the U.S. Government vary with the interest groups and individuals involved, depending largely on their purposes, resources and political sophistication.

The formation of national policy is an endless process into which a particular interest group may choose to enter at any stage as circumstances and opportunity dictate. Lines are often difficult to draw and much overlapping is found, but the methods fall largely into these categories, as illustrated by the case studies which follow:

Committee Testimony. The starting point for many organizations in their attempt to exercise their constitutional right to petition the Government is appearance at hearings by committees of Congress. A specific group may or may not have had a hand in getting the hearings scheduled, and witnesses need not be registered lobbyists. In the case studies, virtually all major interests availed themselves of this opportunity to place their views on record by personal appearance of spokesmen or by submission of statements.

Administrative Hearings. Organized interests promote their positions on the way laws and regulations should be administered at the many hearings by regulatory agencies and executive departments. In most cases, though spokesmen must identify their interests, they need not be registered as lobbyists. Exceptions provided by Congress are witnesses before the Federal Power Commission, Securities and Exchange Commission and the Maritime Administration. (p. 23)

The scope of this activity was suggested by Robert Dechert, representing the American Bar Association in 1965 Senate hearings. He testified that "in today's complex world it is a very important part of the normal practice of law for a great many attorneys to negotiate expropriation insurance provisions with the Agency for International Development, tax issues with the Treasury Department, labor problems with the Labor Department or National Labor Relations Board, antitrust questions with the Justice Department or Federal Trade Commission, and contract clauses with the Defense Department." Such appearances were common in case studies which follow, including those on drugs, education, shipping, trade and sugar.

Judicial Proceedings. While not generally considered part of the lobbying picture, efforts by organized groups to challenge Acts of Congress or executive actions through the courts are a major factor in the whole process of attempts to influence government. Particularly prominent are activities by the American Civil Liberties Union and Ralph Nader's Center for the Study of Responsive Law. The judicial process played a part in the drug and environmental studies below.

Grassroots Lobbying. Increasingly significant in the conflict of pressures are the continuous efforts of organized interests to enlist support from target sectors of the public in their activities to influence Congress and the Executive Branch. Into this category fall much of the vast outpouring of publications, newsletters, pamphlets and television-radio or platform statements, many of which appeal for letters, telephone calls or personal visits to Members of Congress.

Many kinds of groups do this to varying degrees. Nat S. Rogers, president of the American Bankers Association, said in 1970: "As part of proper lobbying activities we try to keep informed about the names of bankers who are best acquainted with their Congressmen and in turn keep them informed about current legislative activities so they may talk intelligently to their representatives. This is the prerogative of all citizens and no innuendo should leave the impression that it is improper when done by the banking community."

Its importance notwithstanding, grassroots lobbying was not covered by the 1946 Lobbying Act as interpreted by the Supreme Court. Congressional sponsors made it clear they intended such activities to be embraced by legislation covering foreign agents.

Use of grassroots lobbying tactics to influence public opinion was prominent in the education, maritime, trade, farm, supersonic transport and environmental lobbying discussed below.

Coalitions. Often closely related to grassroots pressure campaigns is the combining of forces into temporary or more or less lasting coalitions that seek to bend government to their will through the appearance of overwhelming strength. Coalitions can involve teamwork among domestic groups, between domestic and foreign groups with common interests, between elements of the Executive Branch and various groups or between interest groups and political factions. Such activity was marked in the education, maritime, trade, sugar, farm, supersonic transport and environmental case studies.

Trade-off of Support. Frequently a part of coalition formation are negotiations among interest groups and their allies in Congress leading to mutual agreement to support certain legislative goals of the participants. Informal compromises often result which prevent headon collisions in the public arenas. In its extreme form this process is known as logrolling.

Personal Lobbying. The most common concept of lobbying in the minds of public and legislators probably is personally discussing legislation with Members of Congress or staff aides. It is one step closer than committee testimony to the actual process of getting legislation enacted, changed or defeated. Personal contacts by representatives of organized interests also are frequent with executive officials outside formal hearings, although they tend to be disregarded in most Congressional consideration of lobbying.

Personal lobbying by paid representatives, under certain conditions, was the only form requiring registration under the Federal Regulation of Lobbying Act as of 1971. It played an important role in all following case studies.

Selection of Officials. One stage beyond attempts to influence the actions and thinking of persons in public office is the effort by organized interests to retain or replace them with others considered more sympathetic or susceptible. Some pressure groups make determined efforts, directly or indirectly, to influence the outcome of Federal elections to Congress or the Presidency. An *American Medical News* 1970 editorial concerning the American Medical Association's Political Action Committee (AMPAC) stated: "AMPAC is a separate organization with its own Board of Directors. It takes no position on legislation. It is involved in political education and political action, that is, electing people to office."

Also common are groups' attempts to influence the choices of committee and subcommittee chairmen and members, staff personnel and the whole range of executive and judicial appointments by the President. Such activities were conspicuous in the drug, education, maritime and trade studies below.

Pressure from Above and Below. Upon the outcome of elections and appointments can hinge the use, frequently found among some elements of the Washington lobby, of a combination of pressure from within the Government and from outside. A revolving door pattern is often pursued in which individuals switch from interest group to government and back again. This was evident, for example, in drug, trade, maritime and sugar legislation discussed in following pages.

Ignorance: Still a Factor?

By no means do all members of the Washington lobby corps employ every technique of applying pressure on public policy. Many group specialists elect to restrict their activities to reporting on Washington developments to their organizations and arranging for presentation of their positions as the need arises. This can sometimes amount to a defensive strategy. But others are more aggressive.

One reason which Bertram M. Gross gave for writing *The Legislative Struggle* was that "ignorance accounts for the failure of many Americans to do their share in making the law." Gross, in fact, questioned whether many veterans of legislative battles had "any clear idea of the forces that make for victory or defeat."

He said the downtown "office buildings of Washington are filled with organizations that have never penetrated to the inner sanctum....The lobbies of Capitol Hill teem with lawyers, public-relations men, and ex-government officials who accomplish little except to wrest large fees...."

Much has been revealed since Gross' attempt in 1953 to throw light from inside on the legislative process, which he called "a study in social combat." There are indications, however, that the conditions of which he spoke still exist to some degree. Elections and polls sometimes point in that direction.

There can be little question, certainly, that much ignorance persists among supporters of some organized interests concerning the pressures they make possible and their impact on the Government under which they live.

DRUG LOBBY

Librium-Valium Lobbyists Win First Round In Congress

The Swiss-based drug manufacturing firm of Hoffmann-LaRoche Inc., with $40 million to $50 million a year in sales at stake, won a round in 1970 in its long battle against Government regulation of its two top-selling tranquilizer drugs, Librium and Valium.

U.S. officials contended—and the company denied—that the drugs were subject to diversion to black market channels and to misuse by purchasers. The company successfully opposed listing of the two products as subject to controls in legislation enacted by Congress.

Four other drug firms won lobby victories in the course of Congress' most ambitious attempt to stem the tide of drug abuse. Those companies produce amphetamines—stimulants which are used mainly to combat obesity and fatigue by curbing appetite and drowsiness.

The Hoffmann-LaRoche triumph after months of intensive lobbying of Congress was seen in industry circles as a setback for Carter-Wallace Inc., holder of the patent on meprobamate, a competing tranquilizer. It is sold under the brand names Miltown and Equanil. Miltown was described in 1962 drug hearings as the most important product of the Carter-Wallace parent firm.

Meprobamate was brought under Federal controls in mid-1970 when the Supreme Court declined to hear an appeal. Industry sources said that imposition of controls tended to reduce sales of a drug by 20 to 25 percent. The controls included an increase in recordkeeping requirements and tightening up on prescription refills.

Carter-Wallace pushed for similar restrictions on its competition. The controversy extended into a hard-fought lobbying duel in which three prominent Washington law firms were among the forces involved.

Fifteen months after President Nixon sent his proposed revision of drug law to Congress, the contest reached a showdown in a House-Senate conference at the Capitol. The climax came three weeks before the Nov. 3 Congressional elections, which were important to several participants, including:

• The Nixon Administration, interested both in electing more Republicans to Congress and in obtaining pre-election passage of a broad new drug law.

• Sen. Thomas J. Dodd (D Conn.), chairman of the Senate Judiciary Juvenile Delinquency Subcommittee which handled the legislation in the Senate. Dodd was in trouble in his bid for a third term, running as an independent after it became apparent that he would not receive the Democratic nomination following his censure by the Senate in 1967. He lost and died May 24, 1971.

• Sen. Roman L. Hruska (R Neb.), ranking Republican on the Judiciary Committee and on Dodd's Subcommittee and the Administration's Senate spokesman on the drug measure.

• Chairman Harley O. Staggers (D W.Va.) and other members of the House Interstate and Foreign Commerce Committee, responsible for the key sections of the drug legislation. Among these members was Rep. Paul G. Rogers (D Fla.), active in the handling of the drug legisla-

tion and described by *American Medical News,* publication of the American Medical Association, as "usually considered the single most knowledgeable and influential House (Member) on over-all health matters."

• Trade and professional associations led by the Pharmaceutical Manufacturers Association, whose post-election newsletter noted changes wrought by 1970 elections in Congressional committees dealing with drug legislation, and the American Medical Association, which in late 1970 underwent an administrative shuffle in anticipation of major controversy in 1971 over national health insurance.

The AMA is the only organization which ever has exceeded $1 million in its reported annual spending under the Federal Regulation of Lobbying Act of 1946, having spent more than that in 1949, 1950 and 1965, the year Medicaid was enacted over AMA opposition.

As in the case of tranquilizers, authorities reported evidence of widespread diversion to illegal sources and abuse in connection with some amphetamines. A small fraction of the huge output of amphetamines, comprising only liquid-injectable forms of methamphetamines, was made subject to a production quota system in the legislation as enacted. Congressional proponents of broader action said the final bill left untouched the forms from which "speed" is most frequently derived. Speed is a common term for amphetamine-related substances used in search of drug "kicks."

The battle over Librium and Valium, in particular, despite the small proportion of the over-all drug picture it comprises, demonstrates what can take place when a serious attempt is made to reconcile public and private interests where many millions of dollars are involved.

The struggle over the new drug control law signed in 1970 transcended political party lines and offered glimpses into some of the strategies which interest groups used in attempts to influence governmental decisions.

Temporary Victory. The Librium-Valium victory was temporary, though others could follow. As promised, the Bureau of Narcotics and Dangerous Drugs in February 1971 issued a final order aimed at bringing the drugs under the 1970 law. *(p. 70)*

The order said the drugs because of their depressant effect on the central nervous system "have a substantial potential for significant abuse..." It said reliable evidence established that there had been significant abuse of both and that it was reasonable to conclude that the abuse would continue to increase if steps were not taken to curtail it. The Bureau also acted in mid-1971 to place certain amphetamine-type drugs under tighter controls.

The 1970 Act

Proponents of the Comprehensive Drug Abuse Prevention and Control Act of 1970 (HR 18583—PL 91-513), signed by President Nixon Oct. 27, 1970, hailed it as a

(Continued on p. 69)

Drug Industry Lobbyists Include Former Federal Officials

Following is a list of prominent men and law firms with drug industry connections.

Arnold & Porter. Registered April 27, 1970, as Congressional lobbyists for Hoffmann-LaRoche Inc., makers of Librium and Valium. Joseph A. Califano Jr., with the firm until April 1971, was special assistant to the Secretary and Deputy Secretary of Defense, 1964-65, and special assistant to President Johnson, 1965-69. In 1970, Califano was general counsel to the Democratic National Committee. Mitchell Rogovin of the firm was Assistant Attorney General in charge of the tax division, 1966-69. Carolyn Aggers of the firm is the wife of Abe Fortas, former Supreme Court Justice and former assistant to President Johnson.

Clifford, Warnke, Glass, McIlwain & Finney. Represented Hoffmann-LaRoche during several years of administrative hearings concerning Librium and Valium, as well as in Congressional activities. Not registered under lobby law, on grounds that the firm's activities are primarily in regulatory, not legislative, areas. Clark M. Clifford, senior partner, was special counsel to the President, 1946-50, and because of his association with President Johnson was frequently referred to in the press as "the President's lawyer." Mr. Johnson appointed him Secretary of Defense, 1968-69. Partner Paul C. Warnke was general counsel, Defense Department, 1966-67, and Assistant Secretary of Defense, 1967-69. Thomas D. Finney Jr. of the firm, one of those most active in Hoffmann-LaRoche matters, was administrative assistant to Sen. A.S. Mike Monroney (D Okla. 1951-69), 1957-63, and was active in Adlai E. Stevenson's Presidential campaigning. In 1962, Finney was a White House assistant on trade and tariff legislation while on leave from Monroney. He was a key manager in the 1968 Presidential primary campaign of Sen. Eugene J. McCarthy (D Minn.).

Ellis B. Anderson. Vice president, secretary and general counsel of Hoffmann-LaRoche Inc., was introduced at Senate hearings on the 1970 drug bill by Sen. Birch Bayh (D Ind.), who said Anderson "used to be a Hoosier, and I first met him when he was the city attorney for the distinguished senior Senator from Indiana, Senator Hartke, when he was mayor." Bayh was on the Dodd Subcommittee.

Elmer Holmes Bobst. As chairman of the board of Warner-Lambert Pharmaceutical Company, he introduced Richard M. Nixon at a June 27, 1961, luncheon of the Pharmaceutical Advertising Clubs of three cities as the man who "should have been President of the United States." Mr. Nixon, in a speech, criticized a proposed bill as punitive against the drug industry. In 1970, Bobst, then honorary board chairman, was among four sponsors who bought prime television time in nine cities before the Nov. 3 elections to rebroadcast President Nixon's denunciation of campus and urban violence.

Leonard A. Scheele, M.D. A senior vice president of Warner-Lambert, he was a career officer with the U.S. Public Health Service for 23 years, including service as Surgeon General, 1948-56.

Irving W. Swanson. Registered April 10, 1969, as a lobbyist for the Pharmaceutical Manufacturers Association. He was assistant to the Senate Republican minority for several years in the 1960s.

Dr. John Burns. Vice president of research for Hoffmann-LaRoche Inc., he served simultaneously as chairman of the Committee on Problems of Drug Safety for the National Academy of Sciences-National Research Council, a quasi-official agency which provides for research for Government offices. The committee is a major consultant to the Food and Drug Administration on drug efficacy, involving drugs marketed before 1962.

Travis Stewart. Director of governmental relations for Hoffmann-LaRoche Inc., he was one of four regional directors for the Democratic National Committee in the 1968 Presidential campaign of Hubert H. Humphrey. Humphrey returned to the Senate in 1971. In his earlier Senate service (1949-64), Humphrey was the main force behind enactment in 1951 of the Durham-Humphrey Amendment (PL 82-215) which the Pharmaceutical Manufacturers Association (PMA) said in 1970 had resulted in a substantial increase in the proportion of drugs reaching the market as prescription products rather than over-the-counter. Humphrey later conducted continuous subcommittee hearings on the drug industry and related Government agencies regulating it. "Almost certainly he will turn some of his energy in this direction again," the PMA newsletter said after the Nov. 3, 1970 elections. Humphrey had been a pharmacist.

Dr. V. D. Mattia. President of Hoffmann-LaRoche, he was a chairman for New Jersey citizens' committees for Humphrey-Muskie in the 1968 Presidential campaign.

Stephen Ailes. With the firm Steptoe & Johnson, he was an attorney in 1969-70 for S.B. Penick & Company, Merck & Company, and Mallinckrodt Chemical Works. Ailes was Under Secretary of the Army, 1961-64, and Secretary of the Army, 1964-65. In November 1970, Ailes became the chief executive officer of the Association of American Railroads.

John T. Connor. President Johnson's first Cabinet appointee, Connor served as special assistant to Secretary of the Navy James V. Forrestal after World War II, joined Merck & Company Inc. in 1947 as an attorney and was its president and chief executive officer from 1955 to 1965 when he became Secretary of Commerce. He had been vice president and a founder of the National Independent Committee for Johnson-Humphrey, a businessmen's campaign committee. In 1962, Connor told a hearing, "I am another Federal Government alumnus now working in the pharmaceutical industry." He became chairman of the board of Allied Chemical Corporation after leaving the Cabinet.

Theodore G. Klumpp, M.D. President and director of Winthrop Laboratories and a member of the PMA board of directors in 1969, he was chief of the drug division in the Food and Drug Administration, 1936-41.

(Continued from p. 67)
major advance in the Government's efforts to crack down on illicit drugs.

The Act was the product of an attempt to pull together various older laws on the subject and to cope with widespread use of marijuana, speed and other drugs subject to abuse. Among other things, the Act set up machinery by which specific drugs can be brought under supervision of the Bureau of Narcotics and Dangerous Drugs in the Justice Department through administrative proceedings.

The Government's contest with Hoffmann-LaRoche dated from enactment of the Drug Abuse Control Amendments of 1965 (PL 89-74). The amendments strengthened Federal controls over depressant and stimulant drugs. These were defined to include any drug which the Secretary of Health, Education and Welfare designated administratively as having a potential for abuse because of its effect on the central nervous system or its hallucinogenic effects.

President Nixon on July 14, 1969, sent a 10-point program to Congress, followed by introduction of the Administration's Controlled Dangerous Substances Act (S 2637).

Attorney General John N. Mitchell testified that the Bureau of Narcotics and Dangerous Drugs in his Department was faced with administering "two distinct systems of legislation" inherited from the former Bureau of Narcotics in the Treasury Department and the former Bureau of Drug Abuse Control in the HEW Department.

"This has resulted in a great deal of confusion in the regulation of the lawful manufacture of controlled drugs and in inconsistencies in the punishment of illicit drug activities," Mitchell said. He said the system contained loopholes, created "enormous confusion" about registration requirements and made no provision to cancel registrations once granted.

John E. Ingersoll, director of the Bureau of Narcotics and Dangerous Drugs, testified at House hearings in 1970 that the drug trafficker was "perhaps the most sophisticated criminal of our times." He said many of the enforcement tools required updating to meet "current realities."

There were disputes in both the Senate and the House over which committees should have jurisdiction. These in part mirrored a philosophic dispute over whether the new law should confine itself to a law enforcement approach, as originally advocated by the Justice Department and Dodd, or embrace within one piece of legislation educational, research and clinical aspects as insisted upon by Sen. Harold E. Hughes (D Iowa), chairman of the Senate Labor and Public Welfare Subcommittee on Alcoholism and Narcotics, Staggers and an ad hoc group of physicians including some shown by Dodd to hold HEW research grants.

Debate revolved around division of authority between the Justice Department and the HEW Department.

In 1968, Republicans for the most part opposed President Johnson's proposal to center drug law enforcement in the Justice Department while Senate Democrats supported the move. After a change in Administrations, Republican Members were among the most active in pushing for legislation which affirmed the Justice Department's drug regulatory powers. A health-welfare coalition found considerable Democratic support for their drive to vest substantial authority in the HEW Department.

While the public discussion tended to dwell on these factors and on marijuana penalties and the question of "no-knock" entry authority for narcotics agents, behind the scenes the Librium-Valium issue loomed large. One Senate committee source spoke of "tremendous and wild lobbying" as having caused delays in moving the over-all drug control legislation through Congress. At the climax, the Librium-Valium issue alone was said by Dodd and others to have threatened to block final passage of the bill.

Librium-Valium

Hoffmann-LaRoche introduced Librium (chlordiazepoxide) in 1960 and Valium (diazepam) in 1963 as minor tranquilizers. They resulted from research into treatment of mental disorders.

"These drugs have been and are being used by doctors to treat millions of patients with a wide variety of emotional disorders," Dr. V. D. Mattia, president and chief executive officer of the company, said in a 1970 statement for the House Commerce Committee. He said Librium is primarily used to help control excessive anxiety, tension or apprehension. Its uses include the treatment of alcoholism. Valium also has various uses, including as a tranquilizer and a muscle relaxant.

The House Committee considered the advisability of listing Librium and other drugs by name in the 1965 legislation but decided against singling out any drug at that time. That Committee and the Senate Committee on Labor and Public Welfare both expressed an expectation in their reports that the Secretary would take early action to bring Librium and other drugs under controls.

In 1966, the Food and Drug Administration proposed to place Librium, Valium and meprobamate under controls, on the authority of the 1965 legislation. Both Hoffmann-LaRoche and Carter-Wallace asked administrative hearings. After hearings, the drugs were declared by the examiners to be subject to abuse.

Recommendations went to Dr. James L. Goddard, then FDA Commissioner, who took no further action before President Johnson in 1968 issued an executive order which combined agencies and transferred the main regulatory authority to the Justice Department. The proposed control of meprobamate, meanwhile, ran the course of administrative proceedings and judicial review which resulted in the 1970 imposition of controls.

Under the Nixon Administration, the Librium-Valium case was pursued further and the Bureau of Narcotics and Dangerous Drugs on May 19, 1969, issued an order ending the stay of effectiveness announced May 17, 1966, on the listing of Librium and Valium as drugs subject to control under the 1965 amendments. The 1969 order said both "are drugs which, because of their depressant effect on the central nervous system, have a substantial potential for significant abuse...."

Testimony was submitted in administrative hearings that Librium and Valium often were used in suicide attempts, that sample audits of retail outlets disclosed large quantities were missing from inventories without being accounted for, and that, as the bureau put it, there had been "significant use...by individuals on their own initiative rather than on the basis of medical advice...."

Mattia, speaking for Hoffmann-LaRoche, said: "I firmly believe that the experience and evidence accumulated over the past decade, and particularly since the 1965 amendments, clearly demonstrate that Librium and Valium are not subject to abuse by the American public."

Among authorities upon which proponents of control could draw was the President's Commission on Law Enforcement and Administration of Justice. In its 1967 report, "The Challenge of Crime in a Free Society," the commission said concerning Librium:

"Among the other depressants involved in the drug abuse problem are a number of sedative and tranquilizing drugs, introduced since 1950, that are chemically unrelated to the barbiturates, but similar in effect. The best known of these are meprobamate (Miltown, Equanil),...and chlordiazepoxide (Librium). There is strong evidence that abuse of these agents may lead to drug intoxication and physical dependence. Suicide by overdose, and deaths during withdrawal from some of the drugs, have also been reported."

Representing Hoffmann-LaRoche were the firms Arnold & Porter and Clifford, Warnke, Glass, McIlwain & Finney. Thomas G. Corcoran of Corcoran, Foley, Youngman & Rowe represented the interests of Carter-Wallace Inc.

Many other interests were involved in lobbying on the drug legislation. Among them were the American Medical Association, which opposed portions of the Administration bill and contended the HEW Secretary should be responsible for medical decisions on drug classification; the Pharmaceutical Manufacturers Association, made up of 123 companies accounting for 95 percent of the prescription drug products made and sold in the United States, and the American Public Health Association, in which Hoffmann LaRoche and several other drug manufacturers are sustaining members.

Former FDA Commissioner Goddard testified on behalf of the health association that the original Administration proposal would give the Attorney General authority over medicine and medical research which made the bill "intolerable." Proponents countered that the Attorney General already exercised the authority proposed to be incorporated in law.

The original Administration bill made no mention of Librium and Valium. Dodd won a Senate amendment listing them for controls. On Jan. 28, 1970, he took the unusual step of warning the other branch of Congress from the Senate floor of a "concerted lobbying effort" in the House to delete Librium and Valium. The House Committee on Interstate and Foreign Commerce omitted them in its draft, which was passed by the House. With a handful of Senators on the floor during a Presidential television speech on Vietnam, Dodd won reinstatement of the Librium-Valium provision in the Senate.

At the House-Senate conference, Senate conferees agreed to withdraw the amendment, thus deleting Librium and Valium from controls in the final bill. Sen. John L. McClellan (D Ark.), speaking in Dodd's absence, told the Senate Oct. 14, 1970, that the action was taken "with the understanding that administrative action to control these drugs is nearing completion, and that they will likely be brought within Schedule IV by administrative action."

Staggers told the House final administrative action was scheduled within weeks. He said, "The bill provides that, if, upon the completion of these proceedings (including judicial review), these drugs are listed for control, they shall automatically be included within the coverage of the bill and placed in the appropriate schedule."

Dodd, the chief sponsor, said in a statement inserted in the *Congressional Record*:

"As Chairman of the House-Senate Conference, I brought up my amendment to include these drugs as controlled dangerous substances. After I brought up my amendment, after extensive debate, and after having been assured by the Senate conferees that we had the votes to include these drugs, I was shocked and distressed to find that the House conferees bludgeoned the Senate conferees into eliminating these 'killer' drugs by threatening to hold up the reporting of this bill from conference. I was stunned to hear that the inclusion of these drugs with a proven history of criminal diversion, illegal use and multiple fatalities could stop cold the movement of a bill that represents the most far-reaching and comprehensive drug legislation to come before us in 56 years."

Dodd said Hoffmann-LaRoche "annually earns a reputed $200 million from these two drugs alone. It is said in the pharmaceutical industry that once a drug is controlled, its marketing decreases by 25 percent. With $50 million at stake, one can well imagine the pressure that was put to bear on the House conferees. One cannot, however, understand why they have put the economic interests of Hoffmann-LaRoche before that of their constituents, indeed that of the entire country."

Spokesmen for Hoffmann-LaRoche said no undue pressures had been exerted.

The conference decided to add only liquid-injectable forms of methamphetamines to lists of drugs subject to domestic production quotas. "Legitimate U.S. production of this drug is extremely limited," the PMA's newsletter said. The earlier Senate amendment would have made all classes of amphetamine products subject to quotas, extending coverage to 4,000 to 6,000 separate items. The manufacturers who gained most from this change were listed by Sen. Thomas F. Eagleton (D Mo.) as Smith, Kline & French Laboratories; Aeronol Products Corporation; Hexagon Laboratories Inc., and Roehr Chemicals Inc., all of the New York City area.

Staggers told the House: "It is the understanding proceedings will be initiated involving a number of drugs containing amphetamines after the legislation has become law, but exceptions will be made for a number of amphetamine-containing drugs."

Aftermath

Dodd was defeated in the Nov. 3 elections. The winner of a three-way contest for his Senate seat was Rep. Lowell P. Weicker Jr. (R Conn.), whose industrialist father was president of E. R. Squibb & Sons in the 1940s. Hruska won re-election by a narrower margin than had been predicted. All of the House conferees were re-elected.

Beyond buying additional time free from regulation, the net effect of the 1970 Congressional action on Librium and Valium was to switch the struggle from the legislative to the executive arena, perhaps with eventual resort to the judiciary.

The Bureau of Narcotics and Dangerous Drugs published supplemental findings Nov. 24, 1970, stating that evidence shows self-medication and nonprofessional administration of Librium and Valium obtained through legitimate prescriptions, forged prescriptions, suppliers of illicit drugs and from other sources.

On Feb. 6, 1971, the Bureau published its final findings, conclusions and order dated Jan. 30 directing that Librium and Valium should be designated as drugs subject to control under Schedule IV of the 1970 Act when the order became effective in 90 days. The agency earlier had denied a request for new arguments. The order was appealed in June, delaying its effectiveness. A year or more could elapse before final settlement.

EDUCATION LOBBY

Coalition Seeks Increased Federal Funds in 1970

The federal government's first act of direct assistance to education came more than a century ago, but disagreement still exists on continued support.

The question of federal money for education arises at least once each year—when Congress considers the bill making appropriations for the Office of Education in the Department of Health, Education and Welfare (HEW).

The financial pinch felt in the late 1960s by the nation's schools and colleges became a crunch of major proportions by the early 1970s. The nationwide economic downturn, accompanied by inflation, generated a coordinated effort by the education community for full funding of federal aid-to-education programs—and an equally strong determination by the Nixon Administration that federal spending in education, as in other areas, must be held down.

Twice during the first two years of the Nixon Administration these forces collided. The White House won the first round: Congress sustained the President's veto of the Labor-HEW appropriations bill for fiscal 1971 to which the education groups had won addition of more than $1-billion to the Nixon budget request. Despite a concerted "Operation Override," mounted by the coalition Emergency Committee for Full Funding of Education Programs, the House sustained the President's action by a 226-191 roll-call vote.

But later in 1970 the educators were victorious. For the first time, Congress considered education funds in a bill separate from those for the rest of the HEW Department. By this effort Congress hoped to complete action early in the year, so that educators would be able to plan their budgets with knowledge of what amount in federal funds would be available.

Mr. Nixon again vetoed the bill, to which Congress had added more than $500-million to his requests. But this time the education coalition won enough votes to override the veto easily—first in the House, 289-114, and then in the Senate, 77-16.

In 1971, education interests girded themselves for a third full funding campaign. They lost the first encounter. The House refused, 187-191, to add to the fiscal 1972 appropriations bill, a $729-million package amendment backed by the education groups. But the Senate approved the addition of $816-million to the amount approved by the House.

August W. Steinhilber, director of federal and congressional relations for the National Association of School Boards and 1971 chairman of the Emergency Committee for Full Funding, saw this loss as a needed spur. Complacent after the victory in overriding the 1970 veto, the various groups interested in education just did not work as hard on winning the added funds in the House, he said. After that loss, they renewed their effort. The Emergency Committee's leaders said it would be dissolved once full funding was achieved. It became dormant after the 1970 veto was overridden, then came back into action early in 1971.

Federal Aid to Education

The idea that the federal government take some part in the support of education is an old one, dating from the post-Revolutionary years when certain land in every township in the Northwest Territory was set aside by Congress for support of public schools.

But not until 1862 did Congress act again to aid education, then establishing in each state land-grant colleges of agricultural and mechanical arts. In 1867, Congress approved a bill introduced by Rep. (later President) James A. Garfield, creating a non-Cabinet Department of Education. In 1917, Congress authorized federal aid to vocational education.

The federal government made its largest total financial contribution to education through the GI bill (Servicemen's Readjustment Act, 1944) and its successor laws.

In 1950, Congress authorized federal grants for schools in areas where federal activities were adding population while removing property from the tax rolls. But only after the Russians launched Sputnik did Congress pass the National Defense Education Act (NDEA) authorizing $1-billion in federal aid to education.

The decade of the 1960s, particularly the Administration of former schoolteacher Lyndon B. Johnson, brought the greatest extension of federal aid to education through the Higher Education Facilities Act of 1963, the Elementary and Secondary Education Act of 1965 and the Higher Education Act of 1965.

Interest Groups

As Congress enlarged the federal role in aiding education, many education groups set up Washington offices.

The American Federation of Teachers (AFT) moved from Chicago—where it had been chartered by Samuel Gompers in 1916—to Washington. The Association of American Universities (AAU) moved to Washington in 1962 at age 62. The National School Boards Association, founded in 1940, set up a Washington office in 1966.

By 1971, there were hundreds of such groups represented in Washington. Almost every type of institution and teacher was represented, as well as parents, libraries and educational administrators. School librarians and school secretaries each had their own group; as did college governing boards, college registrars and college business officers. In addition, dozens of the colleges and universities had their own Washington representatives. (Partial listing of education interest groups represented in Washington, next page.)

The education community covers a wide spectrum of groups and specific interests from the 1.1-million-member National Education Association and the 10-million-member National Congress of Parents and Teachers to the 56-member Council of Chief State School Officers

A List of Major Education Interest Groups, 1971

Teachers

American Federation of Teachers (AFT)—Union of classroom teachers; established 1916; affiliated with AFL-CIO; represents 250,000 teachers.

National Education Association (NEA)—Largest professional organization in world, representing 1.1 million teachers and educational administrators; established as National Teachers Association in 1857, became NEA 1870; a family of organizations including such affiliates as the American Industrial Arts Association and the Association for Education Communications and Technology, and associated organizations including the American Association of School Administrators, the Association for Educational Data Systems, the National Association of Secondary School Principals.

American Association of University Professors—Established 1915; represents more than 94,000 professors.

Education: General

American Education Lobby—Organized 1967 to oppose federal control (through aid) of education; 10,000 members.

Council of Chief State School Officers—Established 1928; 56 state or territorial commissioners of education.

National Association of School Boards—Established 1940; represents state and local school boards.

National Catholic Education Association—Established 1904; represents all types of Catholic schools.

National Congress of Parents and Teachers—Founded 1897; represents more than 10 million members.

Higher Education

American Council on Education—Established 1918; coordinating organization for higher education groups; represents 312 national and regional associations; 1,343 institutions of higher education, 83 affiliated groups.

American Association for Higher Education—Established 1870 as NEA department, independent in 1971; represents more than 7,000 persons working in higher education.

American Association of Colleges for Teacher Education—Established 1917 as American Association of Teacher Colleges; represents 853 institutions of higher education.

American Association of Junior Colleges—Founded 1920; represents 825 junior colleges.

American Association of State Colleges and Universities—Established 1961 from older organizations; represents 277 state colleges and universities.

Association of American Colleges—Founded 1914; represents about 850 liberal arts colleges; affiliated with National Council of Independent Colleges and Universities, founded in 1971 to speak for private higher education.

Association of American Universities—Established 1900; 46 major universities in the United States and two in Canada.

National Association for Equal Opportunity in Higher Education—Established in 1969 to give visibility to the needs of predominantly black colleges; represents 85 predominantly black colleges.

National Association of State Universities and Land Grant Colleges—Descendant of oldest higher education associations founded in 1885 and 1895; represents 118 major state universities and land grant institutions.

Graduate Education

Association of American Law Schools—Established 1900, represents 124 law schools.

Association of American Medical Colleges—Founded 1876; represents all medical schools, 47 academic societies and 400 training hospitals.

Council of Graduate Schools in the United States—Established 1960; represents 300 graduate schools.

Adult, Vocational Education

Adult Education Association of the U.S.A.—Founded 1951 to further the concept of continuing education.

American Vocational Association (AVA)—Established 1926; represents 50,000 vocational education teachers.

National University Extension Association—Founded 1915; represents 168 universities with extension divisions or divisions of continuing education.

Libraries/Broadcasters

American Library Association—Founded 1876; represents more than 37,000 librarians, libraries, publishing houses, business firms and individuals.

Association of Research Libraries—Founded 1931; represents 89 large research libraries.

National Association of Educational Broadcasters—Founded 1925; professional association of individuals and institutions interested in educational television and radio.

and the exclusive 48-member Association of American Universities.

The men and women who serve as congressional liaison for these different groups come from a variety of backgrounds. There are former government officials, such as Ralph K. Huitt, executive director of the National Association of State Universities and Land Grant Colleges, who served as Assistant Secretary of Health, Education and Welfare for legislation during the Johnson Administration, and Charles V. Kidd, director of federal relations for the Association of American Universities, who served in the Office of Science and Technology in the Johnson Administration.

There are former congressional staff members: John F. Morse, director of the American Council on Education (ACE) Commission on Federal Relations, who in 1962 directed a study of federal involvement in education for Rep. Edith Green (D Ore.), chairman of the House Education and Labor special subcommittee on education; Mary P. Allen, associate for governmental relations to the executive director of the American Vocational Association (AVA), for 12 years a staff aide to Rep. Carl Elliott (D Ala., 1949-1965), a member of the Education and Labor and Rules Committees, and Lawrence Gladieux, assistant director of federal relations for the Association of American Universities, former legislative assistant to Rep. John Brademas (D Ind.), chairman of the House Education and Labor select subcommittee on education.

There are former teachers—Carl J. Megel, former Chicago high school science teacher and coach, for 12 years president of the AFT, and, since 1964, AFT director of legislation. And there are former school officials—John M. Lumley, recently retired after 14 years as assistant executive secretary of the NEA for government relations and citizenship, who came to that position from the post of superintendent of schools in Wilkes-Barre, Pa. And there are parents—the six women volunteers who watch over the legislative concerns of the National Congress of Parents and Teachers.

Emergency Committee: A New Umbrella

No umbrella is large enough to cover all education interest groups although for a brief period in 1970 it seemed that the Emergency Committee for Full Funding might be able to.

But then NEA members reversed that association's position on a matter of educational policy, obligating the NEA to withdraw from active participation in the committee, of which NEA congressional liaison Stanley J. McFarland was serving as chairman.

The National Congress of Parents and Teachers, which works independently for education funds, was advised by its legal counsel not to participate in the committee.

The committee itself, often described as the brain of the second most powerful lobby in Washington, was organized in April 1969 by Lumley, Steinhilber, Kenneth Young of the AFL-CIO and several other educational interest representatives concerned at the cutback in education funds proposed in the last Johnson budget and deepened by the Nixon budget amendments. As Young explained the rationale behind the committee's establishment, "If we can work together on authorizing legislation, why not get together and really work on appropriations?"

From Oregon—to which he had just retired after 13 years' service with Sen. Wayne Morse (D Ore. 1945-1969)—Charles W. Lee was summoned to serve as the committee's director. From 1962 to 1969, professional staff member of the Senate education subcommittee, Lee had a part in the drafting and passage of every education bill during those years. "No one knows more about the Senate and education legislation than Charlie Lee," said Mary Allen of AVA.

From week to week the composition of the committee's membership changes, said Lee. Supported by contributions from member educational institutions and groups, its work was directed by Lee from one crowded suite in the Congressional Hotel across the street from the House office buildings.

From its creation, Lee said, there was a core group of Senators and Representatives willing to work with the committee to win full funding of education programs. "We serve as a free-floating staff" for these persons, said Lee, putting together a package amendment which can be enacted and then providing the information which advocates can use to win votes for that package increase.

The committee's strategy was developed in breakfast meetings—usually held near the offices of member groups, frequently in the cafeteria at One DuPont Circle, the building owned by the ACE and housing many higher education groups.

Lee was the center of a communications network, transmitting timely information about happenings in Congress to member groups so that each could act in the best interests of its constituents. That sort of information —accompanied by suggestions for its use—went out April 9, 1971, two days after the House rejected the $729-million Hathaway (for its House sponsor, Maine Democrat William D. Hathaway) amendment.

Lee sent to member groups a package containing an analysis of the votes cast by about 250 individual Representatives on the Hathaway amendment, the motion to override the 1970 veto, and a previous full funding amendment. Those members whose vote might be changed to favor a conference report containing more funds than those approved by the House were designated. An accompanying memo from Lee encouraged each group to forward this information to its members, asking them to contact their Representative, thanking them for a "yes" vote on the amendment, asking the reason for a "no" vote, and asking absent members how they would have voted.

The committee tries, said Lee, "to cut through the glass that surrounds Congress, to let them know that we are concerned out here, and that we know what is happening."

A Community of Interest

The emergency committee—its creation and operations—cast into relief the difficulty of fusing these diverse groups into an effective cooperating community and the sensitivity of many of them to any suggestion that they were lobbies in the traditional meaning of the word.

Despite a basic common interest, many conflicts arose between groups, related to the various sectors of education which each represented. Black colleges and community colleges often did not benefit from the same programs as do large universities, the all-teacher membership of the AFT might not see things the same way as the teacher-administrator groups within NEA.

Because of these divisions, categorical aid programs —library services and school lunch—were enacted by Congress long before any type of general aid to schools. A proposal for general aid brought out all the contradictions in the educational community—church-state, public-private—while categorical grant programs won support from certain groups without incurring the opposition of others.

In 1971, external threats contributed to an unusual unity within the educational community. The financial crunch produced the cooperative effort of the emergency committee where, Lee said, the groups could hash out their differences and then arrive at a common strategy.

Its "package approach," developing one amendment increasing funding for a variety of education programs, was designed to overcome the fragmentation which had often beset the education community.

The cooperation of the higher education associations working for institutional aid "just shows what the financial bind can do," said one of their representatives. The chief reason that Congress has not approved institutional aid for colleges and universities before 1971, explained Ralph Huitt, was the inability of the higher education groups to agree on the type of program they wanted.

Early in 1971, most of the major higher education groups agreed upon one statement on institutional aid; later they agreed upon the best formula for allocating such aid. This unified pressure won an institutional aid proposal from the Nixon Administration which had said early in 1971 that it would not submit such a bill during the year.

A number of other prominent and often-disagreeing groups united to oppose a program of education vouchers, which was seen as a serious threat to the public school system. The Coalition on Education Vouchers was chaired jointly by AFT's Megel and NEA's Lumley.

Yet the divisions remain, submerged only temporarily. One participant in the biweekly luncheon of the Government Relations Group, the Congressional liaison representatives of the various associations, said that there often was more infighting than communication.

Low-Key Lobby

The NEA and the AFT register their liaison men as lobbyists. But generally, education groups—all tax-exempt nonprofit organizations—shy away from that label.

"I virtually never go to the Hill except on request. I don't walk the halls," said John F. Morse of the American Council on Education. "We lobby by invitation," agreed Huitt of the land grant group. "Our members do the lobbying: it's more effective."

And one primary role for the Washington staff of these groups is to teach their members to do the lobbying. Mary Allen of the AVA has conducted workshops across the country for vocational education leaders. She explained the legislative process step-by-step, pointing out the way in which an individual may make his opinion heard at each step. "When a particular Congressman is the key to a bill or a provision," she said, "we see to it that the folks in his district let him know how they feel about it."

Through newsletters, education groups keep their members informed of legislation under consideration; when the crucial time arrives, a call for action is sent out asking constituents to contact their congressional representatives. These organizations also participate in the formulation of legislation by testifying before Congressional committees, usually represented by persons from their member institutions.

And Federal education officials often consult these interest groups. A hiatus between the Nixon Administration and the education community during 1969 was

ended in 1970 when HEW Secretary Elliot Richardson (formerly Assistant HEW Secretary for legislation 1957-59) restored communication.

The Administration's own education lobbyist, Christopher Cross, Deputy Assistant HEW Secretary for legislation in charge of education, keeps in contact with the education groups.

Some members of Congress criticized the public "high-pressure tactics" of the emergency committee—such as the whip system organized in 1969 to ensure that Representatives who had promised to vote for the committee-backed increase in education funds actually did get to the floor and vote—as out of keeping with the generally low-key behind-the-scenes approach of the education community to Congress. Some of the higher education groups reflected a similar feeling.

Rep. Green, staunch champion of education, questioned in a House speech the propriety of participation in the committee of groups which stand to profit from an increase in education funds, such as federally connected educational laboratories, consulting groups and equipment companies. Lee said that little if any of the group's funds come from such groups.

Rep. William H. Ayres (R Ohio), then ranking minority member of the House Education and Labor Committee, criticized the committee for bringing educators, parents and other citizens to Washington in January 1970 to lobby for overriding the education funds veto. Never in his 20 years in Congress, he said, had he seen "anything as brazen by any group coming here trying to influence legislation."

Commenting on the instructions which the committee issued to these arriving citizens to direct them in talking with their Representative, Ayres noted that the committee instructed the person to tell his Representative that he would be in the House gallery during the vote. Ayres' interpretation of this was "Big Brother will be watching."

And in regard to the committee's note that the constituent might tell the Representative, if he promised to vote to override, that the constituent and his associates would do everything they could to assist him locally, Ayres commented, "in other words, in his next election. By inference, if you do not vote with them, you know what they are going to try to do. I think this is a disgrace to the good name of education." Ayres was defeated in his race for re-election in November 1970.

The NEA was criticized for its lobbying by persons who pointed out that tax-exempt organizations were not allowed to use a substantial part of their funds for legislative efforts.

Lee responded that the emergency committee merely focuses educational concerns and information into each member's office, adding its input to the decision-making process. "Decisions will be made, anyway," he said. "They might as well be made on our input. There's no law against lobbying in the public interest, and that's what we are doing."

Young of the AFL-CIO sees the work of the education community through the emergency committee in a larger context, as part of a long-needed effort to make the appropriations committees more responsive to public needs and concerns. "It was a good fight," he said, "and there ought to be more like it. It was something other groups should have done long ago. The education groups should be proud of themselves."

SHIP BUILDING LOBBY

Subsidies: Persistence and Unity Bring Results

At the end of World War II, the United States had the largest merchant fleet in the world, totaling 3,696 ships. They carried 57.6 percent of the nation's foreign waterborne commerce in 1947.

The fleet declined steadily thereafter. By 1971, it was down to about 750 active ocean ships and ranked fifth in the world on a tonnage basis.

While U.S. trade increased and surpassed that of every other nation, the percentage of that trade hauled by American-flag vessels fell dramatically. By 1971, about 5 percent of the nation's foreign commerce was carried by ships flying the American flag.

By comparison, Russian ships carried 50 percent of the Soviet Union's foreign trade. Comparable percentages for other countries: French ships, 48 percent of France's foreign commerce; Japan, 46 percent; Great Britain, 37 percent; Greece, 53 percent; Norway, 43 percent, and Sweden, 30 percent.

Not only was the U.S. merchant fleet dwindling in numbers, but three-fourths of the ships were at least 20 years old and nearing retirement. The fleets of other nations were younger. The United States, world's largest consumer of petroleum, had fallen to sixth in the world's tanker fleets.

A third of a century after it had enacted the first direct subsidy program to aid the American merchant marine, Congress in 1970 approved a large new program aimed at rebuilding an aging and dwindling fleet. The new program, like the old, authorized payment of government subsidies to qualified shipping interests to offset the lower construction and operating costs of foreign competitors.

1970 Legislation. The enactment of the Merchant Marine Act of 1970 offered an example of legislative persistence, aided in the long run by what Congress seemed to consider a convincing case for identification of private interests with the national interest. Basic disputes still exist. As in the case of U.S. trade policy, with which the shipping industry is intimately related, the question of how to deal with lower-priced foreign competition is a fundamental issue. Another basis of controversy is American ownership of foreign-flag ships.

Designed to build 300 modern ships in 10 years at a gross cost of more than $2-billion matched by more than $3-billion in private funds, the 1970 legislation culminated years of legislative attempts. The earlier efforts were frustrated partly by divisions in the shipping and shipbuilding industries, in the executive branch and in Congress. One Member of Congress counted 11 separate attempts initiated in Congress over a quarter century to enact new maritime legislation before the one that succeeded. President Nixon called the 1970 law "the first significant piece of legislation" in the field since 1936.

The shipping industry's Labor-Management Maritime Committee said in 1968 that policy critics had been deploring the deterioration of the merchant marine for 15 years. The committee estimated that year that Members of Congress themselves "have lamented the state of our U.S.-flag fleet over 550 times during the past year alone." Demanding action instead of more fruitless studies, the committee said, "The American Merchant Marine has been all but 'researched to death'."

Shortly after President Nixon sent his proposal for a new ship subsidy program to Congress amid indications it had broad backing in the industry, Secretary of Commerce Maurice H. Stans was told by Rep. Thomas N. Downing (D Va.) at a House hearing:

"Some day you will have to tell us of all the backroom discussion that went on before this was evolved. I think it would be most interesting."

"I think it may be better if that is just lost to history," Stans replied. "The result is the important thing."

"Whoever was the main force in that backroom discussion I would also like to congratulate," Downing said.

Lost to history or not, "the miracle of the 91st Congress," as some labor sources afterward called the 1970 Act, was marked for its mobilization by merchant marine proponents of the massive forces needed to reverse past defeats in Congress.

Maritime industry leaders pulled dissident factions together at least temporarily in a broad coalition drive. Organized elements of labor and management were among those who pooled their strength on the basic approach despite sharp differences on some aspects.

Labor disputes often have been cited as creating instability in the U.S. maritime industry which helped drive shipping customers to foreign-flag vessels.

Similarities: 1936 and 1970

In the steering of the 1970 legislation through Congress, there were similarities to conditions surrounding passage of the landmark predecessor law, the Merchant Marine Act of 1936.

Besides the unity movement in the face of what many called a crisis, both successful legislative drives were launched and pushed by the President and had the active support of congressional leaders. Both successes found industry representatives involved in the legislative process from beginning to end. Both victories came when the nation's merchant fleet was indisputably in the doldrums despite the past aid of large sums of Government money.

The two successes seemed to support the soundness of advice which a Senator gave the shipping industry on how to deal with Congress. Serious controversy existed at the time over the relative merits of government-versus-private ownership of the merchant fleet—an issue which still crops up.

One thing which Sen. Royal S. Copeland (D N.Y. 1923-38) told the first National Conference on the Merchant Marine Jan. 10, 1928, was this: "You won't get anything for the merchant marine or private ownership unless you kick, and my advice to you is to do that very thing."

(Continued on p. 77)

Key Men: They Switch Between Industry and Federal Posts

In the regulation of maritime affairs, as in the case of many other specialized interests, the principle of self-government underlying the American system is a factor. Here, as with other elements of the national economy, the industries involved take a major hand not only in the writing and enacting of laws governing them but also in their interpretation and enforcement.

Interest groups seek the appointment or election to power of individuals who are acquainted with and sympathetic to their own conditions and problems. Government officials quite frequently are recruited from the industry affected and in time return to the industry in which their qualifications lie. It is not uncommon for talented specialists to switch around through the years from an interest group capacity in which they exert influence on Congress and the executive branch to a legislative position or to an executive agency, as circumstances indicate.

The Men Involved

Many instances of this are found throughout the nation's history in numerous major areas of interest. Examples in the maritime field in recent times include:

James J. Reynolds. President of the American Institute of Merchant Shipping since 1969, he was named by President Truman to the National Labor Relations Board in 1946 and served five years. President Kennedy in 1961 appointed him Assistant Secretary of Labor for labor-management relations, a post in which he was the government's key official in maritime labor disputes. He then became Under Secretary of Labor under President Johnson until Jan. 20, 1969. He registered April 14, 1969, as a congressional lobbyist for AIMS.

Andrew E. Gibson. He was appointed Maritime Administrator by President Nixon in February 1969. The Merchant Marine Act of 1970 which he helped write resulted in his elevation to the new post of Assistant Secretary of Commerce for maritime affairs. He was formerly a senior vice president of Grace Line.

Rocco C. Siciliano. He was Under Secretary of Commerce in the Nixon Administration until his resignation to return to private life as of April 9, 1971. A Labor Department official in the Eisenhower Administration, Siciliano was executive vice president of the Pacific Maritime Association when he took the Commerce post during the push for new maritime legislation.

Ralph E. Casey. Appointed in February 1971 as chief counsel of the House Merchant Marine and Fisheries Committee, Casey was with the General Accounting Office, 1939-55, including duty as associate general counsel in charge of contracts, litigation and maritime activities, 1948-55. He was chief counsel to the House committee, 1955-56, resigning to become president of the American Merchant Marine Institute, holding that post from 1956 to 1968. He was executive vice president of the institute's successor organization, the American Institute of Merchant Shipping, in 1969 and was special counsel to the House committee through 1970 when the new maritime legislation was before Congress.

Robert J. Ables. Chief counsel of the House Merchant Marine and Fisheries Committee, 1969-70, he was general counsel of the Maritime Administration under former Maritime Administrator Nicholas Johnson, afterward spending five years with Coles & Goertner, a law firm whose clients have included the Committee of American Tanker Owners Inc., the Pacific Navigation System Inc., Browning Lines Inc. and the Detroit Atlantic Navigation Corporation, among others. Ables resigned in January 1971 to open his own office.

Peter M. Flanigan. He has been an assistant to the President since 1969. A New York investment banker, Flanigan was president of the Barracuda Tanker Corporation of Liberia before his appointment. He was deputy campaign manager under John N. Mitchell, who became Attorney General, in the 1968 Nixon campaign and in 1960 was national director of Volunteers for Nixon-Lodge.

Smathers, Merrigan & O'Keefe. The firm registered April 29, 1969, as lobbyists for the American Institute of Merchant Shipping. Edward L. Merrigan of the firm appeared at a House hearing in April 1969 as general counsel for AIMS. He registered July 17, 1970, as a lobbyist for Seatrain Lines Inc. George A. Smathers of the firm was U.S. Representative (D Fla.), 1947-51, and U.S. Senator (D Fla.), 1951-69. When he left Congress, Smathers was the second-ranking Democrat on the Senate Finance Committee, which has tariffs, import quotas and taxes among its responsibilities. John J. O'Keefe was Smathers' legislative assistant, 1954-68. William T. McInarnay of the firm was staff counsel, 1958-67, and staff director and general counsel, 1967-69, of the Select Small Business Committee headed by Smathers.

Francis T. Greene. General counsel of the Maritime Administration in the early 1950s, he became executive vice president of the American Merchant Marine Institute and later registered as a lobbyist for Shell Oil Company.

W. Creighton Peet Jr. Secretary of the Maritime Commission, 1937-43, he later became an executive of the Matson Navigation Company and of the Oceanic Steamship Company. In his capacity with Oceanic in 1953, he headed an inter-company committee which hired a consultant to work in the area of operating-differential subsidies.

Earl W. Clark. Co-director of the Labor-Management Maritime Committee, he is a former deputy Maritime Administrator, 1951-54.

Shipyards and Their Parent Corporate Organizations

The Maritime Act of 1970, like that of 1936, requires ships constructed with government subsidies to be built in American shipyards.

The Maritime Administration lists 13 U.S. shipyards as having the physical facilities to build ocean-going cargo vessels under the subsidy program and which might be expected to show interest. Most have existing contracts. Eleven are affiliated with larger corporate groups generally called conglomerates.

Two of the parent organizations are Lockheed Aircraft Corporation and General Dynamics Corporation,

the first and third-ranked defense contractors, respectively, in fiscal 1969. Two other companies which often are among the top defense contractors also are among the parent firms: Litton Industries, ranked 14th in fiscal 1968 and 21st in 1969, and Kaiser Industries Corporation, 18th in 1968 and 45th in 1969. Alabama Dry Dock and Todd Shipyard had few outside connections.

The list supplied by the Maritime Administration to the House Merchant Marine and Fisheries Committee in 1970, with some of the parent group interests, follows:

Shipyard	Parent corporate organization
Alabama Dry Dock & Shipbuilding Co.	——
Avondale Shipyard	Ogden Corp. (non-ferrous metals; foods; race tracks owner)
Bath Iron Works Corp.	Bath Industries
Bethlehem Steel Co.	Bethlehem Steel Corp.
General Dynamics Corp.	General Dynamics Corp. (aircraft; submarines; missiles; electronic equipment; coal; building materials)
Litton Systems Inc., Ingalls Division	Litton Industries (defense and marine systems; business systems; publishing)
Lockheed Shipbuilding & Construction Co.	Lockheed Aircraft Corp. (advanced defense systems & equipment; airport operation; electronics & propulsion)
Maryland Shipbuilding & Dry Dock Co.	Fruehauf Corp. (truck trailers; cargo containers, accessories)
National Steel & Shipbuilding Co.	Kaiser Industries Corp. (worldwide engineering and construction of steel, aluminum, thermal & hydro power; petroleum; minerals; heavy construction projects)
Newport News Shipbuilding & Dry Dock Co.	Tenneco Inc. (natural gas pipelines; oil operation; paper production; manufacturing investments in life insurance, real estate & banking)
Sun Shipbuilding & Dry Dock Co.	Sun Oil Co.
Todd Shipyards Corp.	——
Seatrain Shipbuilding Corp. (former Brooklyn Navy Yard)	Seatrain Lines Inc. (steamship line)

(Continued from p. 75)

Subsidy Background

Government support for American shipping dates from the birth of the Republic. The 1st Congress stipulated in the first tariff act in 1789 that goods imported into the United States on American vessels should get a 10-percent reduction in custom duties and imposed a tonnage tax in favor of American shipping. It was that year, too, that the national policy of reserving all coastwise trade—trade between U.S. ports—to ships owned and operated by U.S. citizens was established.

Mail subsidies began in 1845, with preference given steamships convertible to war purposes if needed. With interruptions and occasional scandals, these continued far into the 20th century.

Other countries have through the years given various kinds of assistance to their own merchant shipping. In the case of the United States, reasons for extending governmental aid were summarized as follows in a study published by the Joint Economic Committee of Congress in 1960:

"Historically subsidies to private shipping interests have been justified on the ground that a large foreign trade fleet giving employment to American citizens and capital contributes to national defense, assures against an interruption of service in time of war and promotes foreign trade by improving the quality of service available to American businessmen and by safeguarding them against discrimination."

Roosevelt Program. President Franklin D. Roosevelt in a message to Congress March 4, 1935, said the time had come for open government assistance to the nation's shipping industry. A former Navy Department official, Mr. Roosevelt said that in the past Congress had many times provided for "disguised subsidies to American shipping."

For example, he said, "The government today is paying annually about $30-million for carrying of mails, which would cost, under normal ocean rates, only $3-million. The difference, $27-million, is a subsidy, and nothing but a subsidy." He proposed a direct subsidy bill to build up the merchant marine.

Dialogue at Hearing Highlights Vote-Getting Tactics

Exchanges between two shipping state Senators and a maritime union officer at a 1970 hearing focused with considerable candor on a long-established technique by which interest groups and their friends in Congress recruit added support. Political scientists call it logrolling. There also was mention of a method sometimes used to kill a bill: overloading it.

President Nixon's original ship subsidy bill made no provision for aid to the Great Lakes shipping industry. Aware of the urgency which backers attached to the maritime legislation, Representatives from Ohio and Michigan criticized the Administration at 1969 House hearings for the omission of what partisans call "the fourth seacoast of the United States."

Secretary of Commerce Maurice H. Stans agreed to study the matter but defended giving priority to buildup of salt-water shipping to increase the U.S. merchant fleet's dwindling share of world trade.

At a Senate hearing March 4, 1970, Paul Hall, president of the Seafarers International Union of North America and president of the Maritime Trades Department, AFL-CIO, expressed regret that the pending Senate version (S 3287) left out the Great Lakes sector. "We think the Great Lakes industry is in a very badly deteriorated condition," Hall said.

Senate Minority Whip Robert P. Griffin (R Mich.) urged Hall to suggest specific language to include the Great Lakes in the same bill rather than try to deal with that area in separate legislation. Griffin, ranking minority member on the Senate Commerce Merchant Marine Subcommittee, said "there is a strong disposition on the part of the Great Lakes Senators that this is the time and we are going to make sure that the Great Lakes region is not brushed aside as it has been too many times in the past."

Hall agreed, adding: "Also I think it would be very helpful if something could be done in this direction because obviously it would create a great deal more interest in the Great Lakes area. The lakes interests would then join a little more with us in the struggle to resolve the questions surrounding this industry generally and from their point of view—particularly the Great Lakes area."

Upon which, Sen. Russell B. Long (D La.), subcommittee chairman, said, "I would think also if we are going to pass a good bill that does justice to the merchant marine we may be needing votes from those Senators from the Great Lakes."

"That is really what I meant," Hall said, "but I did not want to say it that way." Later he said:

"To use the vernacular, no deal can be a good deal unless everybody has a piece going for himself. If we can, as the Senator was saying, get a piece of this action for the Great Lakes, as Senator Long suggested, we will add to the combination and add strength to our fight."

Long promised to see what the committee could do about the various suggestions but cautioned: "I do not want to jeopardize the bill to the extent that we load it down so much that it cannot become law. I am familiar with that technique. I think on some occasions, when I was very much opposed to something, I even participated in helping to load a bill down so much that it could not pass."

Hall suggested a change to permit tax deferred deposits of domestic earnings by coastwise operators to build ships for foreign trade. Long, as chairman of the Senate Finance Committee a key figure in handling the Tax Reform Act of 1969 (PL 91-172) a few months earlier, said:

"I sort of think you fellows should have been here with that suggestion while we had the big tax bill. We had something I think that was every bit as favorable to the railroads in that bill, as is being requested here for the shipping industry. The railroads were successful in winning their fight hands down.

"We had a fight, but they won going away, and I think there are quite a few of us who could have told the railroads at that time we were willing to help them, but they would have to go along with equivalent treatment for shipping. We may have difficulty getting yours now that they already have theirs."

Hall replied: "There is an expression for that, but I will not use that either. Unfortunately there are those who have this attitude in life."

The final version of the Merchant Marine Act of 1970 (HR 15424—PL 91-469) did cover the Great Lakes area, which had "the oldest fleet in the United States by far," according to Maritime Administrator Andrew E. Gibson. The tax deferred shipbuilding fund provision also was broadened in the final bill. The Great Lakes industry also stood to benefit from a provision which forgave payment by the St. Lawrence Seaway Corporation of accrued and future interest ($22.4-million by October 1970) on a loan from the federal government.

As it turned out, World War II erupted just four and a half years later. It required congressional fights in two successive years to enact the Merchant Marine Act of 1936. By then the war was less than four years distant. It took a wartime emergency program to meet the eventual enormous demands for U.S. ships.

Shipping Lobbies. Copeland, who became a key Senate figure in ship legislation, repeatedly urged the shipping industry before and during the depression of the 1930s to organize to protect its interests in Congress. He complained at first of receiving little or no response, but

there were some elements of the industry already on the job. Others eventually put his advice to good use.

The Senator's views on how an interest group may advance its cause in Congress have proved relevant ever since. While acknowledging the value of direct access to the lawmaking machinery through strategic individuals, Copeland urged the necessity of broadening the pressure on Congress.

Congress passed the Merchant Marine Act of 1928 the year Copeland advised his listeners to kick. Among other things, that Act reaffirmed the congressional purpose stated eight years earlier at the end of World War I. It said the United States should have a merchant marine "sufficient to carry the greater portion of its commerce." Evidence was cited several years later in Congress to the effect that shipping interests had spent $150,000 in their efforts to get the 1928 bill passed with features they favored.

In 1931, Copeland urged the shipping conference to "organize a mutual-protective association...to be limited to the one purpose of educating the public in general and the Senate in particular as to the legislative needs of the American merchant marine."

The following year the American Steamship Owners Association did establish a Committee on Shipping Information. At the beginning of 1932, however, Copeland once more had told the annual industry conference: "I am here this year to repeat the scolding....I must say that you do not show 'horse sense' when it comes to legislation...."

His scolding held implications for many other interest groups, with the federal government on the brink of huge expansion which would increase the importance and scope of group relations with the national government. It came as Copeland was rising in seniority and three years before he would head the Senate committee which handled shipping legislation.

"Frankly," Copeland said, "if you did not have Mr. Walker and Mr. Duff (H.B. Walker, president, and E. H. Duff, Washington counsel, American Steamship Owners Association) to fight your battles for you, you would not get anywhere. But why do you leave it all to them? They can tell us how to formulate legislation; they can give some of us instructions as to what are the needs of the American merchant marine, but why do you not help, through your own Senators and Representatives, to make possible the enactment of laws that you want, and, what is more important, prevent the enactment of laws that you do not want?

"You can not blame us—those of us who are interested in the American merchant marine and who fight your battles—if we think we have a right to expect some support from you who are engaged in this great industry, more than simply the good work done by your officers. That work should be supplemented by the personal contacts and acquaintances you have in the Congress of the United States."

In 1935, Copeland became chairman of the Senate Commerce Committee, with responsibility for maritime matters. Across the Capitol, Rep. Schuyler Otis Bland (D Va. 1918-50), longtime chairman of the House Merchant Marine Committee, had practiced law at the shipbuilding city of Newport News, Va., and had been president of the Newport News Chamber of Commerce.

The Roosevelt Administration pushed the new shipping legislation. Within three months of the President's message, the Senate Commerce Committee recommended passage. The committee said the legislation "is a challenge to foreign influence, insidiously at work to prevent the upbuilding of an American merchant marine."

There were charges that the law firm of Ira S. Campbell, counsel to the American Steamship Owners Association and chief lobbyist for the shipping interests, had written the bill. Campbell told Senate probers he did not write the bill but had submitted proposed clauses. He indicated he kept in close touch with Copeland.

The *New York World-Telegram* said in an editorial that Chairman Bland frequently had interrupted the House hearing "to say that Mr. Campbell would not approve of this or that suggestion for new sea safety...."

Amid allegations that the House version contained loopholes favoring the industry, Rep. William D. McFarlane (D Texas 1933-39) hit at the wide discretion permitted regulatory agencies in the bill.

"The lobbyist and the so-called 'high-pressured shipping magnates' would turn the world upside down, if possible, to get weak men on the authority, or to make strong men weak under a wide-open law like this," he said.

The legislation was carried over to 1936. A split between proponents of government and private ownership was marked, accentuated by controversy over public utility holding companies which were not always unrelated to maritime interests. Both interests lobbied heavily.

The Senate Commerce Committee split down the middle in its report on the original version of the Merchant Marine Act of 1936 (S 3500). Sen. Joseph F. Guffey (D Pa. 1935-47) filed a minority report, in which he was joined by nine other Senators, which said: "The bill is framed wholly in the interest of private shipowners and shipbuilders, without any regard for the interests of the taxpayers."

The committee majority, headed by Chairman Copeland, said of a bill (S 4110) pushed by the minority as a substitute:

"The proponents of government ownership in S 4110 have resorted to every device that the outspoken enemies of a government-aided merchant marine can conjure up to hamper, restrict, and prevent private enterprise from constructing ships in American shipyards and operating them under the American flag; and yet they throw down all barriers and open wide the Treasury door to unlimited and unrestricted expenditures in a costly and extravagant scheme of government ownership."

The 1936 Act, which cleared Congress the final day of the session, laid down the policy—unchanged since— that the United States should have a merchant marine "sufficient to carry...a substantial portion" of its waterborne foreign commerce. Congress repeatedly extended the Act thereafter.

Thirty-three years later, James J. Reynolds, former Labor Department official then heading a maritime trade association, testified that the 1936 Act had been successful where properly administered and applied. For example, he said, it had been free in the intervening years of "abuses and scandals by profiteers who while taking high profits, for instance under mail pay contracts, completely ignored the need for fleet renewal through new construction."

1970 Maritime Act

The passage of the 1970 Act, like that of its predecessor, resulted from years of groundwork. This involved, among other things, continuing contacts between the varied elements of the industry and members and staff members on Capitol Hill, as well as with executive branch personnel.

As with other interests, it involved supporting candidates presumed or known to hold sympathetic views. It meant aiding the repeated re-election of selected incumbents which permits the buildup of seniority and power. Much crossing of political party lines occurred. A few examples:

• Records showed that 90 percent of the 1968 campaign funds of Rep. Edward A. Garmatz (D Md.), chairman of the House Merchant Marine and Fisheries Committee, came from shipping donations or maritime receptions for him. In the 1970 campaign, the shipping industry and its unions helped raise a $37,000 campaign fund for Garmatz, including $3,000 from the political arm of the Seafarers International Union (SIU), AFL-CIO. Top maritime officials of the Nixon Administration joined in a fund-raising cocktail party for him. He was unopposed in 1970 for re-election.

A federal grand jury indictment of the SIU and eight individuals in 1970 cited contributions of $40,000 to Republican and Democratic political campaigns in 1968 as part of an alleged plan to spend $750,000 for such purposes over a period of years.

• American President Lines and Pacific Far East Line were fined $50,000 each in federal court in 1970 on their plea of guilty to violation of the Corrupt Practices Act. It was disclosed that Garmatz received $1,000 from the American President Lines and $500 from the Pacific Far East Line in contributions to his 1966 election campaign. Garmatz also received $3,500 from "The Pacific Coast Committee for Re-election of E. A. Garmatz," based at a San Francisco address housing several shipping-related firms who denied knowledge of the committee. Fifteen other Representatives and Senators were reported by the Associated Press to be shown in secret Justice Department files as receiving past campaign contributions from the two steamship lines. They included Sen. Warren G. Magnuson (D Wash.), chairman of the Senate Commerce Committee, whose campaign received $1,000.

Federal law prohibits direct campaign gifts by corporations and labor unions but permits donations by officials as individuals or by special committees set up for political purposes.

• Officials of Litton Industries Inc., parent organization of a major shipbuilding operation among other things, led all individual corporate officer givers in a survey of 1968 campaign gifts by officials of leading government contractors. Eleven of Litton's 29 officers and directors donated $151,000 to Republican candidates, nothing to Democrats. The total included $90,000 from Henry Salvatori, a Litton director, and his wife, and $19,500 from Litton chairman Charles B. Thornton.

• Five officials of Lockheed Aircraft Corporation, which includes major shipbuilding among its interests, contributed $38,880 to Republicans, $1,000 to Democrats in 1968. Nine executives of General Dynamics Corporation, another diversified company with major shipyard facilities, donated $17,265 to Republicans, $1,000 to Democrats.

• Three officials of another corporate parent of shipyard interests—Kaiser Industries Corporation—gave $25,000 to the Democratic party, $8,000 to Republicans. The donation to Democratic fund-raisers came from Edgar F. Kaiser, chairman.

• Joseph Paul Curran, son of Joseph Curran, head of the AFL-CIO Maritime Committee and president of the National Maritime Union, worked for the 1968 campaign of Hubert H. Humphrey, Democratic candidate for President. The next year the younger Curran headed the union's new political action department.

Curran's father in 1968 had called the maritime legislation of the Johnson Administration—in which Humphrey was Vice President—"inadequate, unimaginative and unsatisfactory." Previously, the National Maritime Union had criticized the maritime policies of the Eisenhower Administration, in which Mr. Nixon was Vice President. The *NMU Pilot,* for example, said in 1961 that the Eisenhower Administration "openly invited big business shipping interests to write the nation's maritime policies." On the other hand, Earl W. Clark, co-director of the Labor-Management Maritime Committee who was Deputy Maritime Administrator during the Truman and Eisenhower Administrations, characterized the Johnson Administration in 1969 as "one of the most disinterested and unsympathetic administrations in U.S. maritime history."

• Peter M. Flanigan, investment banker who headed an ocean tanker company, worked as a top aide in the 1968 Nixon campaign. Flanigan had worked in the 1960 Nixon campaign.

Industry Moves. Past efforts to push through a stepped-up shipbuilding and operating subsidy program had foundered partly on disunity in the industry and in government. Strikes disrupted service in the 1960s.

On Feb. 8, 1968, several organizations formed a Joint Unity Committee to pursue common legislative goals. Included were representatives of the National Maritime Union, the International Longshoreman's Association, major steamship companies, the American Merchant Marine Institute, the Labor-Management Maritime Committee, the Maritime Service Company and others.

The Labor-Management Maritime Committee was itself an existing unity movement, composed as Clark said "of major steamship lines and seagoing unions engaged in the foreign commerce of the United States." Co-chairmen were Curran and Manual Diaz, president and chief executive officer of American Export Isbrandsen Lines Inc., a subsidized steamship line. Co-director with Clark was Hoyt S. Haddock, executive director of the AFL-CIO Maritime Committee.

The American Merchant Marine Institute (AMMI) was incorporated in June 1938 to succeed the former American Steamship Owners Association. The AMMI was set up by the same committee which incorporated the earlier trade group, and the founders outlined the same purposes, centered around promoting the American merchant marine.

In addition to steamship companies, the AMMI membership shortly after founding included eight oil companies, involving three of the five AMMI members who paid the top dues of $10,000 a year. Members included Standard Oil Company of California, Union Oil Company of California, Gulf Oil Corporation marine department, Socony-Vacuum Oil Company, Standard Oil Company (N.J.) marine department, United Fruit Company, Atlantic Refining Company, Sun Oil Company and Tide Water Associated Oil Company. The oil companies made up nearly one-fifth of the 43 AMMI members.

Nixon Program. Mr. Nixon had pledged during his campaign to do something about the merchant marine. With his election, a series of moves toward that end occurred. An early one involved the industry itself.

The month after the 1968 election, the AMMI and other groups merged in a new trade association called the American Institute of Merchant Shipping (AIMS). James

J. Reynolds, the number two official in the Labor Department in the Johnson Administration, was named to head AIMS. He had been a key figure in maritime disputes in 1961, 1964 and 1965. Reynolds once said this gave him some familiarity with collective bargaining—"the same familiarity that a shuttlecock has with a couple of badminton rackets."

At a House hearing April 16, 1969, three months after he left the Labor Department, Reynolds referred to the recurring disputes between shipowners, shipbuilders, operating unions and building unions, congressional committees and executive departments.

"In recognition of the need for unity," he said, former members of AMMI, the Committee of American Steamship Lines and the Pacific American Steamship Association, among others, organized AIMS. The Committee of American Steamship Lines was an association of 13 U.S.-flag steamship companies which had operating-differential subsidy contracts with the government.

At its founding, AIMS contained 39 companies which owned and operated 539 U.S.-flag ships making up 62 percent of all active previously owned tonnage registered under the U.S. flag. Reynolds said AIMS was an association "which for the first time in the history of this nation can speak for at least a substantial portion of most of the sections of the merchant marine, the subsidized and the unsubsidized and the tankers and bulk carriers and the coastal carriers."

Ralph E. Casey, president of the old AMMI, became AIMS executive vice president. The new maritime trade group thus had, in Reynolds, the foremost government official involved in attempts to settle some of the labor disputes of the 1960s and, in Casey, the key negotiator for the industry at the time.

Albert E. May, an executive of the Committee of American Steamship Lines, became vice president of AIMS. Named treasurer was Parker S. Wise, who was with Socony-Mobil Oil Company Inc., 1929-62, including a period as general manager of its marine transportation department, 1953-62. Wise was chairman of the American Petroleum Institute's central committee on transportation by water, 1960-61, and was an executive of AMMI from 1963 until its merger into AIMS in December 1968.

The board of directors of AIMS also included a vice president of Texaco Inc. The Natomas Company, whose varied holdings included oil interests, had a voice in AIMS through its control of American President Lines Ltd., American Mail Line and Pacific Far East Line Inc. The AIMS board of directors included Worth B. Fowler, president of American President and American Mail, and Leo C. Ross, president of Pacific Far East. The Pacific Far East Line was sold in mid-1969 to Consolidated Freightways Inc.

Ralph K. Davies, chairman of Natomas and of American President Lines and a director of the Bank of America, N.A., was senior vice president of the Standard Oil Company of California, 1935-46, and deputy petroleum administrator, Petroleum Administration for War, during World War II.

President Nixon appointed as Maritime Administrator Andrew E. Gibson, a former senior vice president of Grace Line. The President named Rocco Siciliano, executive vice president of the Pacific Maritime Association, as Under Secretary of Commerce. Peter Flanigan became a White House assistant. The President appointed Mrs. Helen

Delich Bentley, maritime editor of the *Baltimore Sun,* as chairman of the U.S. Maritime Commission.

Changes also took place at the Capitol as the year 1969 progressed. Robert J. Ables, former general counsel of the Maritime Administration, became chief counsel of the House Merchant Marine and Fisheries Committee. Sen. Russell B. Long (D La.), described by the AFL-CIO's Haddock as "a stout friend of the merchant marine," moved up in 1969 from his former sixth-ranking Democratic spot on the Senate Commerce Merchant Marine Subcommittee to the chairmanship.

Pressures. Pressures for action persisted from various directions. These included speeches, statements, resolutions and publications urging interested constituents to contact members of Congress and executive officials. The National Maritime Union's national council in a statement in March 1969 said, "We are dependent on foreign flag ships today to carry about 95 percent of our foreign commerce." It called this "the height of folly."

Curran was among those present at a meeting between the AFL-CIO executive council and Mr. Nixon with several Cabinet members in May 1969. Curran said he reminded the President that when Curran visited the Soviet Union in 1960, Premier Nikita S. Khrushchev boasted to him that the Soviet Union would be the world's greatest maritime power by 1975.

A series of publications went out in mid-1969 from the Labor-Management Maritime Committee to members of Congress, executive officials and others. Stating that the committee embraced major steamship companies representing 70 percent of all ships in the liner trade and seagoing longshore unions covering some 268,000 maritime workers, the committee climaxed that phase of its activity with a 12-page brochure entitled, "Maritime Program Imperatives: A Time for Deeds—Not Words."

Clark and Haddock followed up in 1970 with a book reviewing the nation's recent maritime history. It was called: *The U.S. Merchant Marine Today: Sunrise or Sunset?*

The Transport Workers Union of America, AFL-CIO, asked all its local presidents to write their Senators and Representatives asking action to rebuild the merchant fleet and correct what was called "this shameful condition."

Support came from non-maritime groups, including some labor unions and the American Legion, which was interested from a national defense viewpoint. The legion's *Advance* published an appeal to all legion posts to contact Congress urging maritime legislation.

The published appeal said the legion had expressed its position to the White House, adding: "By making its views known to decision makers in the executive and legislative branches of government and through its educational programs, the American Legion strives earnestly to assure the future of our merchant marine."

As months passed without submission of the promised legislation by the White House, a note of impatience appeared here and there. The AFL-CIO Maritime Committee prodded the Administration. It issued a statement during the national AFL-CIO convention in October 1969 saying the United States required a merchant marine capable of carrying at least 50 percent of its foreign waterborne commerce. Noting that the Nixon program had not yet been introduced, the statement said:

"Continuing delays have brought to the forefront many abuses of rich foreign flag shipowners and conglomerates who have gotten rich on evading U.S. taxes." It said, "While the President's promises of an adequate merchant marine gather political moss, the American conglomerates such as Walter Kidde are milking the treasuries of such organizations as the United States Lines."

The Kidde interests later asked government permission to sell the United States Lines, for years the largest government-subsidized operator, to another conglomerate, the R.J. Reynolds tobacco interests which already were involved in containerized shipping.

On Oct. 23, 1969, President Nixon sent a message to Congress announcing a new maritime subsidy program which he said "will replace the drift and neglect of recent years and restore this country to a proud position in the shipping lanes of the world."

Both houses held brief hearings on the proposal within days after the President's announcement, but because the bills (S 3287, HR 15424) were not actually introduced until late in December, no action was taken on them in 1969.

Meanwhile, many prolonged discussions of the legislation took place behind the scenes. Casey and other representatives of AIMS had registered in 1969 to lobby on maritime legislation. At the beginning of 1970, when Congress was due to get down to cases on the new Act, Casey left his AIMS post to become special counsel for the House Merchant Marine and Fisheries Committee. He was listed the first six months of 1970 as head of the committee's 11-member "investigations committee staff." His salary of $35,000 throughout 1970 equaled that of chief counsel Ables. Casey had served an earlier stretch on the committee's staff during the Eisenhower Administration. *(Box p. 24)*

AIMS President Reynolds testified Feb. 5, 1970, that meetings and discussions had occurred between the Administration and groups involved in the proposed legislation.

"The Maritime Administrator and members of his staff responsible for the drafting of the bill have graciously made themselves available for prolonged and detailed discussions," Reynolds said. "There are a great many technical details. There are a great many nuances of interpretation in the draft legislation which required very detailed examination with Mr. Gibson...I understand that he has, indeed, met with other groups, as I say, management, labor and shipyard interests, so that they, too, might be better informed concerning the legislation."

Reynolds later made it clear that the discussions occurred after the legislation was drafted and submitted to Congress, rather than before.

On March 2, 1970, after the various unity movements in an industry known for friction, Chairman Magnuson of the Senate Commerce Committee said: "With the putting aside of historic disagreements and enmities, and the cooperation of all the parties involved, we can have a new law and program very shortly."

Congress cleared the legislation (HR 15424—PL 91-469) on Oct. 7, 1970. In spite of unity appeals by Magnuson and others, a number of sharp disputes occurred before that time. Disagreements over details of the legislation produced harsh words at times, though some industry sources tended to discount their significance afterward. There were charges of favoritism and of un-

due influence from the National Maritime Union against the shipbuilders' lobby, the oil interests, the Seafarers International Union and some of the unsubsidized operators. An NMU official said, nevertheless, that he felt labor elements of industry agreed more often than not.

Aftermath

Few in the industry considered the 1970 Act would solve all the problems besetting the U.S. merchant marine. Many of these were of long standing. The success of the shipbuilding program authorized by Congress would be vitally affected in the next decade by the future actions of the varied elements who, despite differences, pulled together long enough to make the legislation possible.

Mrs. Bentley told the 50th anniversary luncheon of the Shipbuilders Council of America on March 3, 1971:

"Certainly, the major problems of United States shipbuilding enterprise can be traced, in the main, to the lack of long-term government commitment to our merchant marine and shipyard industries. But should we not also admit that some of the woes are entirely the fault of the industry?"

Among controversies yet to be solved were:

• Cargo—Many industry spokesmen said the generation of cargoes, which would make the new ships profitable, was all-important. As Edwin M. Hood, president of the Shipbuilders Council of America, who was credited by Mrs. Bentley with playing a major part in developing the 1970 policy changes, put it, "Cargoes are the name of the game."

• Labor-Management Relations—Unions tended to blame elements of the industry who transfered major shipping operations to ships operated by American-owned subsidiaries under flags registered in Liberia, Panama and Honduras to escape high labor costs, taxes and other costs faced under U.S.-flag operations. Owners of foreign-flag ships, on the other hand, criticized unions as running up costs through excessive demands, making it impossible to compete with cheaper foreign competitors. Work stoppages, sometimes initiated by small groups, were cited by owners as driving customers to more dependable lines. The foreign shipping operations financed by U.S.-based companies, including oil interests, were called flags of convenience, flags of necessity, or runaway flags, depending on who was talking.

• Passenger Service—The 1970 Act made no provision for American passenger shipping, also in disrepair in the face of foreign competition.

Casey became chief counsel of the House Merchant Marine and Fisheries Committee in February 1971. Government agencies and some unions and management groups announced drives to promote greater reliance on U.S.-flag ships by shippers in hopes of increasing the cargo hauled. The AFL-CIO Maritime Committee and the National Maritime Union, among others, opened a push for congressional action to revive passenger service.

The union's chosen method of exerting pressure in the latest campaign was to bring union seamen to Washington to confront Senators and Representatives from their own states and districts.

"This method has proven to be the most effective kind of confrontation, requiring each legislator to come face to face with the facts and take a position on the question," the *NMU Pilot* said. "It is a method far superior to mass demonstrations."

FOREIGN TRADE LOBBY

1970 Trade Bill: Stakes Big, Lobbying Heavy

Foreign and domestic interests in 1970 engaged in an all-out pressure fight over U.S. foreign trade policy. Matching some of the powerful forces that clashed in 1962 when trade last arose as a major issue in Congress, the 1970 confrontation was seen by some as holding possible significance in the Presidential and Congressional elections of 1972.

The struggle involved many months of intensive lobbying and grassroots efforts to influence American public opinion. Many influential lobbyists, including a number of present and former Government officials and prominent law firms, took part.

The leverage at every level was money.

A major stake was the continuance of a freer U.S. trade policy—a process set into motion in a sharp policy turnaround in 1934 and given momentum by the Trade Expansion Act of 1962 (PL 87-794). President Kennedy called that Act "the most important international piece of legislation...affecting economics since the passage of the Marshall Plan."

Carl J. Gilbert, longtime Gillette Company executive who headed the leading free trade pressure group in the fight which gave Mr. Kennedy a major legislative victory of 1961-62, became President Nixon's Special Representative for Trade Negotiations. The ambassador-rank post was established by the 1962 Act empowering the President to negotiate trade pacts.

The Committee for a National Trade Policy of which Gilbert was president was as prominent in the 1970 trade struggle as it was in 1962.

A new factor took on importance—the multinational corporation. The 1970 contest found some of the largest U.S.-based international business concerns, including a faction which contains three of the top five U.S. defense contractors and 10 of the top 25, throwing their substantial weight against tariffs, quotas and other trade barriers.

Most of the main factions active in 1962 held positions generally similar to those they held before. Others had revised their stands in the light of recent developments. The AFL-CIO, for example, had shifted its stance to favor tighter reins on imports which were shown to damage U.S. industries.

The pressure on Congress and on President Nixon came from within the United States and from without. U.S. trade legislation invariably draws foreign attention, as shown by the many trade-related registrations with the Justice Department under the Foreign Agents Registration Act of 1938.

This was accentuated in 1970 by the strength of pressures in the United States for restraints against certain imports from abroad. Some domestic interests said heavy imports injured them, even threatened their survival.

The House passage (Nov. 19, 1970) of a bill (HR 18970, the Trade Act of 1970) legislating quotas on textile and footwear imports and simplifying executive restric-

tions, as asked by some U.S. interest groups, came amid organized opposition at home and from foreign governments and trade associations. Equal opposition met the Senate Finance Committee's approval of the bill with important changes. The bill subsequently died in last minute Senate maneuvers.

Retaliation Warnings

Many warned of retaliation. Mr. Nixon wrote Sen. Hugh Scott (R Pa.), Minority Leader, in a letter made public Dec. 10, 1970, that textile quotas were needed "in view of our inability to reach negotiated agreements" with foreign suppliers, but that the Senate Committee's bill "could trigger international trade practices destructive of the economy of the entire Free World."

The Chamber of Commerce of the United States issued a press release Dec. 15, 1970. It said chamber branches in 31 countries warned "serious retaliation... will be swiftly invoked by foreign governments if Congress enacts import quotas." Proponents of restraints called retaliation unlikely.

Some contended—others denied—that the struggle revived the decades-old contest between "protectionist" and "liberal" trade policies. The fight came against a background of unrest over rising unemployment and inflation—possible issues in 1972, when Mr. Nixon was expected to seek a second term.

The New York Times reported from London that European reaction added up "to the most intensive international lobbying seen in years against a piece of domestic American legislation." Equal pressure came from Latin America and the Far East, especially export-conscious Japan, target of many U.S. critics.

Foreign officials and trade spokesmen did not hesitate to speak or act in attempts to sway Congress and the President. Their American agents—some of them working for U.S. import-export interests at the same time—vied with lobbyists of American pressure groups for the attention of Senators and Representatives.

Rep. Paul Findley (R Ill.) said Nov. 18, 1970, as the House began trade debate: "In attempting to get to the floor today I had to elbow my way through a swarm of lobbyists in the corridors. It was all I could do to get to the floor. These lobbyists are well represented, I am told, elsewhere in this chamber. No doubt they are here to serve what they think are the best interests of the textile industry, of the shoe industry, of the mink industry or whatever it might be...."

In a letter dated the next day, Hendrik S. Houthakker, Amsterdam-born Harvard professor on the President's Council of Economic Advisers, reminded Findley that "within the last few days the European commission has again put the soybean tax on its agenda, but a decision has been postponed until after the fate of the trade bill is clear." Illinois, largest U.S. producer of soybeans, depended heavily on exports.

(Continued on p. 85)

Trade Council: Largely Financed by Japanese Government

The United States-Japan Trade Council drew criticism at 1970 House foreign trade hearings. As a result, it changed its statement identifying Japanese backing at Senate hearings later.

Rep. John W. Byrnes (R Wis.), ranking Republican on the House Ways and Means Committee, said the council's witness failed to make clear—as Byrnes put it—that the council was "a front for what is fundamentally a Japanese government-financed operation."

Nelson A. Stitt of Stitt, Hemmendinger & Kennedy said he did not feel he had misled the Committee. He said the United States-Japan Trade Council, "just because it is largely financed by the Japanese government, does not take a Japanese government position."

Stitt told Committee Chairman Wilbur D. Mills (D Ark.): "I think many of your witnesses, Mr. Chairman, I suspect, are also being substantially financed from abroad but have not been as meticulous as we in reporting our activities and our financing to the Department of Justice as required by law."

U.S. Groups. The Committee hears only U.S. citizens or spokesmen for corporations incorporated in the United States. When Stitt testified in opposition to U.S. import quotas May 19, 1970, he identified himself as director of the United States-Japan Trade Council, "an association of approximately 800 firms doing business in the United States and interested in promoting a growing healthy trade between the two countries."

Noel Hemmendinger, Stitt's partner, testified June 2, 1970, as counsel for the American Importers Association's Footwear Group, made up of 26 companies which import footwear from Europe and the Far East. He opposed across-the-board quotas on footwear.

Hemmendinger is counsel for the United States-Japan Trade Council. There was no mention of the council during Hemmendinger's appearance, but the published hearings contain a statement he resubmitted from a 1969 Senate hearing which said, "Our firm also represents a number of Japanese associations of companies that are engaged in the production of footwear and exportation to the United States."

On June 11, 1970, Byrnes said it had come to his attention that the United States-Japan Trade Council received—as he put it—98 percent of its financing from the Japanese government and 2 percent from membership dues. Byrnes said it seemed to him "that the Committee was intentionally misled as to who Mr. Stitt really was appearing for on May 19."

Stitt said in a reappearance: "It is entirely true that about 95 percent of the financing of our council emanates in Japan and emanates from the government of Japan." But, he said, "we are definitely not a propaganda arm of the Japanese government." He said council positions decided by himself, Hemmendinger and one other officer often varied from those of the Japanese government. The council's emphasis was on liberal trade policies, he said.

Foreign Agent. Stitt noted that among material given the Committee was a label approved by the Justice Department under the Foreign Agents Registration Act. The label said the council was a trade association "with a membership of over 700 (said by Stitt to be out of date) firms in the United States interested in fostering trade relations between the two countries. Because a substantial contributing member, the Japan Trade Promotion Office, 111 Broadway, New York, N.Y., is financed from Japan, the council is registered...as an agent of such foreign principal."

Stitt said "the Foreign Agents Registration Act... says any foreign agent which appears before a committee of the Congress must supply the committee with the most recent copy of its registration statement.

"This was so done and handed to a member of your staff before I took the stand....So, we have complied with the law. We have openly disclosed." Byrnes said the information "was not written into the record...except in the very small print presented to the Committee."

Stitt said about 150 members were Japanese trading firms also incorporated in the United States. He said the Japan Trade Promotion Office had a staff of two and obtained its money from the Japanese government. He accepted Byrnes' figuring that the Japan Trade Promotion Office gave the trade council $339,772 in 1969, while member companies paid about $14,000 in dues. The larger sum was listed in a report for the Justice Department as intended "for promotion of U.S.-Japan trade." Of dues paid the preceding six months, the trade council report said: "This sum was not received to be used in the interests of the foreign principal, but is reported here in order to make full disclosure of receipts."

Supplementary Report. In a supplementary report filed with the Department early in 1970, the Japan Trade Promotion Office listed receipts of $259,986 and transmittal of $231,992 to the United States-Japan Trade Council in the preceding six months.

In a six-month report in mid-1970, the trade council reported receiving $170,215.57 from the Japan Trade Promotion Office under an agreement calling for payment of $316,407 for the fiscal year.

When Stitt testified Oct. 9, 1970, before the Senate Finance Committee, the label on his testimony said the Japan Trade Promotion Office "is financed by the Japanese government..." and he stressed this factor to the Committee. The press release on his testimony bore the old label.

Stitt, Hemmendinger & Kennedy had active registrations under the Foreign Agents Registration Act in 1970 on behalf of these foreign principals:

Japan Chemical Shoes Industrial Association; Embassy of Japan; Japan General Merchandise Exporters' Association; Japan Rubber Footwear Manufacturing Association; Japan Stainless Steel Exporters' Association; Japan Trade Center; United States-Japan Trade Council; Japan Woolen & Linen Textiles Exporters Association; Nippon Kokan Kabushiki Kaisa; Nippon Steel Corporation, Suminoto Metal Industries Ltd and Japan Iron and Steel Exporters Association.

Swarm of Lobbyists

Trade lobbyists were noted by Rep. John B. Anderson (R Ill.). Like Findley, he opposed the bill submitted by Rep. Wilbur D. Mills (D Ark.), chairman of the Ways and Means Committee, and subsequently passed by the House.

Referring to "the forces of protectionism," Anderson said that during Committee hearings "the representatives of special, parochial interests—company officials, labor union leaders, local government spokesmen—had streamed endlessly into this city. One by one they came forward with their pleas for protection: the manufacturers of scissors and shears, toys, umbrellas and novelties; the producers of glue, flowers, candles and sporting goods; the makers of pins and fasteners, mushrooms, honey, footwear and textiles and apparel....

"These groups worked hard. They collared and buttonholed. They turned out a torrent of facts, figures, charts and memorandums....They gained an enormous amount of support."

Mills, from a cotton state, was cited by President Kennedy for helping pass the 1962 law. At 1970 hearings, Mills cited evidence that unrestricted imports were injuring some industries, especially in textiles and footwear which employ many low-skilled workers. Mills said to a spokesman for Japanese interests:

"I have said repeatedly that I didn't get to be chairman of the Ways and Means Committee to preside over the destruction of any segment of our American industry, and I mean it."

Rep. W. J. Bryan Dorn (D S.C.), secretary of the unofficial House textile committee, spoke of an "unprecedented volume of misleading propaganda" from opponents of import curbs. He said people from his area favored reciprocal trade, adding: "But we have become disillusioned with reciprocal trade as administered in Washington."

Dorn said "the fact is clear...that the jobs of the 2½ million people of the textile apparel and fiber industries are in grave danger."

The AFL-CIO held that current trade conditions chiefly aided multinational companies. AFL-CIO Legislative Director Andrew J. Biemiller (U.S. Rep. D. Wis. 1945-47, 1949-51) testified:

"The choice is not between free trade and protectionist theories. Free, competitive trade relations hardly exist any longer in this world of managed national economies and the large-scale operations of foreign subsidiaries of U.S. companies."

Biemiller said AFL-CIO members "have no intention of becoming isolationists....We oppose the promotion of private greed at public expense or the undercutting of U.S. wage and labor standards."

Rep. John H. Dent (D Pa.), referring to the "Jekyll and Hyde nationalism" of multinational companies, told the House Aug. 12, 1970:

"The best financed lobby the world has ever seen is represented by these huge multinational corporations and their counterparts in foreign countries. The import-export lobby cannot be outbid, it must be outsmarted and outvoted."

Trade Policy Background. U.S. trade policy since the 1930s has aimed at reducing or eliminating tariffs and quotas or other non-tariff barriers between nations.

The Smoot-Hawley Act of 1930 raised U.S. tariffs to their highest level in history. The high tariffs and the depression had worldwide repercussions. Restrictions on trade multiplied everywhere. The House Democratic Study Group said Smoot-Hawley "raised tariffs so much that it eliminated over half of the value of American trade within three years and precipitated a major worldwide protectionist trade war."

The Trade Agreements Act of 1934 authorized the President to make tariff cuts of up to 50 percent of the Smoot-Hawley rates, in return for equivalent concessions. The Trade Expansion Act of 1962 continued the free trade policies, as did Mr. Nixon's proposed Trade Act of 1969.

In the 1968 Presidential campaign, Mr. Nixon pledged to act to prevent further injury to U.S. textile and clothing industries from underpriced imports. After House hearings presenting 377 witnesses and filling more than 4,600 pages, the Mills bill emerged. Its provisions were tighter than the President had asked. So were those of the Senate version. The President was brought under pressure to veto the bill.

Multinational Corporations

Emergency Committee for American Trade. Among forces exerting pressure for free trade provisions in 1970 were spokesmen for corporations which operate across national boundaries. Involving leading U.S. firms, these enterprises had admirers and critics. Their foremost organization was the Emergency Committee for American Trade (ECAT).

ECAT was formed by a few companies in 1967 "to oppose the surge of protectionism," ECAT Chairman Donald M. Kendall told House hearings May 18, 1970. Kendall was president and chief executive officer of PepsiCo Inc., was a client of Mr. Nixon's former law firm and had been chairman of the National Alliance of Businessmen. Arthur K. Watson, longtime IBM executive who became Ambassador to France, said ECAT—which he helped found—contained producers of nearly 10 percent of the U.S. gross national product.

Grown to about 51 companies, ECAT said Mr. Nixon's trade message to Congress (Nov. 18, 1969) seemed to offer "precisely the right prescription for the United States at this juncture."

Ellison L. Hazard, board chairman and president of Continental Can Company Inc., who testified for ECAT, devoted a 1970 speech largely to what he called a "very important concept: the idea that peace can be best brought about, not by nation-states balancing force with force, but by businessmen constructing interlocking channels of trade and finance, throughout the world."

Hazard said "company after company has found it desirable to export its knowledge and skills to a local base of operation, instead of shipping products over long distances." As a result, he said, "we see emerging today, many companies of various national origins, with operations in a multiplicity of countries....

"These companies are unlike any of the great international companies of the past—companies that were by design and objective extractive and exploiting enter-prises....To name a few—Goodyear and Unilever, Phillips, Sony and IBM, Singer, ICI and Honeywell—these all serve to illustrate today's 'multinational' corporation."

Hazard said a multinational corporation had these characteristics:

"First, a significant and growing portion of its operations and resources are located outside its country of incorporation.

"Second, its management is truly multinational in character.

"Third, and perhaps most important, it uses its skills and resources to promote the growth of the economies in all the areas in which it operates."

George W. Ball, who as Under Secretary of State helped obtain enactment of the 1962 trade bill, said in a speech May 15, 1970:

"The multinational corporation may prove a valuable instrument to set the pace of progress. Almost certainly, as our great enterprises become increasingly de-nationalized, they will evolve into entities where Japanese and American, British, French, Germans and other businessmen can work together within a common institutional framework for a common purpose."

Kendall testified that "restrictions breed restrictions" and that when nations retaliate with trade barriers, "the results cancel each other out on a downhill race." He said ECAT was not prepared to discuss oil quotas "because it is a defense issue."

ECAT ran a full-page advertisement in *The Washington Post* July 13, 1970, half filled by the words: "Congress: Please don't declare a world trade war!" It bore the names of chairmen or presidents of these firms, among others: Boeing Company, National Biscuit Company, Honeywell Inc., Caterpillar Tractor Company, Bendix Corporation, American Motors, McDonnell Douglas, McGraw-Hill Inc., Ford Motor, Sperry Rand, Bristol-Myers, W. R. Grace & Company, United Aircraft;

Texas Instruments Inc., Lockheed, Continental Can, H. J. Heinz, Deere & Company, Hewlett-Packard, International Paper, Borg-Warner, Standard Oil (N.J.), IBM World Trade Corporation, PepsiCo Inc., Singer, Time Inc., American Metal Climax Inc., Cummins Engine Company Inc., Lever Brothers, Bell & Howell, Bank of America;

Kaiser Aluminum & Chemical, General Motors, Chase Manhattan Bank, Quaker Oats, Litton Industries Inc., Chrysler, American Export Isbrandtsen Lines, Xerox and First National City Bank.

Three ECAT members—Lockheed, United Aircraft and McDonnell Douglas—were among the top five U.S. defense contractors in fiscal 1968 and fiscal 1969. Others among the top 25 defense contractors included Boeing, GM, Litton, Sperry Rand, Ford, Honeywell and Standard Oil. A number also are prime contractors for the National Aeronautics and Space Administration. ECAT represented a large segment of the U.S. industry.

Rep. Dent told the House the companies in the ad "have foreign affiliates in 108 countries, and 32 of the companies have ownership in Japanese firms, many producing the same goods abroad they once produced in the United States." He supplied a partial list of the companies' overseas connections.

Sen. Ernest F. Hollings (D S.C.), from a textile state, said in the Senate Dec. 4, 1970: "The members

of ECAT are intent upon preserving their foreign investments, and they do so by opposing policies which might incur the wrath of their foreign benefactors. They speak in terms of the virtues of free trade, but act obviously with as much self-interest as any other group in our society."

AFL-CIO Position. The AFL-CIO's Biemiller said the U.S. position in world trade has deteriorated in recent years.

"The basic causes are major changes in world economic relationships during the past 25 years," he said. These included "the skyrocketing rise of investments of U.S. companies in foreign subsidiaries and the mushrooming growth of U.S.-based multinational corporations." Biemiller said multinationals "now account for about one-half of U.S. exports." He told the Mills Committee:

"Multinational companies attempt to use a systems approach to global production, distribution and sales. With plants and other facilities spread through numerous countries, multinational firms can and do juggle the production of components and assembly operations, license and patent agreements, distribution and shipping and sales arrangements to maximize the gains of the firm....

"A multinational corporation can produce components in widely separated plants in Korea, Taiwan and the United States, assemble the product in a plant in Mexico and sell the goods in the United States—with a U.S. brand name.

"Moreover, when such goods are sold in the American market, they are sold at American prices. So the American worker loses his job and the American consumer pays the same price or close to it. The beneficiaries are the U.S.-based multinational companies."

Other Liberal Trade Lobbies

Committee for a National Trade Policy. The CNTP has described itself as a nonprofit "business league." It is incorporated with a board of directors and other "supporters" who donate funds. The chairman and general counsel was Charles P. Taft, former mayor of Cincinnati, 1955-57, and a State Department official in 1944-45. He was the brother of the late Sen. Robert A. Taft (R Ohio 1939-53). "For 16 years we have been leading advocates of generally freer trade in the over-all public interest," Taft said in generally supporting the President's bill.

Of 31 companies named on the CNTP board of directors list, 12 were also supporters of ECAT. Five of the company executives were on both groups' lists.

Gilbert, Mr. Nixon's trade negotiator, was president of CNTP during the 1962 trade battle. Taft was general counsel. Then as now, the executive director was John W. Hight.

The CNTP issued a statement (Sept. 18, 1970) signed by 4,390 economists opposing the trade bill then pending in the House and urging a Presidential veto if necessary. It said Congress appeared on the verge of making "another massive mistake" of the nature of Smoot-Hawley. Sponsors included four former chairmen of the Council of Economic Advisers: Gardner Ackley, Walter W. Heller, Leon H. Keyserling and Raymond J. Saulnier. Sen. Philip A. Hart (D Mich.) brought the CNTP statement to the attention of the Senate three months later as it took up trade matters. Calling the Senate Committee's version "a serious attack upon the antitrust policy of the United States," the chairman of the Senate Judiciary Antitrust and Monopoly Subcommittee said:

"Both tariffs and quotas offer domestic competitors havens from the rigors of foreign competitors or the foreign subsidiaries of domestic competitors." He said the Senate should examine "the historical relationship of high trade barriers to the creation of domestic trusts and international cartels."

Chamber of Commerce of the United States. As in 1962, the Chamber supported continued trade expansion policies. The Chamber includes more than 37,000 companies and individuals in the United States and abroad. Among its constituents are businesses which are sensitive to heavy import competition as well as those who belong to the CNTP or ECAT.

Chamber representatives emphasized that almost four million American jobs depend on exporting and importing and warned against legislative restrictions "which will almost surely provoke retaliation." Chamber publicity highlighted the possibility of retaliation and singled out specific U.S. export items and countries. For example, the Dec. 15 release timed to coincide with Senate consideration of the trade bill said:

"Italy—likely to retaliate against U.S. corn, aircraft, soybeans, electronic products, laminated steel, mechanical steel, optical precision instruments, various chemical products and others....1969 U.S. exports to Italy of these products were, as follows: corn, $30 million a year; soybeans, $50 million; coal, $40 million; laminated iron and steel, $35 million; airplanes and parts, $60 million.

"Spain—Retaliation appears certain against U.S. soybeans, corn, tobacco, tallow, protein meals and cakes, wood of various kinds, cattle hides, live cattle, poultry, pulses (beans, lentils, peas), seeds, cotton, frozen meats and many manufactured products. The U.S. trade surplus with Spain was $502,900,000 in 1969."

As with the material issued by other interest groups, this message was aimed equally at Members of Congress and Americans involved in affected products at every level. Standard procedure in campaigns to build pressure on Congress includes efforts to mobilize broad support among the constituents back home.

The chief representative at House hearings for the Chamber was Walter S. Surrey of the law firm Surrey, Karasik, Greene & Hill. Identifying himself as a member of the Chamber's International Committee, Surrey supported the Administration bill, with qualifications.

Surrey was chief of the State Department's division of economic security controls, 1946-47. He was consultant to the Economic Cooperation Administration, 1948-59, and to the State Department, 1950-53. Other members of the firm had held posts in the State, Justice and Defense Departments. The firm was registered under the Foreign Agents Registration Act on behalf of the Associated Sugar Producers of Guadeloupe and Martinique, interested in promoting sales of sugar cane, and on behalf of an Italian manufacturer of helicopters, motorcycles and components.

American Farm Bureau Federation. The AFBF says it is "the world's largest general farm organization,"

with a record membership of 1,943,181 families at the end of 1970.

Considered conservative on some issues, the AFBF favored lowered trade barriers largely because—as President Charles B. Shuman said—"The production from approximately one acre out of four is exported." The Farm Bureau is sensitive to talk of foreign reprisals.

"We believe that American agriculture, more than any other segment of our economy, would be seriously injured by legislation imposing import restrictions on individual industrial and agricultural products," Shuman testified May 22, 1970.

AFBF representatives pursued that position in their contacts with Congress, as well as that expressed by Shuman at the AFBF's annual meeting Dec. 7, 1970. He said:

"Agriculture has far more to gain from trade expansion than from protectionism. However, we do need to continue the escape clause provisions to permit the President to impose quotas or higher tariffs when imports threaten to destroy an industry or when other nations subsidize production to dump on our markets."

Protectionist Lobbies

Nation-Wide Committee on Import-Export Policy. O.R. Strackbein, president, who founded the predecessor National Labor-Management Council on Foreign Trade Policy in 1950, said the organization "is composed of industries, companies, associations, agricultural growers and some labor organizations that have in common the problem of import competition." Agriculture was brought in in 1953 to form the present group.

Strackbein was an economist with the AFL, 1933-37, and an economist in the Commerce Department, for the Tariff Commission and in his own consulting firm.

Strackbein, long a fighter for protective measures for American industry, coordinated the lobbying for the bill with import quotas. He expressed pleasure at having elements of organized labor on his side this time.

Trade Relations Council of the United States. The council grew out of the American Protective Tariff League, founded in 1885 to protect infant industries which sprang up in the industrialization after the Civil War. In a series of name changes, the group broadened its purpose to concern itself with protective devices such as quotas and subsidies. It also takes positions on foreign aid and other foreign economic matters.

General counsel Eugene L. Stewart told Congress that 10 basic industries in 1969 "experienced a net balance of trade deficit in their products of $6,200 million." He said the contentions of some that inflation or other short-term factors were responsible were inaccurate.

"The reality is that we have reduced our tariffs so low and the competitive advantage of countries whose industries have the same technology, and workers that are as highly motivated as ours, is so great that this situation will continue to grow worse," he said.

The council has been critical of the Executive Branch's administration of trade laws.

Its president was Richard C. Rose, secretary of Allegheny-Ludlum Steel Corporation. James M. Ashley, vice president of Libbey-Owens-Ford Company, was chairman.

Others

Many specialized groups were involved in the 1970 trade fight. Like the others, they sent representatives to appear at House or Senate hearings, issued printed statistics and statements furthering their positions, and lobbied Members of Congress through their regular lobbyists and through locally influential sympathizers from Members' home areas.

Specialists said more than 100 basic U.S. industries stood to be affected by the trade legislation.

Among groups working for import restraints were the American Textile Manufacturers Association, the National Cotton Council of America, the American Footwear Manufacturers Association and the National Machine Tool Builders Association. One which opposed trade restrictions was the American Importers Association.

The interests of domestic and foreign clients of lobbyists at times coincided to a marked degree without public notice being taken of it in Committee hearings or on the floor of House or Senate. For example, Michael P. Daniels appeared as general counsel of the American Importers Association's Textile and Apparel Group. He also accompanied the president of the American Association of Woolen Importers before the House Committee.

A Ways and Means Committee spokesman said it has no requirement that a witness appearing for an American organization supply information concerning any foreign clients he might also have.

Hence, the published hearings contain no mention that Daniels' law firm, Daniels & Houlihan, was registered in 1970 as an agent for these foreign principals: Japan Lumber Importers Association, Japan Trade Center, Japan Woolen and Linen Textiles Exporters Association, Japan Chemical Fibres Association, Embassy of Japan, Vorort des schweizerischen Handels und Industrie-Vereins (Swiss Union of Commerce and Industry) and Cocoa, Chocolate and Confectionery Alliance of Great Britain.

The decision is made within a committee on including in the public record supplemental material provided by witnesses. In 1968, for example, the Senate Finance Committee published Daniels' cover letter when he submitted a statement on behalf of the Swiss Union of Commerce and Industry for a collection of papers reviewing U.S. trade policies. Then associated with the firm of Stitt, Hemmendinger & Daniels, he said in the cover letter that he was registered with the Justice Department as an agent of the Swiss organization and that a copy of his registration was on file.

In his 1970 appearance for the American Importers Association group, Daniels opposed legislated quotas on textiles and apparel and said "our position is that there has been no case of injury or threat thereof for the textile and apparel products industry on an over-all basis." He said:

"The fact that international negotiations on wool and manmade fiber textiles have not yet produced an agreement is due to the rigid insistence by the United States upon a comprehensive arrangement covering all textile products without proof or demonstration of injury. The impasse in these negotiations is not due to the attitude of foreign nations, but rather to the inflexibility

and unreasonableness of the United States position up to now, insofar as we know....

"We ask you, Mr. Chairman, and this Committee, if it is interested in negotiation, to make it clear to the Administration that negotiation does involve meeting the other party halfway, or at least part of the way.... How could we expect Japan to relax its own barriers to trade and investment when we demanded control of textile exports at the same time?"

Daniels said, "All Presidential candidates are vulnerable to demands by protectionist industries....We believe the essential task for this Committee is to insulate legislators and the Executive Branch from this kind of pressure and to preserve a legal framework within which these problems can be solved in an orderly and equitable manner."

Foreign Government Comments

Official foreign comments as U.S. trade legislation awaited action by Congress in 1970 included:

Norway. Foreign Minister took a note to State Department Nov. 17 expressing fears regarding the trade bill's consequences for world trade.

Japan. Ambassador took a note to State Department Nov. 16 saying bill would "have serious adverse effects on both the cause of free trade as well as the future trade relations between Japan and the United States." It said the Japanese government "reserves the right to take necessary measures to safeguard its interests...."

Denmark. Embassy in a note left at State Department Nov. 13 said certain provisions "cannot but create the impression that the United States is actually withdrawing from its previous position as a firm advocate of freer world trade."

Sweden. Embassy in a note left at State Department Nov. 13 mentioned countermeasures, saying "the prospect of a trade war is an alarming one...."

Switzerland. Ambassador gave note to State Department Nov. 12 expressing concern regarding certain amendments "and the harmful consequences they would have for the world-wide exchange of goods and services."

Canada. Government in a note delivered to State Department Nov. 6 said the bill "could have serious adverse implications for Canada" and could "affect the willingness of other nations to continue their own efforts toward liberalization."

Latin America. Members of the Special Committee for Consultation and Cooperation of the Inter-American Economic and Social Council adopted a resolution Nov. 3 expressing concern over "protectionist tendencies" in the United States.

Europe. The Council of the European Economic Community adopted a statement Oct. 27 saying "the adoption of protectionist measures by an important industrialized country...could unleash a cumulative process of trade restrictions."

Italy. Foreign Trade Minister told the press Aug. 1 that a step back to protectionism would mark "the beginning of the end of American world economic and political leadership."

SUGAR LOBBY

Foreign Producers Lobby for Share of U.S. Market

Congress set out in 1971 once again to reshuffle the sugar quotas allocated to foreign and domestic producers under the U.S. sugar program.

Extension of the 1948 Sugar Act touched off some of the hottest lobbying activity of the Washington scene in 1965, and 1971 was no exception.

The United States depended upon imports for about 40 percent of its sugar and provided a premium worth between $290-million and $342-million each year to foreign suppliers. Competition among foreign producers seeking larger shares of the U.S. sugar market lured agents and lobbyists, some of whom have held positions of influence in government.

Lobbyists testifying during House Agriculture Committee hearings early in 1971 included former Rep. Harold D. Cooley (D N.C. 1934-66), who was chairman of the House Agriculture Committee for 16 years and sponsored much sugar legislation; former Senate Republican Whip Thomas H. Kuchel (R Calif. 1953-69); former Rep. Charles H. Brown (D Mo. 1957-61), and Thomas Hale Boggs Jr., son of House Democratic Leader Hale Boggs (D La.).

Rep. Paul Findley (R Ill.), a critic of the U.S. sugar program, denounced the high fees paid to lobbyists and foreign agents. Fees reached a high of $50,000 in 1965, but in 1971, one firm received $180,000. *(Chart p. 91)*

The competition among foreign countries in 1965, the last time the Act was extended, gave the House Agriculture Committee the reputation as the "little State Department" as members of the Committee doled out "trade not aid."

Although the Act answered the needs of a great many interest groups, its renewal touched off considerable debate in 1971. Domestic producers, seeking larger quotas for mainland cane or beet production, fought a move in Congress to cut subsidy payments to growers. Thirty-eight countries sent representatives to petition for quota increases. Some foreign countries faced efforts by members of Congress to cut their quotas for political or economic reasons—apartheid in South Africa and expropriation of U.S. property in Ecuador and Peru.

The Administration, which earlier in 1971 hinted it might not want any sugar bill at all, asked for a short extension of the Act, leaving the way open for major reassessment of the U.S. sugar program and the world sugar situation as international sugar agreements come up for renewal in the next two or three years.

Background

The U.S. government has had an interest in sugar production since 1789 when sugar tariffs brought a substantial portion of government revenues. The government relied on tariffs and bounties to protect domestic sugar production until the Jones-Costigan Act of 1934 initiated the sugar quota system. The Sugar Acts of 1937 and 1948 followed and have been renewed many times, most recently in 1965 when the 1948 Act was extended until Dec. 31, 1971.

The key feature of the system was division of the U.S. sugar market, by means of quotas. The aim was to prevent oversupply and depression of prices and to guarantee domestic producers a share of the market despite lower-cost competition from foreign countries. In addition to placing mandatory limits on the amount of sugar that could be marketed by each group of producers, the Sugar Act permitted the Secretary of Agriculture to place acreage limitations on domestic beet and cane growers under a triggered system if he thought unrestrained production was likely to produce a surplus.

Consumption in the United States increased from 6.575 million tons in 1934 to 10.9 million tons estimated for 1971.

By limiting the amount of sugar that could be placed on the U.S. market, the quota system usually kept the U.S. price for sugar higher than the world market price. This made a share of the U.S. market highly profitable for foreign sugar producers.

Until mid-1960 when President Eisenhower suspended the import of sugar from Cuba, Cuba had supplied about one-third of the total U.S. sugar consumption, about two-thirds of the foreign supply. In 1946, the United States signed a treaty with the Philippines providing a base annual quota of 952,000 short tons.

In 1961, Congress extended the Sugar Act of 1948 until June 30, 1962, making a temporary allocation of the Cuban quota to other countries. Meanwhile, domestic beet and cane sugar interests campaigned for enlargement of domestic quotas.

In 1962, the Kennedy Administration agreed to a larger quota for domestic interests and eliminated country-by-country quotas in favor of a first-come-first-served system. Preference under the global system was given to Western Hemisphere countries and those purchasing U.S. agriculture commodities, and an import fee equal to the full amount of the difference between the U.S. price and the world price was put on foreign sugar entering the United States.

In 1964, the global quota system and import fee provisions expired. Controversies in Congress, primarily over the share of the sugar market going to domestic producers and the fight by foreign countries for a share of the Cuban allocation, stalled renewal of the Sugar Act until 1965. The Secretary of Agriculture set foreign quotas administratively in 1965, without an import fee and on a country-by-country basis.

The key feature of the 1965 Sugar Act amendments was an increase in the share of the U.S. domestic producers from 60 percent to about 66 percent of consumption. However, the major controversy, in the 1965 Act focused on the activities of foreign lobbyists. The House and Senate agreed that domestic quotas should be increased but engaged in a dispute over the size of individual foreign quotas.

The Johnson Administration approach, backed by the Senate, was that quotas should be based on deliveries to the United States during the sugar crisis years of

1963-64, thus rewarding countries that had stuck by the United States at the time when the world price had gone up. The House approach was that quotas should be based upon deliveries during more normal years such as 1962 and upon other factors. These included a nation's ability to produce enough to meet its quota reliably and to carry reserves for emergencies; the need for ready availability of sugar from nearby sources (Mexico and the

Sugar Quotas, 1971

(Short tons, raw value)

Production area	Basic quotas	Total quotas and prorations [1]
Domestic beet area	3,263,333	3,263,333
Mainland cane area	1,186,667	1,186,667
Hawaii	1,180,000	1,180,000 [2]
Puerto Rico	1,140,000	1,140,000 [2]
Virgin Islands	15,000	15,000
Total domestic areas	**6,785,000**	**6,785,000**
Philippines	1,126,020	1,126,020 [2]
Mexico	229,862	476,527
Dominican Republic	224,807	466,048
Brazil	224,807	466,048
Peru	179,310	371,729
British West Indies	89,804	164,079
Ecuador	32,710	67,811
French West Indies	28,249	51,614
Argentina	27,655	57,331
Costa Rica	26,465	54,865
Nicaragua	26,465	54,865
Colombia	23,789	49,317
Guatemala	22,302	46,234
Panama	16,652	34,522 [2]
El Salvador	16,355	33,905
Haiti	12,489	25,892
Venezuela	11,300	23,426
British Honduras	6,542	11,953
Bolivia	2,676	5,548
Honduras	2,676	5,548
Australia	107,051	194,965
Republic of China	44,604	81,235
India	42,820	77,986
South Africa	31,520	57,406
Fiji Islands	23,492	42,784
Thailand	9,813	17,872
Mauritius	9,813	17,872
Malagasy Republic	5,055	9,206
Swaziland	3,866	7,041
Ireland	5,351	5,351 [2]
Bahamas	10,000	10,000
Total foreign	**2,624,320**	**4,115,000**
Total	**9,409,320**	**10,900,000**

1 Proration of the quotas withheld from Cuba and Southern Rhodesia.
2 Direct-consumption limits in tons: Hawaii, 37,278; Puerto Rico, 163,500; Philippines, 59,920, Panama 3,817; Ireland, 5,351.
SOURCE: House Agriculture Committee Print, "The United States Sugar Program."

Western Hemisphere countries), and the need to aid friendly nations.

Critics of the House quotas said lobbyists for foreign countries exerted undue influence upon the deliberations of the House Agriculture Committee. Unsuccessful efforts were made on the House floor to write an anti-lobbyist amendment into the bill. Ultimately, the House prevailed on most individual country quotas.

Rep. Paul Findley (R Ill.) unsuccessfully introduced an amendment that would have canceled the quota of any foreign country that employed a lobbyist to help it obtain sugar act quotas.

Findley said in 1965 that the Sugar Act cost U.S. consumers $700-million a year in hidden subsidies. In March 1971, he called the Act "the worst outrage on the American taxpayers and consumers being perpetrated by the federal government."

Former Rep. Cooley became known as "sugar king" when the Act was up for renewal in 1964-65. Cooley maintained an open door policy and talked to each foreign interest that sought a quota. Some attributed his defeat in 1966 to the spate of publicity he received during the sugar legislation controversy.

Cooley practiced law in Washington, D.C., and in 1971 registered as a foreign agent for Liberia, which was seeking a sugar quota for the first time, and Thailand, which was seeking an increase in its quota.

Looking back on his years as sponsor of sugar legislation, Cooley said: "I participated in every sugar act in the last 35 years and I don't regret any position I ever took on it. If I had to pick out a program that had been enacted by Congress, this would be the best of all. The taxpayers of America have made millions on it.

"The people who criticize the sugar program don't know anything about it. Without it there would be no domestic production," Cooley said. "The sugar bill is so involved and complicated there is not a man living who can discuss it without notes.

"Everybody called me sugar czar, but all the quotas were written by the full committee," Cooley added. "There was no undue influence on anybody."

Poage's Policy

Chairman W. R. Poage (D Texas) of the House Agriculture Committee sent a letter March 4, 1971, to all lobbyists or agents registered on behalf of foreign countries seeking sugar quotas.

Poage outlined the criteria the committee would use in allocating new quotas. He wrote that it would not be possible for him to meet with everyone and it would be appreciated if representatives of foreign countries "would not seek a personal or private discussion." Some other members of the committee followed his example.

Poage wrote that the committee, in allocating quotas, would consider the following:

• Friendly government to the United States, including non-discrimination against U.S. citizens in the quota country and indemnification for property owned by U.S. citizens in cases of expropriation.

• Dependability as a source of sugar supply as reflected by the country's history in supplying the U.S. market, its maintenance of sugar inventories and its potentials for supplying additional sugar upon call during critical periods of short supply.

(Continued on p. 92)

Foreign Sugar Producers and United States Agents

Country[1]	Agent	Fee[2]
Argentina	William R. Joyce Jr., Alejandro Orfila	$1,000 per month, $12,000 per year
Australia	Robert C. Barnard, Cleary, Gottlieb, Steen & Hamilton	Bills for services
Bahamas	Hugh C. Laughlin	No amount listed[3]
Bolivia	Blake Franklin, Coudert Brothers	$10,000 per year
Brazil	Albert S. Nemir, A.S. Nemir Associates	$180,000 per year
British Honduras	Arthur L. Quinn, Arthur Lee Quinn	$10,000 per year[2]
Central America	Thomas H. Boggs, Jr., Patton, Blow, Verrill, Brand & Boggs	$36,000 to $50,000 per year
Columbia	Tom Kuchel	$200 per hour (in last six-month period reported $13,156)
Costa Rica	Dina Dellale	$15,000 per year
Dominican Republic	James N. Juliana, James N. Juliana Associates, Inc.	$3,000 per month
Ecuador	Arthur L. Quinn, Arthur Lee Quinn	$25,000 per year[2]
England	Daniels & Houlihan	$18,000 per year
Guadeloupe, Martinique	Walter S. Surrey, Surrey, Karasik, Greene & Hill	$12,500 per year
Fiji	Charles H. Brown	$2,000 per month
Haiti	Philip F. King	Expenses only
India	Michael P. Daniels, Daniels & Houlihan	$25,000 per year
Ireland	George W. Bronz	Bills for expenses
Liberia	Harold D. Cooley	$10,000 fee plus $1,000 per month
Malagasy Republic (Madagascar)	Walter S. Surrey, Surrey, Karasik, Greene & Hill	$25,000 per year
Malawi	Jerry Collier Trippe	$15,000 per year
Mauritius	W. DeVier Pierson, Sharon, Pierson & Semmes	$25,000 per year
Mexico	Dennis O'Rourke, Sutton & O'Rourke	$4,000 per month
Panama	Arthur L. Quinn, Arthur Lee Quinn	$18,000 per year[2]
Paraguay	Sheldon Z. Kaplan	$500 per month
Peru	Prather, Levenberg, Seeger, Doolittle, Farmer & Ewing	$15,000 per year[4]
Philippines	John A. O'Donnell	$3,750 per month (does not include bonuses in recognition of services. Last reported bonus was $6,000)
Republic of China	George C. Pendleton, Culbertson, Pendleton & Pendleton	$600 per month
South Africa	John Mahoney, Casey, Lane & Mittendorf	$20-$65 per hour (reported $48,573 receipts for past year)
Swaziland	Justice M. Chambers	$20,000 per year
Thailand	Harold D. Cooley	$15,000 per year
Uganda	Andreas F. Lowenfeld, Fox, Flynn & Melamed	$16,000 per year
Venezuela	Edward L. Merrigan, Smathers & Merrigan	$50,000 per year[2]
West Indies	Arthur L. Quinn, Arthur Lee Quinn	$35,000 per year[2]

1 Includes private and government interests.
2 Fee includes expenses.
3 Laughlin is not listed as a foreign agent because he represents a U.S.-owned firm. No amount was listed under his lobby registration with the House Clerk.
4 From lobby registration filed with house Clerk.

SOURCE: Foreign Agents' registrations, Justice Department

(Continued from p. 90)

• Reciprocal trade as reflected by purchases of U.S. products and services, as contrasted with sales to the United States.

• Need of the country for a premium priced market in the United States including (a) reference to the extent it shares in other premium priced markets such as the United Kingdom, (b) its relative dependence on sugar as a source of foreign exchange and (c) present stage of and need for economic development.

• Extent to which the benefits of participation in this market are shared by factories and larger land owners with farmers and workers together with other socio-economic policies of the quota country.

The Agriculture Committee devoted about 10 days to hearing the prepared statements of the 38 representatives of foreign countries.

Lobby Fees

It has been the policy of the Agriculture Committee for years to prohibit foreign nationals from testifying; thus, foreign countries interested in having their views heard must hire lawyers or lobbyists.

In 1965, lobbyists' fees in some cases were based on the size of the quota received, but a 1966 amendment to the Foreign Agents Registration Act eliminated this aspect of competition. Fees in 1965 ranged from $3,000 from the Republic of China up to $50,000 from Mexico and Venezuela, but the average was about $20,000. *(Box p. 91)*

According to official reports, A.S. Nemir Associates, Washington, D.C., will receive an annual fee of $180,000, including expenses, this year from the Brazilian Sugar and Alcohol Institute, a quasi-governmental organization which represents the Brazilian sugar industry. Arthur L. and Arthur Lee Quinn, Washington, D.C., will receive a total annual fee of $84,000, including expenses, to represent sugar interests in British Honduras, Ecuador, Panama and the West Indies.

Some of the agents appearing before the committee in 1971 had represented the same countries in 1965: John A. O'Donnell, Philippines; Arthur L. and Arthur Lee Quinn, Panama, Ecuador and British Honduras; Edwin H. Seeger, Peru; Albert S. Nemir, Brazil, and John Mahoney, South Africa.

Registrations filed under the Foreign Agents Registration Act revealed the connections lobbyists had within government and Congress—some of them related to sugar legislation.

Cooley, former chairman of the Agriculture Committee, registered for Liberia and Thailand; former Republican Senate Whip Kuchel registered on behalf of Colombian sugar interests; former Rep. Brown registered for the Colonial Sugar Refining Company Ltd. of Australia, represented Fiji; and Boggs, son of the House Democratic Leader, represented Central American sugar interests.

Domestic sugar interests also have their representatives. One is Horace D. Godfrey, a former administrator of the Agriculture Department's Agriculture Stabilization and Conservation Service which administers the Act. Godfrey represents the Sugar Cane League of the United States of America and the Florida Sugar Cane League.

According to the House Agriculture Committee's associate counsel, Hyde H. Murray, the best way to deal with lobbyists and with the various interests at work is by public disclosure.

"Somebody has to cut the slices," Murray said. "If it weren't the committee it would be the bureaucrats in State, Agriculture or the Executive behind closed doors over coffee.

"If it takes place in public where the press and others can see who is there and know who is represented, then it will be in the record, and it will have to be defended in the forum of floor debate."

The Agriculture Committee contains strong interests in domestic sugar production; it includes representatives from Louisiana and Hawaii as well as from states where refineries or processors are located or sugar beets grown.

Five members of the committee visited Africa in November 1970 using counterpart funds:

Representatives Poage, Thomas G. Abernethy (D Miss.), George A. Goodling (R Pa.), Wiley Mayne (R Iowa) and Eligio de la Garza (D Texas).

The Representatives traveled to Upper Volta, Niger, Chad, Central African Republic, Uganda, Malawi, Mauritius, South Africa, Congo, Liberia, Mauritania and Surinam for about two weeks studying agricultural development, including sugar.

South Africa and Mauritius have requested quota increases, and Uganda, Malawi and Liberia have requested quotas for the first time.

Other trips made by members of the committee in 1970 to countries concerned with sugar production included: Graham Purcell (D Texas) traveled to Australia and New Zealand in December at his own expense; Committee Chairman Poage went to India to attend an agriculture meeting and Australia in April-May 1970 at the expense of the Department of Agriculture; Charles M. Teague (R Calif.) also traveled to India and Australia in April 1970 on committee business.

Purposes of Act

The purposes of the Sugar Act of 1948 as amended are to assure consumers of adequate supplies of sugar at reasonable prices, to maintain the domestic sugar industry and to promote U.S. export trade.

Main features of the Act include:

• Determination each year by the Secretary of Agriculture of the quantity of sugar needed to supply the nation's requirements at reasonable prices that will be fair to producers.

• Division of the U.S. sugar market among domestic and foreign supplying areas by the use of quotas.

• The allotment of these quotas among the various processors in each domestic area.

• The adjustment of production in each domestic area to the established quota.

• The levying of an excise tax of 53 cents a 100 pounds of refined sugar paid by manufacturers on the processing of all foreign and domestic sugar, the proceeds of which are used for payments to augment the income of producers.

• The levying of a tariff on all foreign sugar entering the United States amounting to 62.5 cents per 100 pounds of sugar raw value. (Under a U.S.-Philippines trade agreement of 1946, the Philippines now pay 40 cents per 100 pounds raw value.)

TAX-EXEMPT INTERESTS

Foundations: New Activism Raises Tax Law Questions

Although not technically lobbyists, powerful tax-exempt foundations and other non-profit groups can exert wide influence on public policy and legislation.

Tax-exempt groups were placed under strong restrictions by Congress in 1969, the final year of a decade in which many foundations exchanged their traditional roles of charity and education for a new activism.

Throughout the 1960s—a decade of war, crusades for human rights and new pressures for social welfare—tax-free foundations had moved from relatively uncontroversial charitable grants to gifts with well-defined legislative and political purposes.

Such activities attracted the concern of Congress, particularly after charges of impropriety against some foundations in 1968 and 1969. Members criticized some foundations as "holding companies" for out-of-power Government officials and charged that the influence of powerful foundations constituted a sub-government that swayed the thinking of legislators and Executive Branch officials.

Some writers, such as Kevin P. Phillips, contended that major tax-exempt groups were alliances for liberal causes. Phillips wrote April 17, 1971: "The leaders of the top universities, fashionable churches, big name foundations and concerned coalitions are increasingly forthright spokesmen these days—along with the media and corporate knowledge industry—for a viewpoint that can be called ecology-urban crisis-disarmament-brotherhood liberalism."

However, some of the most heavily endowed foundations and tax-favored study groups, such as Freedoms Foundation, Institute for American Strategy and the National Institute for Law/Order/Justice Legal Assistance Fund, advocated ideas which would commonly be called conservative.

Congress in 1969 acted to restrict the moves of foundations with the Tax Reform Act, which imposed a 4-percent excise tax on foundations and limited direct legislative and political acts.

Although foundation officials tended to play down the effects of the bill (the Ford Foundation announced in January 1970 that it was continuing to make grants in line with normal procedures), many observers said foundation effectiveness had been handicapped by the law. They were particularly concerned about the prospects for political activism.

William Watts, former Ford Foundation official and in 1971 head of Potomac Associates Inc., a Washington, D.C., consulting firm, said the 1969 law "had seriously damaged foundation work as an innovative, creative force. Economic development programs, for example, such as minority or ghetto projects, may be very vulnerable areas."

Other critics said that traditional charitable activities would experience few difficulties but that new types of social experimentation might encounter obstacles under the new code. "Experiments frequently fail, and the Internal Revenue Service now is taking a much more conservative view toward this type of philanthropy," said Mitchell Rogovin, chief counsel of the IRS during the Johnson Administration.

Individual Influences

The new law notwithstanding, foundations continue to exercise their power through individual contacts by foundation officers with high Government officials.

"The personal contacts just cannot be discounted," said Watts, one-time member of the National Security Council staff of Henry Kissinger, President Nixon's foreign policy adviser. "The degree of interplay is just fantastic. You are dealing with highly motivated people, who go to the foundations because they are more interested in making government act rather than in making money."

Few Government officials or Members of Congress sever foundation connections when entering government. Foundation links with officials are numerous, at every level of government. National administrations for decades have drawn upon foundations for high-level appointees, including Cabinet rank. Some examples:

John Foster Dulles was chairman of the trustees of the Carnegie Endowment for International Peace when President Eisenhower named him Secretary of State. Dean Rusk in 1952 resigned as Assistant Secretary of State to become president of the Rockefeller Foundation, and remained there until President Kennedy appointed him Secretary of State in 1960. In 1969, the Rockefeller Foundation issued the retiring Rusk a one-year "transitional grant" to afford him time to compile his papers.

W. Willard Wirtz served simultaneously as Secretary of Labor for both Presidents Kennedy and Johnson and as a trustee of the Stern Family Fund. Clifford M. Hardin, a Rockefeller trustee, became President Nixon's Secretary of Agriculture. Arthur F. Burns, counselor to Mr. Nixon and then chairman of the Federal Reserve Board, remained a trustee of the 20th Century Fund. C. Douglas Dillon, President Kennedy's Secretary of the Treasury, is on the Rockefeller Foundation Board.

John Connally, Mr. Nixon's Treasury Secretary, served the Sid W. Richardson Foundation while Connally was Governor of Texas. New York Mayor John V. Lindsay (Republican Member of the House from 1959-65) was a trustee of the Carnegie Endowment for International Peace.

In Congress, Sen. George McGovern (D S.D.) is a trustee of the Danforth Foundation. Sen. Edward W. Brooke (R Mass.) is a trustee of the Council on Religion and International Affairs. Sen. Edward M. Kennedy (D Mass.) is a director of the Pan American Development Foundation, as is Rep. F. Bradford Morse (R Mass.). Rep. Jonathan B. Bingham (D N.Y.) is a trustee of the 20th Century Fund. Rep. John P. Saylor (R Pa.) was trustee and secretary of the Accokeek Foundation, which worked to persuade Congress to acquire and preserve part of the Maryland shoreline on the Potomac River.

"When a foundation funds or sponsors a conference to which a group of Congressmen or Governors or department officials are invited, the thinking of those people is going to be influenced," said Watts. "A skull session of university professors and policymakers almost always affects the direction of government programs."

Foundations can contribute to policy in other ways, from actual writing of legislation for Members of Congress or the White House staff to giving grants that will result in policy changes. The W. K. Kellogg Foundation of Battle Creek, Mich., financed the building of a Washington, D.C., office building that houses most of the major education lobby groups in the capital.

Background

Modern philanthropic foundations have their roots in the late 19th and early 20th centuries, when American businessmen and industrialists amassed tremendous wealth through corporate profits. The Peabody Education Fund, created in 1867 by investment banker George Peabody to assist the war-stricken South, was called the "beginning of the foundation as we know it today" by Warren Weaver in his 1968 book *U.S. Philanthropic Foundations.*

Another major foundation, the General Education Board, was established by John D. Rockefeller in 1902.

This was followed by the Carnegie Foundation for the Advancement of Teaching in 1905 (founded by steel magnate Andrew Carnegie), the Russell Sage Foundation in 1907, Carnegie Corporation of New York in 1911 and the Rockefeller Foundation in 1913.

"A clear majority of the big American foundations were created by rich men who had the good sense, late in their careers, to realize they were but one short step ahead of either outraged public opinion, their own uneasy consciences, or the tax collector," said Joseph C. Goulden in *The Money Givers,* a 1971 book. "Piety and piracy are well-documented parallel characteristics of the American industrialist."

Benefits Realized. Imaginative philanthropy has made thousands of worthwhile contributions in the public interest, among them public libraries, the conquest of hookworm, the discovery of insulin, the successful war against polio and yellow fever, reform of medical education, improved agricultural techniques, cultural benefits, better salaries for college teachers, space exploration and educational television.

Congress fostered the notion of favorable tax treatment for American foundations, believing that groups which gave money for improving the public welfare should receive some consideration from government.

The Revenue Act of 1894 provided for an income tax but exempted "corporations, companies or associations organized and conducted solely for charitable, religious or educational purposes." Although the act later was held unconstitutional, many of its provisions, including the

---

Other Types of Tax-Exempt Groups and Holdings

Many tax-exempt organizations—aside from foundations—carry on political education among their members and in the public forum and publicize results of research and study on national issues.

Veterans groups, fraternal orders, labor unions, public interest law firms, legal defense funds, environmental groups and a melange of other charitable or nonprofit organizations qualify under various provisions of the Internal Revenue Code for some form of tax exemption. Other forms of favorable tax status are available to colleges and universities, churches and hospitals.

According to *The Pluralistic Economy,* by Eli Ginzberg, the nonprofit sector of the American economy accounted in 1970 for at least one-third of all employment and controlled great wealth. Assets held by religious organizations have been estimated at $110-billion, and all tax-exempt real estate in the United States has been valued at $600-billion—one-third of the total real property valuation.

In *The Free List,* a 1971 book, author Alfred Balk found that tax-free property in Washington, D.C., accounted for 52.3 percent of the total tax valuation, much of it held by government agencies but a substantial amount taken by the tax-exempt headquarters of many national lobby groups.

Contributions to organizations that come under Section 107(c) of the Internal Revenue Code are deductible by taxpayers. More than 135,000 of these groups are listed in a 600-page biennial cumulative list, Publication No. 78 of the Internal Revenue Service. Some of these groups register as lobbyists at the Federal or state level.

Among the better known groups with Congressional influence are the following:

Center for the Study of Responsive Law, Brookings Institution, Resources for the Future, Environmental Law Institute, National Planning Association, American Enterprise Association for Public Policy, Conference on Economic Progress, World Federalist Educational Fund, League of Women Voters Education Fund, Institute for Policy Studies, Lawyers Committee for Civil Rights Under Law, Citizens' Advocate Center and American Freedom from Hunger Foundation, all of Washington, D.C.

American Red Cross, United Fund, Council on Foreign Relations, Foreign Policy Association, National Audubon Society, NAACP Legal Defense and Educational Fund, Twentieth Century Fund, American Assembly, Committee for Economic Development, the Tax Foundation, the Population Council, Public Affairs Committee, National Health Education Committee, National Institute for the Prevention of Drug Addiction and the National Educational Television and Radio Center, all of New York, N.Y.

Center for Advanced Study in the Behavioral Sciences, Palo Alto, Calif.; Joint Council to Improve the Health Care of the Aged, Chicago, Ill.

charitable exemption, reappeared in the 1913 and 1917 Internal Revenue Acts. In 1934, Congress adopted the exempt organization provision—Section 501(c)(3)—in its present form. *(Box, this page)*

Private foundations have proliferated since 1930, many for charitable or educational purposes, but some of the smaller or "family" foundations have been created as a method of reducing tax liability. Referring to the growth in the number and assets of foundations, Leo Eagan, writing in *The New York Times* March 1, 1954, said, "All authorities agree that the number has risen rapidly since 1939 and is still on the increase. It is likewise agreed that extremely high income and inheritance taxes on big incomes and estates have been a major factor in promoting this growth."

A list of foundations in the United States compiled in 1968 by the Internal Revenue Service and reprinted by the House Select Committee on Small Business contained 30,262 entries. However, that report was disputed by the Foundation Center, the trade organization for foundations, which in 1968 listed 22,000 foundations, with total assets of approximately $20.5-billion, at market value, and annual expenditures of $1.5-billion. About 7 percent of tax-exempt organizations control 90 percent of all assets held by private funds.

Congressional Investigations

The first assessment of tax-exempt groups authorized by Congress began in 1912 and resulted in a three-year investigation by a committee headed by Kansas City, Mo., lawyer Frank P. Walsh.

The Walsh Committee report, issued in 1916, concluded, "The domination by men in whose hands the final control of a large part of American industry rests is not limited to their employees but is being rapidly extended to the control of the educational and social services of the nation." However, little action was taken toward foundations by Congress.

Another study was approved by Congress in 1952, when the Select Committee to Investigate Tax-Exempt Foundations and Comparable Organizations was established and headed by Rep. Edward E. Cox (D Ga. 1925-52). But the first comprehensive inquiry into tax-exempt groups by Congress was in 1954 by the Special Committee to Investigate Tax-Exempt Foundations and Comparable Organizations, headed by Rep. B. Carroll Reece (R Tenn. 1921-31; 1933-47; 1951-61). Findings of the year-long study were issued in a special report by the committee (H Rept 2681, 83rd Congress).

Patman Inquiries. The longest and most thorough study of tax-exempt groups by any branch of government began in 1961, when Rep. Wright Patman (D Texas), acting as an individual Member of Congress, sent inquiries to more than 500 foundations requesting information on their activities. Patman since has become the nation's leading critic of foundations, and his Select Small Business Subcommittee on Foundations produced more than 6,000 pages of evidence and testimony as a result of his investigations from 1961 to 1970. Patman concluded that many "philanthropic" foundations abused their tax exemptions to gain control of businesses.

The House April 27, 1971, passed a resolution (H Res 320) transferring the foundations subcommittee to the

---

Internal Revenue Code

Title 26 of the U.S. Code defines the qualifications for tax exemption of an organization as follows:

Section 501 (c)(3)—Corporations and any community chest, fund or foundation, organized and operated exclusively for religious, charitable, scientific, testing for public safety, literary or educational purposes or for the prevention of cruelty to children or animals, no part of the net earnings of which inures to the benefit of any private stockholder or individual, no substantial part of the activities of which is carrying on propaganda, or otherwise attempting to influence legislation, and which does not participate in, or intervene in (including the publishing or distributing of statements), any political campaign on behalf of any candidate for public office.

Internal Revenue Service regulations, compiled in 1971 by the Treasury Department, interpret the tax code on legislative and political involvement by private foundations as follows:

1.501(c)(3)-(b)(3) Authorization of legislative or political activities. An organization is not organized for one or more exempt purposes if its articles expressly empower it:

(i) To devote more than an insubstantial part of its activities to attempting to influence legislation by propaganda or otherwise; or

(ii) Directly or indirectly to participate in, or intervene in (including the publishing or distributing of statements), any political campaign on behalf of or in opposition to any candidate for public office; or

(iii) To have objectives and to engage in activities which characterize it as an "action" organization.

(c)(3) "Action" organizations. An organization is not operated exclusively for one or more exempt purposes if it is an "action" organization.

An organization is an "action" organization if a sub-part of its activities is attempting to influence legislation by propaganda or otherwise. For this purpose, an organization will be regarded as attempting to influence legislation if the organization:

(a) Contacts, or urges the public to contact, members of the legislative body for the purpose of proposing, supporting or opposing legislation; or

(b) Advocates the adoption or rejecting of legislation.

House Banking and Currency Committee, of which Patman is chairman, and extending the subcommittee's authority.

Patman accused foundations of wholesale tax law violations and abuse of the privilege of tax exemption. In 1962, he said that non-operating foundations should be broken up so that control of American industry would "tend to be redistributed among wider groups in the population." Non-operating foundations are those that are engaged chiefly in giving financial grants to charities rather than operating their own charities.

Patman said in March 1969, "I have nothing against the foundations. I just think it is unfair for people generally to pay taxes while some few have special privileges and don't have to pay taxes.

25 Largest Foundations

Following are the 25 foundations whose holdings as of 1969 distinguished them as the largest of all such organizations in the United States. Total assets of the 25 foundations in 1969 were $10,406,-000,000.

Information on foundations, principal officers, and assets was compiled through use of the *Foundation Directory*, annual reports and tax return forms filed by foundations.

Foundation	Assets 1969 *(Millions of dollars)*
1. **Ford Foundation**, New York, N.Y., McGeorge Bundy, president.	$2,922
2. **Rockefeller Foundation**, New York, N.Y., J. George Harrar, president.	890
3. **Duke Endowment**, New York, N.Y., and Charlotte, N.C., Thomas L. Perkins, chairman.	629
4. **Lilly Endowment,** Indianapolis, Ind., Eli Lilly, president.	580
5. **Pew Memorial Trust**, Philadelphia, Pa.	541
6. **Charles Stewart Mott Foundation**, Flint, Mich., C. S. Harding Mott, president.	413
7. **W. K. Kellogg Foundation**, Battle Creek, Mich., Emory W. Morris, president.	409
8. **Kresge Foundation**, Detroit, Mich., William H. Baldwin, president.	353
9. **John A. Hartford Foundation**, New York, N.Y., Harry B. George, president.	352
10. **Carnegie Corporation of New York,** New York, N.Y., Alan Pifer, president.	335
11. **Alfred P. Sloan Foundation**, New York, N.Y., Nils Y. Wessell, president.	329
12. **Andrew W. Mellon Foundation**, New York, N.Y., Charles S. Hamilton Jr., president.	272
13. **James Irvine Foundation**, San Francisco, Calif., N. Loyall McLaren, president.	250
14. **Bernice P. Bishop Estate**, Honolulu, Hawaii, Edwin P. Murray, president.	234
15. **Longwood Foundation** (duPont), Wilmington, Del., Henry B. duPont, president.	226
16. **Rockefeller Brothers Fund**, New York, N.Y., Laurance S. Rockefeller, chairman.	222
17. **Houston Endowment**, Houston, Texas, J. Howard Creekmore, president.	214
18. **Moody Foundation**, Galveston, Texas, Robert E. Baker, executive administrator.	200
19. **Danforth Foundation**, St. Louis, Mo., Merrimon Cuninggim, president.	173
20. **Emily and Ernest Woodruff Foundation** (Coca Cola), Atlanta, Ga., Boisfeuillet Jones, president.	167
21. **Richard King Mellon Foundation**, Pittsburgh, Pa., Robert E. Willison, director.	164
Commonwealth Fund, New York, N.Y., J. Quigg Newton, president.	145
Sarah Mellon Scaife Foundation, Pittsburgh, Pa., James M. Bovard, chairman.	145
24. **Cleveland Foundation**, Cleveland, Ohio, John Sherwin, chairman.	130
25. **Carnegie Institution of Washington**, Washington, D.C., Caryl P. Haskins, president.	111

"I just think we should all be treated alike. If Ford and Mellon and Rockefeller have their foundations, I think we should all be able to have foundations," he said.

Later Criticisms

Charges of quasi-political activities and impropriety by some foundations in 1968 and 1969 precipitated increasing public awareness of the influences of non-taxed organizations.

The Ford Foundation, founded in 1936, is the largest tax-exempt foundation, with assets in 1970 of more than $3-billion, and an income estimated at nearly $1-million a day. In late 1968, it was revealed that Ford gave grants totaling $131,000 for "travel and study" to eight members of the staff of the late Sen. Robert F. Kennedy (D N.Y. 1965-68). The disclosure brought criticism from a number of Members of Congress.

The Ford Foundation also was criticized for giving a grant to the Cleveland, Ohio, chapter of Congress of Racial Equality, one-seventh of which—$25,000—was used in 1967 to assist a voter registration drive among the city's East Side Negroes. After Carl B. Stokes became the first black man elected mayor of a major city later that year, the role of the Ford funds was the subject of controversy.

Foundation involvement with Supreme Court justices came to light in 1969. A disclosure that Justice Abe Fortas had accepted $20,000 from a charitable foundation controlled by the family of Louis E. Wolfson resulted in Fortas' resignation from the Court. The American Bar Association's ethics committee said Fortas' conduct was "clearly contrary" to the Canons of Judicial Ethics.

Controversy arose in 1969 concerning Justice William O. Douglas and his association with the Albert Parvin Foundation. Douglas was president of the foundation and accepted a $12,000 annual payment for his services. Critics contended that Douglas may have given the foundation legal advice on tax matters while he was president and the only paid officer of the foundation.

Sierra Club Case. In 1966, the Internal Revenue Service began an investigation of the Sierra Club's exemption from tax. The club, founded in 1892 in California, concerned itself with conservation and environmental issues, and sponsored films, wilderness outings and widely distributed newsletters and books. The organization employed a professional legislative representative in Washington, D.C.

The IRS officially revoked the Sierra Club's exemption in August 1968, concluding that the club's legislative activities went "well beyond any permissible limits of such endeavors for Federal income tax purposes." Tax investigators found that as a regular and important part of its function the club formulated an official position on proposed and pending legislation, and that the position adopted became an official objective to be accomplished through club action.

1969 Tax Law Restrictions

A number of forces, including persistent opposition by Patman and adverse public reaction to charges of foundation impropriety, merged into strong demands in many quarters for increased government supervision of foundations and restrictions on their activities.

A CHANGE IN THE TAX FORM

Form **990** Department of the Treasury Internal Revenue Service	**Return of Organization Exempt From Income Tax** Section 501(c) of the Internal Revenue Code	**1970**

For the calendar year 1970, or other taxable year beginning ...., 1970, and ending ...., 19.......

Name of organization	Employer identification number (See instructions)

SOMETHING NEW—For the first time in 1970, all tax exempt organizations used the same tax form, No. 990, to report their financial status to the Internal Revenue Service. The new form replaced Forms 990 (SF), 990-A and 990-A(SF).

12 Net worth . . . .

	Yes	No
13 Have you engaged in any activities which have not previously been reported to the Internal Revenue Service? If "Yes," attach a detailed description of such activities		
14 Have you during the year (1) attempted to influence any national, State, or local legislation, or (2) participated or intervened in any political campaign? If "Yes," attach a detailed description of such activities and copies of any materials published in connection with such activities		

SOMETHING DELETED—Originally, Line 14 of Form 990 required groups such as labor unions and business trade organizations to file detailed descriptions of lobbying and political activities. However, the IRS Feb. 11, 1971, decided to change the provision, making it apply only to foundations and charitable organizations exempted under Section 501 (c)(3) of the U.S. Code. A label was pasted on the printed form with the new instructions.

The Congressional response in the House Ways and Means Committee and the Senate Finance Committee was a series of provisions in the 1969 Tax Reform Act (PL 91-172) related to foundations. A controversial provision was the establishment of a 4-percent excise tax on the investment income of foundations.

The tax act prohibited or limited a host of legislative and political activities. For the first time, "private foundations" were separated from other charitable organizations exempted from tax under Section 501(c)(3) of the Internal Revenue Code. The Act defined rules prohibiting foundations from:

• Carrying out propaganda or lobbying campaigns to influence legislation.
• Influencing the outcome of any specific public election or carrying on any voter registration drive.

• Influencing legislation through grass roots campaigns to affect the opinion of the general public.
• Influencing legislation through communication with members or employees of any legislative body, or any other government official, who may participate in the formulation of the legislation (except technical advice or assistance provided to a governmental body or committee in response to a written request).

The law provided strong penalties, in the form of extra taxation, for violation of the legislative and political prohibitions.

The mood of Congress toward foundations was seen in the report (S Rept 91-552) of the Senate Finance Committee in its version of the tax reform bill. The Committee said:

"In recent years, private foundations have become increasingly active in political and legislative activities. In several instances called to the committee's attention, funds were spent in ways clearly designed to favor certain candidates. In some cases, this was done by financing registration campaigns in limited geographical areas. In other cases contributions were made to organizations that then used the money to publicize the views, personalities and activities of certain candidates."

Patman, Bundy Testimony. The influence of testimony by two witnesses before the House Ways and Means Committee, Patman and McGeorge Bundy, president of the Ford Foundation, probably helped effect a stronger tax law for foundations.

Patman, testifying Feb. 18, 1969, scored the activities of some foundations in his remarks. An excerpt:

"While the Congress and the Administration searched feverishly for funds to finance essential urban rebuilding programs, the Richard King Mellon Foundation sent $50,000 to Ireland for the 'preservation of historical buildings.' While thousands of Puerto Rican youngsters drop out of New York schools because they can't master English, one of the 13 Rockefeller-controlled foundations sends $11,280 to Japan to 'improve English-language teaching in Japanese schools.'

"The Rockefeller Foundation spent $1,693,762 in India but not a penny in Arkansas. It spent half a million dollars in Uganda but not a cent in Idaho. It spent more than $1-million in Nigeria, but it could bring itself to spend only $1,000 in Kentucky."

In an appearance Feb. 20, Bundy, former national security adviser to Presidents Kennedy and Johnson, defended controversial Ford grants in a manner which some committee members described as "arrogant" and displaying a "total lack of humility." After passage of the tax measure, some observers said the harsh Congressional treatment of foundations was due in large part to Bundy's attitude before the Committee. The Ford Foundation itself had received public criticism for several years for its action-oriented grants, quarters and salaries.

Lobbying on Tax Bill

A well-planned and widely reported lobbying campaign succeeded in eliminating a Senate Finance Committee amendment that would have required foundations after 40 years to distribute all assets to charity or to pay a regular corporate tax on income.

Strategy to oppose these provisions during Senate floor action on the bill was laid at a Nov. 28, 1969, meeting of foundation officials with Sen. Walter F. Mondale (D Minn.), in Mondale's office. Representing the foundations were Bundy and Alan Pifer, president of the Carnegie Corporation of New York. The meeting had been arranged by David Ginsburg, a Washington, D.C., lawyer with long government experience.

It was agreed that Mondale would sponsor an amendment to eliminate the 40-year rule. Three co-sponsors were selected, spanning the geographical and political spectrum: Senators Carl T. Curtis (R Neb.), Ernest F. Hollings (D S.C.) and Charles H. Percy (R Ill.).

Mondale's amendment deleting the 40-year rule was adopted Dec. 9 by a 69-18 roll-call vote.

Impact of Tax Bill. By the time the tax bill was signed into law on Dec. 30, 1969, there was little in it that foundations were unable to live with, according to tax attorneys, foundation lobbyists and the foundations themselves.

The Act's 4-percent tax on the net investment income of foundations produced estimated Federal revenues of $35-million in calendar 1970, and was expected to rise to about $55-million per year eventually.

But precise assessments of the bill's effects on foundation activity awaited implementation and use of the provisions for several years and preparation of regulations by Internal Revenue Service tax law specialists. Some foundations—particularly those promoting reform causes—felt the IRS was at a crossroads in determining the scope of their activities. One foundation executive, quoted anonymously in *The Wall Street Journal* March 31, 1971, said "There's a totally different atmosphere at foundations today. There's a genuine fear the government could clamp down anytime."

New Tax Form. One result of the tax Act was a new income tax return form, No. 990, which combined previous report forms for all tax-exempt organizations—charitable groups, foundations, labor and business groups, churches and hospitals.

Question number 14 on the new form asked for a detailed description of all lobbying and political activities carried on by the groups. Labor and business groups (to which donations are not deductible) objected to the new form, saying they had not previously been required to report such activities. The IRS relented and recalled the form. When it was re-issued, a label was pasted with new instructions for labor and business groups to disregard the question. *(Tax form, preceding page)*

Future of Tax-Exempt Groups

Actions in Congress during the early part of the 92nd Congress indicated that both the House and Senate would continue close surveillance of foundation activities.

On March 30, Sen. Edmund S. Muskie (D Maine) introduced a bill (S 1408) "to allow tax-exempt charitable organizations to advocate the public interest directly before Congress on an equal basis with private business." Muskie said his bill, similar to a House measure (HR 8176) introduced by Rep. James W. Symington (D Mo.), would benefit civil rights organizations, consumer and environmental groups and public interest law firms. Under the IRS code, Muskie said, such groups "have their voices stifled."

The House April 27 approved by voice vote a resolution (H Res 320) transferring the jurisdiction of the Select Small Business Foundations Subcommittee to the Banking and Currency Committee.

In calling up the measure for floor consideration, Rep. Richard Bolling (D Mo.), a member of the Rules Committee, called the resolution "an entirely non-controversial matter." Another Rules Committee member, Republican James H. (Jimmy) Quillen of Tennessee, supported the resolution, saying "the interested parties agree that this change is desirable and we know of no opposition to the resolution."

One of those "interested parties" was Rep. Patman, who engineered the transfer of jurisdiction. Patman agreed to give up his Select Small Business Committee assignment, but he remained chairman of Banking and Currency and the Domestic Finance Subcommittee, which took over the duties of the former foundations subcommittee.

In supporting the change, Patman said the jurisdiction of the subcommittee should be expanded beyond small business interests. "We now feel it is appropriate that a broader look be taken at the impact of foundations and other tax-exempt organizations on the national economy."

Shortly after passage of the resolution, Patman's staff put into production a comprehensive report on the stock holdings and financial assets of the 15 largest foundations, the result of more than a year's research.

Said Patman of the report: "We believe this is a pioneering effort which will assist Congress and the Executive Branch in evaluating the effectiveness of the new statutory rules on foundations and the need for future action to ensure that foundations function exclusively in the public interest."

Goulden, at the conclusion of *The Money Givers,* offered some advice to tax-exempt groups. "What the rich do with their money in private is their own business. But once they claim the privilege of tax-exemption, each of us acquires an interest in the dollars involved, and we deserve to know how and why they are being spent. Most of us would quickly be bored silly and go away, but the foundations would operate in the constant knowledge that someone could ask at any minute: 'What have you done for America recently?'"

Foundations, too, seem prepared to investigate themselves. A foundation-sponsored study by the Commission on Foundations and Private Philanthropy in 1969-70 recommended creation of consortiums of small foundations with professional staffing, retaining investment counsel to increase income, larger payouts of income annually, IRS audits of all foundations by 1973, annual publication by IRS of a complete foundation statistical report and establishment of an Advisory Board of Philanthropic Policy.

The commission was headed by Peter G. Peterson, who was formerly president and chief executive officer of Bell & Howell Company. In February 1971, he was named Assistant to the President for international affairs.

ENVIRONMENTAL LOBBYING

Pressure Groups Disagree on Fighting Pollution

In the early 1970s the national focus on pollution and on the threatened eventual exhaustion of such resources as pure air, clean water, food and living space touched off vigorous jostling for position among many conflicting or overlapping interests. So great and varied were the stakes that broader struggles could lie ahead.

President Nixon told Congress in his State of the Union address (Jan. 22, 1970): "Restoring nature to its natural state is a cause beyond party and beyond factions." Whether the new political activism and debate of policy, along with the traditional pursuit of financial advantage on many fronts, lead to prolonged conflict hinged initially on current efforts to unify Americans in what Mr. Nixon called "a cause as fundamental as life itself."

Proposed solutions raised issues which were equally fundamental. Some signs suggested that the projected war on pollution, before it could become reality, must overcome a pitfall met by earlier ambitious projects, including the war on poverty: the prospect of becoming a new arena for combat among many familiar forces over familiar issues given a new sense of urgency.

Early battles in which environmental issues figured prominently included congressional election campaigns, timber-cutting proposals and the recurrent conflicts over funding of the supersonic transport (SST). *(Timber cutting lobbying p. 102)*

Both proponents and opponents of development of an American SST to compete with flying models built by other countries cited technical studies to support positions in which they were diametrically opposed. Foes contended the SST posed serious dangers to the environment; SST supporters disputed the claim. *(SST p. 108)*

Major Issues

The environmental crisis involved the welfare not only of all Americans but also of many of their institutions and of basic elements in the nation's economy. While many vested interests agreed on the need for action, much room for disagreement existed on what should be done, how it should be done and where the power of decision should rest.

Just reaching general agreement on a definition of the pollution problem and of the scope of corrective actions required presented controversy.

A paramount issue was who should pay the cost, estimated by some at $300 billion to end pollution in the United States by the end of the century. Some have pointed to such basic industries as the oil and automotive. On the other hand, many companies in those and other fields publicized heavy spending on efforts to clean up their operations.

The Chrysler Corporation called environmental pollution "the number one concern in this country today" and added: "Much of what is printed and said about pollution leaves the impression that little is being done by industry and business to combat this problem. This simply is not true." Chrysler said it had spent millions to that end.

John E. Swearingen, chairman of Standard Oil Company of Indiana, said in 1970:

"A society capable of interplanetary travel can surely devise the technology to control its own wastes. But broad public support of the necessary steps and a willingness to share in the costs are indispensable. This is one more counter at which no free lunch is available, and the sooner the public faces up to that fact the sooner we will be on our way. Public enthusiasm for pollution control is matched by a reluctance to pay even a modest share of the cost. All members of society have created the problem and all will have to be party to the solution."

The huge financial stakes directly involved the interests of thousands of companies with millions of employees and stockholders, each affected by the corporate well-being. As citizens, they were affected by deteriorating environment along with other people. Some labor unions introduced pollution control as a factor in collective bargaining. New antipollution companies came into existence, and existing companies set up new antipollution enterprises as part of their diversification programs. The field ranked among "glamour-stocks" on stock markets as the decade of the 1970s opened.

A task force report on air pollution prepared by Ralph Nader's Center for Study of Responsive Law spoke of "the new gold rush" and found irony "in the fact that many of the giants preparing to move into the environmental control field are themselves major polluters."

The cost of pollution control cannot be figured in dollars alone, just as the effects of pollution cannot. Beyond differences of opinion based on grounds of financial self-interest, sweeping though they are, other differences carried into the decision-making arenas by organized interests stem from political and ideological factors. Questions of individual and corporate freedoms are involved, as well as of governmental jurisdictions at various levels up through that of national sovereignty.

International Pressures. The environmental crisis crosses national boundaries. Pressures for the United States to join in raising to an international basis the attack on environmental problems come from inside and outside this country. Much lobby activity on Capitol Hill and elsewhere is not inconsistent with the position of the United Nations' U Thant, who said in 1970: "For the task of saving the environment, nothing less than a new step toward world order will do." He called for "a global authority" and said, "It should be able, if necessary, to police and enforce its decisions."

Controversial Areas. Major questions upon which interest groups differed widely in the search for environmental solutions were:

• The degree to which reliance should be placed on the profit system or, alternatively, on "collective responsibility," as some put it.

Sources of Pollution Varied; Results May Be Drastic

Suggestions of the far-ranging interests affected by antipollution proposals, presenting many openings for potential collision between conflicting forces, are found in analyses of the sources of environment damage.

For example, Rolf Eliassen, professor of environmental engineering at Stanford University, told the Senate Public Works Subcommittee on Air and Water Pollution July 9, 1968:

"These three realms are inevitably linked in urban areas: pollution of the air from municipal refuse dumps and outmoded incinerators; pollution of surface waters from industrial dumps, mill tailings, floating debris, and with the runoff from uncontrolled garbage dumping and filling areas; pollution of ground waters by infiltration of contaminated water from mineral dumps and refuse landfills; and desecration of the landscape by strip mines, tailings ponds and piles from the processing of coal and minerals."

President Nixon told Congress (Feb. 10, 1970) that the fight against pollution "is not a search for villains." He said the damage to environment has resulted, "not from malign intention, but from failure to take into account the full consequences of our actions." Other excerpts from Mr. Nixon's message on environment:

"Water pollution has three principal sources: municipal, industrial and agricultural wastes....

"Most air pollution is produced by the burning of fuels. About half is produced by motor vehicles....Industries, power plants, furnaces, incinerators—these and other so-called 'stationary sources' add enormously to the pollution of the air....

"New packaging methods, using materials which do not degrade and cannot easily be burned, create difficult new disposal problems....While our population grows, each one of us keeps using more of the earth's resources. In the case of many common minerals, more than half those extracted from the earth since time began have been extracted since 1910."

The Chrysler Corporation said in a report: "There is no method known today by which even the most simple product can be manufactured without producing waste....

"But there is a favorable side to the problem—the very high proportion of industrial wastes, scrap, and emissions that are cleaned up, reclaimed, recycled, disposed of, and otherwise prevented from fouling the environment. It is good housekeeping as well as good business to conserve natural resources and re-use metals, liquids, chemicals, and other materials..."

Undefined Boundaries. Some individuals and groups define both the problem and the solution in terms which recognize few if any limitations.

Leonard Woodcock, successor to Walter P. Reuther as president of the United Auto Workers union, told a 27-nation symposium (June 15, 1970) cosponsored at Onaway, Mich., by the UAW and the United Nations that poverty and deprivation are among the most dangerous forms of pollution. Woodcock said that "without a vigorous push for an economy of equal opportunity and distributive justice, the chances for environmental sanity may well be lost."

U Thant, Secretary General of the United Nations, said in a Texas speech printed in the *Congressional Record* (June 3, 1970): "This is the first time in its history that mankind faces not merely a threat, but an actual world-wide crisis involving all living creatures, all vegetable life, the entire system in which we live, and all nations large or small, advanced or developing. It is a crisis which concerns literally everyone, and involves, directly or indirectly, almost everything."

Asserting that solutions required that nations "depart radically from the hitherto sacred paths of national sovereignty," U Thant said "we face a rapidly increasing imbalance between the life-sustaining systems of the earth and the demands, industrial, agricultural, technological and demographic, which its inhabitants put upon it....If we fail to meet that challenge, it could become an unthinkable disaster for our children."

• The types of incentives, including tax policy, and compulsion which should be used in motivating antipollution action.
• The degree and character of Federal jurisdiction, in compliance with Congress' declaration that U.S. policy is "to create and maintain conditions under which man and nature can exist in productive harmony...."
• The specific form which Federal involvement should take, including the jurisdiction and makeup of various existing or proposed agencies.
• The jurisdiction of various committees in Congress concerning what could become an area of enormous and high-priority Government spending, holding the prospect of enhanced political leverage for certain Members. Lobbies have invariably sought, with success, to lodge regulatory and legislative authority over their field with individuals they consider sympathetic to their interests. Formation of a new joint committee for environmental affairs is among proposals advanced.

• The degree and nature of international involvement and the corresponding effects on sovereign interests of the United States and other nations. This could be an issue both directly and as a backdrop to other areas of controversy, such as that of war and peace.

President Nixon sought to ease the way for reconciliation of differing views through broad representation at high levels of policy planning—in effect, a form of institutionalized interest group participation in the making of Government policy often used by Presidents in the past. At the international level, the United Nations planned a Conference on Human Environment in Stockholm, Sweden, in June 1972.

Defining the Problem

An initial hurdle which must be crossed in any war on pollution is to achieve agreement among a multitude of interests, involving a vast sector of the U.S. population, on the nature and scope of the problem. A wide disparity of views exists on what the terms pollution and environment embrace. As in the cases of poverty and human rights, opinions on the solutions are as diverse as the assessments of the problems from which they are derived.

Frank M. Potter Jr., executive director of the Environmental Clearing House, said in a report published by the Center for the Study of Democratic Institutions at Santa Barbara, Calif.,"We have never seriously set out to define what we mean when we talk about an 'optimum' or 'livable' environment....The tennis-shoed little old lady may grieve for the Redwoods or a threatened brook without realizing that bigger and more serious problems may threaten much more basic values—perhaps life itself."

Some advocate far greater Government controls over industry and individuals. Others concur with the need for action but see dangers of over-reaction to the environmental crisis equal to the risks of inaction.

Steven Cotton, spokesman for Environmental Action, national coordinating group for "Earth Day" in 1970, said "war and the environment are not two distinct issues....environment does not mean just pollution—rather, making the world a livable place." Many leaders in the environmental "teach-in" April 22 had taken part in protests against U.S. involvement in the Vietnam war. A primary aim of student groups and other antiwar demonstrators has been a change in priorities of Government spending from defense to other purposes, including the environment.

Among those who lobbied in the Senate for proposals aimed at ending U.S. military involvement in Southeast Asia was former Sen. Joseph S. Clark (D Pa. 1957-69), president of World Federalists USA and chairman of the Coalition on National Priorities and Military Policy. The coalition, which included Americans for Democratic Action, said it was a group of "national organizations working for arms control and disarmament agreements, reductions in military spending, and a reordering of national priorities."

Samuel Z. Klausner, director of the Center for Research on the Acts of Man at the University of Pennsylvania, has noted that an earlier writer once said the growth of monopoly industry under U.S. capitalism was paving the way for socialism by creating bureaucratic structures subject to takeover by a central authority. Klausner wrote in *The Annals* of the American Academy of Political and Social Science (May 1970): "The current environmental interest may be leading us in the same direction...by preparing public attitudes and model legislation for the extension of bodies of law designed to constrain the individual actor to be sensitive to the requirement of general welfare as he uses or enjoys some environmental resource."

In the speech cited by Magnuson, U Thant listed among many broad questions he said should be re-examined in the light of the environmental crisis "the whole system of profits, of sales promotion and of the nature of commercial enterprise, as part of a national way of life," in some countries.

Herbert D. Doan, president of Dow Chemical Company, said (March 1970), "The search for profit must be recognized as a motivator, a useful social tool. If we can define a market in environmental control, I am convinced that the search for profit and competition will provide useful low-cost solutions."

The welfare of innumerable individuals and groups is at stake in the decisions which will come in the months and years ahead. The repercussions will be felt in Congress, the Executive Branch, at the state and local levels and in

International Groups

David R. Brower of Berkeley, Calif., former chief officer of the Sierra Club, in September 1969 announced activation of two internationally based organizations plus a subsidiary: Friends of the Earth (FOE), its subsidiary League of Conservation Voters, and the John Muir Institute for Environmental Studies. Brower had been crowded out of his Sierra Club post previously in a management dispute which involved his view that environment should be dealt with on an international basis.

The Institute and FOE are located at the same San Francisco address (451 Pacific Ave.). Brower is director and vice president of the nonprofit, tax-deductible Institute and is president of the FOE. Max Linn of Albuquerque, N.M., public relations director for Sandia Laboratories, is president of the Institute and a vice president of FOE along with Stewart M. Ogilvy of Yonkers, N.Y. The FOE's executive director is Gary A. Soucie, who also was formerly with the Sierra Club.

The FOE registered in 1970 as a Congressional lobby organization "to promote legislation to preserve, restore and encourage rational use of the ecosphere." Among its three registered lobbyists is Soucie.

Brower said the FOE was not made tax-deductible because it would concentrate on legislative and political action and planned "to be extremely aggressive and noncompromising in our activities." When Brower headed the Sierra Club, the Internal Revenue Service took the unusual step of revoking the clubs' privilege of receiving tax-deductible contributions because of its activities in blocking two new dams in the Grand Canyon.

Rep. Morris K. Udall (D Ariz.), looking back over the fight later, said of the conservationist faction led by the Sierra Club, "I can't think of any group in this country that has had more power in the last eight years," and he credited Brower with "cleverly exploiting it."

The John Muir Institute was founded with a $80,000 gift from board chairman Robert O. Anderson of Roswell, N.M., chairman of the Atlantic Richfield Company and chairman of the Aspen Institute for Humanistic Studies at Aspen, Colo. His company in June 1970 began marketing a lead-free gasoline in what Anderson called an effort to help automobile engineers "to bring an essentially pollution free internal combustion automobile from the drawing boards to the general public without undue delay."

elections as faction leaders resort to the various weapons in their arsenals to advance or defend what they construe to be the interests of their constituents.

The internationally based Friends of the Earth was among groups which successfully backed Rep. Paul N. McCloskey (R Calif.) in 1970. He later announced readiness to run against President Nixon on the war issue.

FOE won 11 of the 12 House races and one of the three Senate contests in which it took positions. It played a part in the defeat of Rep. E. Ross Adair (R Ind.), ranking

Republican on the Foreign Affairs Committee, and successfully backed Sen. Philip A. Hart (D Mich.), chairman of the Commerce Energy, Natural Resources and Environment Subcommittee. Environmental Action won five of its 10 House endorsements. *(Election results p. 45)*

One area in which differing viewpoints on environmental questions figured prominently in Congressional activity involved timber cutting proposals. The study below details the many forces and factors affected even by a relatively uncomplicated piece of legislation involving the environment.

Struggle Over Timber

Timber industry attempts to outflank conservationists by enlisting urban support for a bill to increase timber cuts from national forests were blocked when the House Feb. 26, 1970, refused to take up the measure.

By a 228-150 roll-call vote, the House rejected the rule under which the National Forest Timber Conservation and Management Act (HR 12025) was to be considered. Most Representatives from northern urban districts voted against the bill, despite supporters' arguments that more lumber from Federal lands is needed to meet housing shortages felt most acutely by the inner-city poor.

The lumber industry's tactics, which included alliances with builders' associations and urban lobby groups, turned what started as another in a series of confrontations with conservation organizations into a debate over which of two national needs—adequate housing or preservation of the environment—should be given priority.

The controversy found the House Agriculture Committee, with only nine of 33 Members who voted for the 1968 Housing and Urban Development Act, urging adoption of a bill its report described as one answer to housing conditions that "...are a disgrace to this nation, degrading to our citizens, costly to our economy and extremely dangerous to the health of the country."

Opponents, led by an ad hoc alliance of 10 conservation groups called the Conservation Coalition, rejected the housing argument as an industry attempt to lend moral weight to a measure to its own economic benefit. High interest rates, not lack of lumber, hinder housing construction, they argued.

"The sudden solicitude that the timber industry is showing for the ill-housed urban ghetto dweller is transparent," wrote Michael McCloskey, Sierra Club executive director, in the Dec. 13, 1969, *New Republic.* "The industry really wants to promote markets for its products.... Housing goals can be met without any increase in timber production."

The bill, which was endorsed by Secretary of Agriculture Clifford M. Hardin and Secretary of Housing and Urban Development George Romney, directed the U.S. Forest Service to develop "optimum timber productivity" on the 97 million acres of commercial timber in the national forests.

"Without the substantial increase in timber production which the enactment of this legislation will encourage, it will be difficult, it not impossible, to build the homes America needs," Romney said Feb. 12.

Some Members of Congress were skeptical about claims that more intensive harvesting of national forests would help realize the 10-year goal of 26 million units of new and rehabilitated housing set by the 1968 housing act. In dissenting views to the House Agriculture Committee's report on HR 12025, Rep. Charles M. Teague (R Calif.) said the bill would lower lumber prices and encourage housing construction "...only incidentally, if at all."

Rep. James H. Scheuer (D N.Y.) said Feb. 26 that the bill "... is not only a poor conservation measure, but it is also a poor housing measure." He suggested that alternative materials to replace wood were the answer to housing problems.

At least one Member from an urban district—Rep. John Conyers Jr. (D Mich.)—voted against the bill after first endorsing it. In a statement in the Feb. 4 *Congressional Record,* Conyers said he originally thought HR 12025 offered "...a solution to a major aspect in the problem of insufficient and inadequate housing. If the principal drawback to increased home construction was the lack of lumber, then HR 12025 would go a long way toward solving our housing problems."

"It now appears," Conyers added, "that much of the blame for the present low level in new housing starts can be attributed to the spiraling rates of financing and other costs rather than to a lack of lumber."

Other Members, including Rep. Wayne N. Aspinall (D Colo.), chairman of the House Interior and Insular Affairs Committee, opposed consideration of the bill until the Public Land Law Review Commission completed its study of existing public land policies. Its report after five years of work was submitted to Congress and President Nixon on June 23, 1970.

The bill, prompted by timber shortages that drove prices up between 1967 and 1969, was supported by industry, housing and urban groups led by the National Forest Products Association and the National Association of Home Builders.

The Conservation Coalition that directed opposition to the measure was composed of the Sierra Club, Friends of the Earth, Citizens Committee on Natural Resources, the National Rifle Association and other conservation groups. The United Auto Workers Union also opposed the bill.

Timber Prices

A primary reason for introduction of the timber supply bill was pressure on the timber industry from the housing industry in late 1968 and early 1969 after a shortage of timber drove prices up.

There were both temporary and long-range reasons for this tight situation. Temporary reasons included a dry summer in 1967 that caused a shut-down of some logging operations due to fire hazard, heavy snows in the Northwest in January 1969, a boxcar shortage and an East Coast dock strike that slowed deliveries. A long-range reason was the export of logs—primarily to Japan. Exports to Japan and other nations represented nearly 7 percent of the total domestic production of softwood saw logs and veneer logs.

In March 1969, prices began to go down, a phenomenon which the National Association of Home Builders attributed to the "present slowdown in housing, particularly the drop in single-family housing."

History of the Timber Bill

Sen. John J. Sparkman (D Ala.) introduced S 1832, the first version of a timber supply bill, on April 18, 1969,

Supporters and Opponents

Major supporters of HR 12025 included:

National Association of Home Builders, whose members build approximately 75 percent of all homes and apartments constructed by professional builders.

National Forest Products Association, a federation of 19 associations incorporating 1,500 individual forest products industries, including such large companies as Weyerhauser and Boise Cascade.

National Association of Housing and Redevelopment Officials, composed of 1,700 local public agencies and 7,000 individuals administering public housing, urban renewal and housing codes throughout the nation.

The United Brotherhood of Carpenters and Joiners.

Western Governors' Conference. Some 79 percent of the National Forest lands covered by the act lie within their state boundaries.

Associated General Contractors of America.

American Forest Institute.

Major opponents of HR 12025 included:

Citizens' Committee on Natural Resources.
Izaak Walton League of America.
National Audubon Society.
National Rifle Association.
Sierra Club.
Trout Unlimited.
The Wilderness Society
Wildlife Management Institute.
National Wildlife Federation.
Friends of the Earth
United Auto Workers

after hearings March 19-21 of his Subcommittee on Housing and Urban Affairs on the prices of lumber for housing.

S 1832 was referred by Sparkman's Subcommittee to the full Senate Agriculture Committee, whose chairman, Allen J. Ellender (D La.), said that he would not release it unless the House acted favorably.

The Subcommittee on Forests of the House Agriculture Committee held hearings May 21-23 on a proposed timber supply bill (HR 10344). On June 10, Subcommittee Chairman John L. McMillan (D S.C.) offered a new bill (HR 12025) said to incorporate suggestions made at the hearings by conservation groups and the Forest Service.

Conservation Lobby Against Bill

Vigorous lobbying by 10 conservation groups contributed to House refusal to consider HR 12025. Early this year the ad hoc Conservation Coalition began an intensive campaign against the bill, stressing that the emphasis in the measure was on logging at the expense of all other uses of the national forests.

W.R. Poage (D Texas), who abstained when the House Agriculture Committee—of which he is chairman—favorably reported HR 12025, said on Feb. 5, "Frankly, I'm going to vote against it, as I see the bill now. I think it opens the door to destroy multiple use."

The members of the Conservation Coalition, who joined forces to fight the timber measure, were: the Sierra Club, the Izaak Walton League of America, the National Audubon Society, The National Rifle Association, Trout Unlimited, the Wilderness Society, the Wildlife Management Institute, the National Wildlife Federation, Friends of the Earth and the Citizens' Committee on Natural Resources.

Eight of the national conservation organizations sent a telegram Jan. 28 to all Members of Congress contending, among other things, that the bill "threatens America's national forests, scuttles historic multiple-use practices and undermines prospective parks, wilderness, open space and recreation areas."

Volunteers and officers of five of the organizations—the National Audubon Society, the Sierra Club, the Wilderness Society, Friends of the Earth and Trout Unlimited—were active in canvassing Congressional offices. They operated out of a room in the Rayburn Building. Workers for the Sierra Club delivered an information kit Dec. 21 to Members of Congress. The kit contained articles on the environmental impact, the housing effect and the forestry implications of the bill.

In addition, Brock Evans, Northwest representative of the Sierra Club and the coordinator of the fight against the bill, said that he had visited 25 to 30 Congressional offices. The Sierra Club, which took the lead in the effort against the measure, lost its tax-exempt status in August 1968. A limitation in the Internal Revenue Code provides that "no substantial part of the activities" of tax-exempt organizations may be devoted to "carrying on propaganda, or otherwise attempting to influence legislation." Many conservation organizations are wary of violating this provision and thus losing their right to receive tax-deductible contributions.

Friends of the Earth, an organization founded by David Brower, former president of the Sierra Club, declined tax-exempt status in order to be able to directly influence legislation.

Three organizations—the Izaak Walton League of America, the National Rifle Association and the Wilderness Society—as well as the Sierra Club, sent information to members and urged them to write their Representatives. A Sierra Club newsletter Feb. 20 told club members: "A vote for HR 12025 will be a vote for raiding the national forests. Phone or telegraph your Representative today—and get others to do likewise."

Sierra Club Executive Director Michael McCloskey said Feb. 27 that the House vote not to consider HR 12025 demonstrated that conservation groups could "compete in the legislative arena." He predicted that a similar Conservation Coalition would be active in the near future on issues such as spending for water pollution control and the establishment of new wilderness areas.

Supporters of Measure

Lobbying in support of HR 12025 was led by the National Forest Products Association and the National Association of Home Builders. *(Box this page)*

E. F. Behrens, executive assistant to Agriculture Secretary Clifford M. Hardin, was employed by the National Forest Products Association from 1958 to 1967. His last position with the association was manager for general operations.

The two trade organizations agreed to make a united effort to increase national forest timber cutting a joint meeting at Houston, Texas, in 1969. Several legislative proposals developed at the meeting were part of HR 12025.

Arguments on Timber Bill

Supporters of the timber bill argued that the nation's chronic housing shortage was due in large part to a recent shortage of timber.

Opponents maintained that the housing shortage was a result of high interest rates, high land prices and high labor prices.

Supporters said the worsening housing situation justified emphasizing increased timber production. Opponents contended that HR 12025 would sacrifice the national forests to maximum timber cutting without regard for protection of watershed, fish and wildlife, grazing or scenic and recreation values.

Supporters of the measure held that almost any wood substitute required the development of depletable resources and the production of water and air polluting wastes in the manufacturing process.

Opponents argued that the timber industry, whose real worry is that wood will be displaced by lower-priced substitutes, was trying to hold on to the construction material market.

Supporters argued that curtailing the export of timber to Japan would shift the balance of trade to the disadvantage of the United States.

Those in favor of the timber supply bill argued that higher levels of management would benefit national forest land in that proper harvesting would enhance a forest's watershed capacity by preventing compacted soil and controlling erosion.

Opponents contended that the largest increase in logging under the bill would occur in the virgin timber of the Pacific Coast and Rocky Mountains where, they said, the mountainous terrain is ecologically fragile. Further, they said, the Forest Service was already selling timber at a rate about 50 percent in excess of that which can be sustained while maintaining good forestry.

Supporters of HR 12025 maintained that under the bill the Forest Service would be able to protect areas which should be left as wilderness. Opponents said that a provision requiring intensive forestry on all land capable of supporting marketable timber would make it possible to withdraw the six to eight million acres which have their highest value as wilderness.

Supporters of HR 12025 said that the bill would increase the funds available to the Forest Service. Opponents said it would not alleviate the Forest Service's funding problems because the Service would still have to go through the appropriations process every two years.

The Forest Service favored having at its disposal proceeds from timber sales rather than having to rely entirely on appropriations from the general Treasury. The agency estimated that under the bill it would have received $229 million from the timber fund in fiscal 1971 for reforestation and forest management. The bill required, however, that unused funds be transferred to the Department of the Treasury after two years.

On Jan. 28, 1970, the two associations jointly published a 36-page booklet, "Housing Goals and the Future Course for the National Forests," urging adoption of HR 12025. Ralph N. Hodges Jr., vice president of the National Forest Products Association, said 5,000 copies were mailed to Members of Congress, newspaper editors, editorial writers and radio and television journalists. He estimated the cost of printing and mailing the publication at $2,000.

The National Forest Products Association also urged urban lobby groups to support HR 12025. The National Urban League, the National Association of Housing and Redevelopment Officials and the National Housing Conference all endorsed the measure.

A letter from Whitney M. Young, Jr., National Urban League president, to Rep. Catherine May (R Wash.) voicing the organization's support for the bill was circulated among Members.

After the House voted Feb. 26, 1970, against considering HR 12025, Hodges said the next day that the bill was dead—a conclusion which proved correct. Although the measure remained on the House calendar, it would have required more strength than supporters demonstrated in the original vote for them to revive it. The bill died at the end of the 1970 session.

Nevertheless, Hodges said "the housing problem is not going to go away" and Congress would have to act on a new proposal when pressure built up again for more housing and more timber. Hearings were held in 1971 on new legislation.

Land Commission Report

The Public Land Law Review Commission on June 23, 1970, recommended that stringent controls over the environment on the 755.3 million acres of Federally owned public land—one third of the nation's land area—be put into effect without delay.

The Commission recommended that enhancement and maintenance of the environment, with rehabilitation where necessary, be defined as objectives for all classes of public lands. It said Federal standards for environmental quality should be established. Until Congress enacted such legislation, it said, state standards should be enforced.

It recommended that public lands be managed under statutory guidelines "to enhance the quality of the environment, both on and off public lands" where feasible. Thus, public land users would not only be required to meet high standards in removing resources such as timber and minerals from public lands but also in processing them off public lands.

"For example," the commission said, "public land timber may supply a woodpulp mill causing air and water pollution and the degradation of landscape esthetics. Smelters processing public land minerals may cause similar adverse environmental impacts....The granting of public land rights and privileges can and should be used, under clear Congressional guidelines, as leverage to accomplish broader environmental goals off the public lands."

Congress should require land management agencies to classify public lands for environmental management into four basic categories: water, air, biosystem and quality of experience, the commission said.

FARM LOBBY

New Coalition Challenged Administration in 1970

A new farm lobby emerged in 1970 to challenge attempts by the Nixon Administration to change the direction of farm policy.

The lobby—the Coalition of Farm Organizations—was not able to scuttle the Nixon Administration's major farm bill, as it had hoped. But it did succeed in blocking House action on the bill until it had wrung concessions from the Administration on several features of the plan. The Agricultural Act of 1970, which cleared Congress Nov. 19, bore the imprint of the coalition lobbying.

The Administration wanted to ease Government controls on farming and adjust price supports to a free market. The coalition argued that farm income could be maintained only with high Government supports and tight production controls.

Thirty-two farm commodity groups and cooperatives joined the coalition to fight the Administration proposals. The only major farm group not a member was the American Farm Bureau Federation, which was recommending a five-year phase-out of price supports and production controls.

The battle between the Administration and the coalition over the farm bill was fought largely behind the closed doors of the House Agriculture Committee during the early months of 1970.

After public hearings in 1969, the Committee went into executive sessions on the farm legislation. An omnibus farm bill was cleared by the Committee on July 23, 1970, but not before the coalition had received enough support for its position to effect changes in the original Administration proposal.

After the Administration had compromised on several points to reflect coalition demands, the bill appeared headed for Committee approval. In a surprise move on June 2, however, a majority of Committee members substituted a major coalition plank for a previously approved Administration provision on feed grains. The Committee vote culminated a series of maneuvers between the Administration and the coalition that had been going on since the coalition organized in July 1969 to fight the Administration plan.

The coalition favored the permanent extension of existing farm programs, which included government support payments and production controls, acreage allotments and marketing quotas. The only changes coalition members wanted were higher support guarantees and stronger production controls. Coalition leaders said they preferred no bill at all to the Administration measure.

If the coalition and its supporters in Congress had succeeded in blocking the Administration bill without passing a bill of its own, farm programs would have reverted to pre-1965 support levels. From 1966 through December 1970, farm programs operated under provisions in the 1965 Food and Agriculture Act.

Background. In 1965, Congress passed a four-year farm program providing acreage reduction and price support payments for cotton, wheat and feed grains, which are the major farm commodities. The Food and Agriculture Act of 1965 (PL 89-321) also included programs for wool, dairy products, rice, tobacco and peanuts.

Although President Johnson had requested permanent extension of the farm program in 1968, Congress provided only for a one-year continuation through Dec. 31, 1970 (PL 90-559). Members argued that a new Administration should be given an opportunity to recommend its own program.

During his 1968 Presidential campaign, Richard M. Nixon called the 1965 Farm Act "a patchwork of older legislation unsuitable for the long term." He did support a temporary extension of the Act, however, to give farmers adequate time to plant their crops while a new Administration worked out details for a new farm program.

The new Secretary of Agriculture, Clifford M. Hardin, did not appear before the House Agriculture Committee with a draft plan until September 1969.

Farm Population

The number of farms in operation in the United States was lower in 1969 than at any other time in the past 100 years.

The Department of Agriculture estimated that a total of 2,895,000 farms were worked in 1969—a decline of 3 percent from 1968 and a 28-percent drop from the 1959 total. The Census Bureau had estimated that there were 2.7 million farms in 1870.

Although the number of farms had been declining, the amount of land actually farmed had dropped off by a much smaller percentage—5 percent from 1959 to 1969. The figures suggest increasing concentration of farm ownership.

Although there were fewer farmers in the country, agriculture still was one of the nation's largest industries. It employed 4.6 million workers. Farmers were first in spending for equipment, the total averaging close to $5.5 billion annually. Agriculture was first in assets with $307 billion and fourth in sales with around $47.4 billion a year. Three out of every 10 jobs in private employment were related to agriculture.

Farm groups used these figures to illustrate the importance to the nation of sound agricultural policies. They also stressed that the American consumer had to spend only about 16.5 percent of his disposable income for food.

Yet the farmer continued to suffer from low income, the farm groups argued. While 1969 farm prices were only two percent higher than the 1947-49 base, the price of goods purchased by farmers, interest, taxes, and wage rates had increased 50 percent.

Hardin said the Department wanted to work closely with the Committee in developing specific proposals out of a number of possible options for farm programs. A series of Monday night meetings between the Committee and Department officials followed, alternating with public hearings.

Administration Farm Plan

While the Administration did not propose dismantling the existing structure, it did call for easing Government restrictions on planting and for giving the Agriculture Secretary greater authority for basing price supports on market prices rather than on parity.

The parity formula established a commodity price to maintain the producer's purchasing power at a par with what he would have realized had he been growing the same crop during a 1910-1914 base period. Parity relates the price the farmer receives to his cost of production.

The Administration recommended elimination of the existing floor under per-pound and per-bushel support rates for major crops. Instead, the Secretary of Agriculture was to be given discretionary authority to set price supports between zero and 90 percent of parity to encourage more farmers to sell in the market.

A major feature of the Administration proposal was a "set-aside" plan for limiting crop production. Under the set-aside, after the farmer had agreed to keep a certain number of acres out of production, he would be free to plant whatever crop he wished on the remainder of his land. The coalition argued that the plan would increase production, not limit it.

Coalition of Farm Groups

When the outlines of an Administration plan began to appear in the summer of 1969, about 20 farm groups met under the sponsorship of the National Farmers Union and the National Grange. The aim of the meeting was to seek consensus and develop strategy for proposals to counter the Administration bill.

The coalition was the first effort by farm organizations to ban together for a joint purpose. National Farmers Union officials explained that a number of the farm groups had worked together in the past in shifting alliances on different pieces of farm legislation, but no major concerted effort previously had developed on a major farm bill.

Although the coalition got off to a slow start in its lobbying in 1969, it began to bring increasing pressure to bear on the Agriculture Committee and House Members in the spring of 1970.

A key figure in the maneuvering was Committee Chairman W. R. Poage (D Texas).

Poage was insistent that no farm program would pass an urban-dominated House without strong Administration support. Republicans had in the past challenged farm programs which contained strong Government controls and supports. They argued that farmers would realize a better income if their commodities competed in an open market.

Poage said he needed to join Republican votes with those of rural Democrats to move a farm bill through the House. Urban Members had become increasingly discon-

How the Program Works

The purpose of the 1965 Food and Agriculture Act was to maintain farm income through a system of relatively generous price supports and direct payments combined with production controls. The following is a description of how the program worked for the three major crops of wheat, feed grains and cotton.

Cotton. The system was based upon a national minimum acreage allotment of 16 million acres. Individual farm acreage allotments were based on this minimum.

A farmer participating in the program qualified for price-support loans at 90 percent of the world market price on all the cotton he produced. He also received direct payments on the portion of his production grown on his domestic allotment. The farmer averaged 65 percent of parity from the combination of the two benefits.

The parity formula established a commodity price that would maintain the producer's purchasing power at a par with what he would have realized had he been growing the same crop during a 1910-1914 base period. A parity ratio of 80, for example, meant that the prices the farmer received were less favorable in relation to his costs than they had been in the base period.

Wheat. Farmers planting within their acreage allotments were eligible for a return equal to 100 percent of parity on about two-fifths of their crop— the portion needed for domestic human consumption. On the remainder of their production, they would get the market price.

On wheat produced for domestic consumption, the farmer received a combination of price supports, direct payments and marketing certificates to bring his return up to 100 percent of parity. In 1969, he sold his wheat for the market price ($1.25 a bushel) or obtained a price-support loan for about that amount, plus a direct Government payment of 63 cents and a special bonus payment of 75 cents a bushel. The bonus payment was made by millers purchasing wheat to be processed for human consumption; they were required to redeem, at the 75-cent rate, "certificates" distributed by the Government to wheat farmers participating in the program.

Farmers who chose to reduce wheat acreage below their permitted allotments could also receive special diversion payments.

Feed Grains. To participate in the program, a farmer had to retire at least 20 percent of the feed grain acreage. If the farmer chose to divert additional acreage, up to a total of 50 percent of his base, he would receive diversion payments for that additional acreage. The payment in 1969 was 45 percent of the total price support times the projected yield.

Farmers who agreed to divert the 20-percent-minimum acreage were eligible for price-support loans plus direct subsidy payments. The Secretary of Agriculture was authorized to set the price-support loan at less than 65 percent of parity as long as the combined rate of loans and payments was at least 65 percent.

tented with the costs of farm programs. The fiscal 1970 Department of Agriculture budget was $7.5 billion. Subsidy payments totaled $3.7 billion of the total.

One reason for the quickened activity by the coalition in 1970 was an April 8 vote in the Agriculture Subcommittee on Livestock and Grains. Subcommittee Chairman Graham Purcell (D Texas), sponsor of the coalition bill in the House, was voted down 9 to 8 when the Subcommittee voted to scrap parity as a basis for determining loan levels for wheat and feed grains. The provision adopted by the Subcommittee set loans at 80 to 100 percent of average world market prices, instead of relating loan levels to parity. Under the existing law, supports for domestic wheat were set at 100 percent of parity.

The proposal had the support of the Administration and the deciding vote was cast by Poage.

The steering committee of the coalition met the next day and called the Subcommittee's recommendation "completely unacceptable" and a "sell-out" of the nation's grain producers. Passage of the provision, said NFU President Tony Dechant, "would plunge farmers into a depression that could threaten the entire economy." Coalition members feared the recommendation could become a pattern for other commodities.

Two days before the Subcommittee vote, more than 500 leaders of the coalition met in St. Louis. They adopted a resolution calling on Congress "to make a renewed commitment to the preservation of family agriculture and the attainment of parity prices for agricultural producers." Price protection for the farmer, said the coalition, had to be related to the concept of fairness. "Fairness is not possible unless costs of production are considered," it said.

Poage had to leave Washington in early May for a two-week conference in Australia. Purcell said the break in Committee meetings during Poage's absence gave the coalition enough time to build up pressure once again for the coalition bill. Lobbying efforts intensified.

By the time Poage returned and Committee meetings resumed, the Administration was ready to make some concessions on its farm bill—to continue existing price-support loans and direct support payments on wheat and feed grains for three years.

Total price support for wheat intended for the domestic market—the combination of loans and supplemental direct payments—were to be tied to the full parity price for the crop. The compromise plan also called for a minimum support payment guarantee for corn.

Coalition support for the Administration bill was not won, however, by the compromises. The coalition continued to press for higher support guarantees tied to the farm parity standard.

But coalition leaders thought they would have to take their fight to the House floor. A final Agriculture Committee vote was set for June 2 to approve the separate proposals in the bill for wheat, feed grains and cotton and to ratify previous Committee votes on subsidy limitations, food stamps and other agriculture provisions.

But the Committee unexpectedly reversed itself and threw out the compromise support plan for wheat and feed grains. By a 17-14 vote, the Committee adopted an amendment to tie price supports for feed grains as well as wheat to the parity level.

As a result of the Committee's action, Chairman Poage postponed any further work on the farm bill. Since

House Agriculture Committee

The 35-member House Agriculture Committee considered the farm bill for more than a year with almost no public attention.

In an increasingly urbanized America and a Congress which reflects that population change, agriculture has a limited audience.

But the powerful Agriculture Committee controls a billion-dollar program. With the help of well-organized farm interests, the Committee shepherded agricultural legislation through an increasingly hostile Congress.

The Committee was, however, sharply divided in 1970 on how the farm programs should operate in the future. Members of the Committee represented diverse constituencies—not all of them farm districts. Assistant Committee Counsel Hyde Murray estimated that only about 10 members of the Committee were from farm districts, another 10 from urban areas and the remaining 15 from rural districts in which farming was not the predominant industry.

Philosophies on the Committee ranged from the conservatism of a Thomas G. Abernethy (D Miss.) to the liberalism of the newest member, Allard K. Lowenstein (D N.Y.), who was defeated for re-election in 1970.

the feed grain amendment was unacceptable to the Administration, he said, the farm bill could not pass as it then stood.

No more Committee sessions would be held, Poage said, unless someone produced a substitute plan that could receive Administration support and pass the House.

Final Action

Coalition leaders were pleased by the June 2 Committee action, they said, because it meant they had convinced at least 17 Members not "to cut the guts out of farm programs." They were also pleased in the progress they had made, they said, in moving the Administration toward the policies the coalition favored.

In a statement issued after the June 2 vote, Agriculture Secretary Hardin said he was disappointed by the action. He said he was still hopeful, however, that a bill could be produced which would receive general support.

By the time the farm bill cleared both Houses, it had been modified to include floors under price supports for wheat and feed grains. On the loan level for wheat, conferees on the bill adopted a Senate provision for a minimum of $1.25 per bushel compared to House language which had given the Secretary of Agriculture flexibility to set the level between zero and 100 percent of parity.

The final bill also contained a Senate provision for a floor of $1 per bushel on the loan level for corn. Conferees accepted the House provision for a floor of $1.35 per bushel in price support payments for corn, but added a 70-percent-of-parity guarantee as well.

The farm coalition may not have been able to pass its own bill in the 91st Congress, but it was at least moderately successful in changing the Administration's to meet its demands.

SUPERSONIC TRANSPORT

Failure of Intensive SST Lobbying Campaign

An 11th-hour crash lobbying program by industry, labor and Administration officials failed to save the controversial supersonic transport (SST) program in 1971.

The Senate voted 51-46 March 24, 1971, to discontinue Federal funding of the 300-passenger, 1,800-mile-an-hour plane. The House voted March 18 to end Federal financing of the SST effective March 30.

In 1964 Congress first considered legislative proposals to terminate the SST project; they were defeated, and the debate concerning the plane simmered until 1970 when the Senate voted to delete $290-million in appropriations for work on the plane in fiscal 1971.

After the House and Senate reached a compromise funding level ($210-million through March 30), the Administration, aided by a new lobby group, the National Committee for the SST, launched an intensive campaign to save the aircraft and obtain the full $290-million appropriation. Meanwhile, the Coalition Against the SST—an alliance of political and environmental groups—continued its attempt to convince Congress the project should be scrapped.

Interest Groups

The critics, including the coalition, had claimed that the plane would significantly alter the earth's atmosphere, produce intolerable noise levels on take-off and create sonic booms over land and sea. SST backers replied that the noise problems had been solved, the plane would not be permitted to fly over land areas, and the atmosphere would suffer no more change from SST flights than it did from natural causes.

Following Congressional hearings on the SST, one House Member, who voted against the plane in 1970, said, "The environmental issue has been put to rest." The Library of Congress' Science Policy Research Division released an SST study March 1 which concluded: "The environmental aspects of the SST...have received the bulk of attention of critics. Yet...most of these postulated effects are found to be trivial."

The discussion shifted more to economics. SST proponents asserted that the plane was necessary to assure a favorable balance of trade and that production of the SST would provide jobs for 50,000 workers. Opponents argued that if the plane had merits it would not need public funds.

Sen. William Proxmire (D Wis.), who led the fight against the SST in 1970, said Jan. 2 that it should be no surprise if sponsors of the plane never resumed their campaign for full SST funding.

After that date, the Administration intensified its lobbying efforts to obtain funding for the SST by sending Cabinet members, agency heads, and aerospace scientists to Capitol Hill. And, in February, aerospace management and unions joined forces by setting up a committee called Industry and Labor for the SST which promoted the airliner in Congress and with the public.

By March 3, Proxmire's earlier prediction seemed irrelevant. "The chances (now) of defeating the SST in Congress are at best 50-50," he told a group of state legislators.

Organizations opposing the supersonic jet joined the Coalition Against the SST. One of its members, Friends of the Earth, coordinated the coalition's public information and Congressional activities.

But the coalition was worried about the outcome of the SST debate. George Alderson, director of the anti-SST forces, told Congressional Quarterly March 12 that he had "hoped the pro-SST lobby would defeat itself on environmental issues."

In addition to environmental and economic issues, the question of who was spending how much on lobbying activities entered the discussion.

The coalition March 12 reported receiving $20,600 in contributions from private donors.

The National Committee for the SST announced Feb. 23 that it had set up a $350,000 goal to fight for the plane. But the group's executive director John O'Shea said March 11 that the committee was hoping for one-third that amount and that he doubted the full $350,000 could be spent.

Reasons for SST Defeat

Why did Congress—generally sympathetic to development of the SST in previous years—curtail all funds for the project? Several explanations could be offered, including the new teller vote procedure by which the House—which had always supported the aircraft—voted the SST down March 18.

A result of the 1970 Legislative Reorganization Act (PL 91-510), the procedure required Members of the House to be recorded by name on amendments crucial to major legislation. Previously, amendments were disposed of by non-record votes which enabled Members to vote without making their positions public.

Sidney R. Yates (D Ill.), who offered the amendment to delete funds for the SST from the Department of Transportation's fiscal 1971 appropriations, said after the vote, "I think the recorded (teller) vote made the difference." And Silvio O. Conte (R Mass.), another SST opponent, said, "The Members no longer could duck under parliamentary guise." New Members also had an effect on the outcome. Of the 56 freshmen, 37 voted for the Yates amendment.

In the Senate, the vote of Clinton P. Anderson (D N.M.) offered a clue to the SST defeat, which environmentalists claimed as a victory. Anderson, who had previously supported SST development, voted against the plane March 24 to the astonishment of many. Later he said, "I read my mail." On the morning of the Senate vote, he had received 78 telegrams and letters against the SST, eight in support.

Of 11 new Senators, the Administration won the votes of only four, a ratio matching the votes of their

1967 and 1970 supported the SST by a 54 to 28 margin
on the teller vote. Thirteen Senators from states which
received more than $1-million in contracts favored the
SST, but 26 voted against the project. *(Box p. 111)*

President Nixon received word March 9 from
the two Republican leaders, Sen. Hugh Scott (Pa.)
and Rep. Gerald Ford (Mich.), that because the Administration had expressed determination to solve
environmental problems relating to the SST, the plane's
chances in Congress had been helped.

Environment. In a departure from 1970, scientists
who support the SST defended the plans publicly in 1971.
Accompanying Magruder to Congressional hearings,
three scientists, two of them Government employees,
denied that the SST was a threat to the environment.

Dr. Fred S. Singer, a physicist and chairman of
DOT's SST environmental advisory committee, stated,
"There is no question that the SST is going to release
some pollutants into the atmosphere, but it is doubtful
whether they will be of any significance. In the balance,
I believe the question of whether we should or should not
have an SST must be decided on the basis of economics
and national priorities...."

Another physicist, Dr. William W. Kellogg, associate director of the National Center for Atmospheric
Research, testified that he had found no environmental
basis for delaying the SST program. "The best estimates
we have today regarding the climatic aspects of large-
scale SST operations indicate the effects will be generally imperceptible and trivial compared to changes we
experience from natural causes," he said.

Discussing noise levels, Dr. Leo L. Beranek, chairman of the SST Community Noise Advisory Committee,
told Congress that there were no technical reasons why
a commercial SST could not be built.

He said that enlargement of SST engines and noise
suppression advances have eliminated the argument that
the SST on take-off would disturb citizens living up to
15 miles from airports.

However, this raised another argument. The addition of anti-noise devices added 50,000 pounds in take-off
weight to the SST, raised eventual purchase prices to
the airlines, increased operating costs and shortened the
jet's range.

Economics. Rep. Henry S. Reuss (D Wis.), an
SST opponent, said March 2 that Federal financing for

SST Subcontracts, 1967-1970

The following table shows the amount by state of
first tier subcontracts awarded by the two SST prime
contractors, Boeing and General Electric.

Specific Prototype Subcontracts Awarded By:

	Boeing	General Electric	Total
Alabama	$ 11,924	$ 97,015	$ 108,939
Alaska	——	——	——
Arizona	13,503,733	914,062	14,417,795
Arkansas	306	——	306
California	82,959,797	23,063,164	106,022,961
Colorado	117,152	16,673	133,825
Connecticut	4,966,925	8,510,622	13,477,547
Delaware	40,444	45,242	85,686
Florida	85	915,772	915,857
Georgia	708,215	121,253	829,468
Hawaii	——	——	——
Idaho	862	——	862
Illinois	1,770,277	6,958,795	8,729,072
Indiana	518,593	6,918,692	7,437,285
Iowa	104,134	12,581	116,715
Kansas	32,045,885	1,440	32,047,325
Kentucky	22,152	855,293	877,445
Louisiana	——	480	480
Maine	——	——	——
Maryland	12,036,749	1,428,352	13,465,101
Massachusetts	1,742,738	5,540,331	7,283,069
Michigan	765,516	16,988,333	17,753,849
Minnesota	198,856	2,553,117	2,751,973
Mississippi	35,040	——	35,040
Missouri	1,909	71,298	73,207
Montana	——	——	——
Nebraska	——	8,099	8,099
Nevada	78	18,367	18,445
New Hampshire	1,146	133,277	134,423
New Jersey	372,027	3,728,738	4,100,765
New Mexico	——	26,540	26,540
New York	31,667,822	5,544,434	37,212,256
North Carolina	1,045	228,871	229,916
North Dakota	——	——	——
Ohio	15,777,206	20,326,968	36,104,174
Oklahoma	6,901,975	104,720	7,006,695
Oregon	50,063	1,251,931	1,301,994
Pennsylvania	1,641,978	2,539,972	4,181,950
Rhode Island	141,593	13,019	154,612
South Carolina	——	——	——
South Dakota	——	——	——
Tennessee	902,202	1,515,674	2,417,876
Texas	2,579,353	994,242	3,573,595
Utah	82	——	82
Vermont	250,000	63,350	313,350
Virginia	1,167,257	25,922	1,193,179
Washington	3,351,513	5,702	3,357,215
West Virginia	11,035	43,472	54,507
Wisconsin	73,835	1,313,903	1,387,738
Wyoming	25	——	25
Canada	2,848	——	2,848
TOTAL	**$216,444,375**	**$112,899,716***	**$329,344,091***

*Does not include $5,485,963 which cannot be allocated by states due to a
feature of General Electric's computer program.*

SOURCE: Department of Transportation

the SST should be ended because "it will establish a precedent which could haunt the Federal Government for years." Reuss asserted that foreign SSTs "are not as formidable a competitive threat as has been claimed," and a delay in the program would permit the SST "to be financed by private money in response to a true market demand."

A week later, Connally, appearing before the Senate Appropriations Committee, argued the Government's side of the economic controversy.

"We dare not be so timid as to not produce an SST on an experimental basis," Connally said.

Conceding that any forecast in balance-of-trade levels has uncertainties, Connally, nevertheless, expressed optimism that the United States net gain on trade over the next 20 years "would be some $17-billion to $22-billion" with a reduction in imports and an "SST to sell."

From the Commerce Department, Robert McClellan, Assistant Secretary for domestic and international business, told Congress that 76 percent of all jet aircraft in operation throughout the free world is built in the United States. "Of DOT's total market estimate of 500 American SSTs by 1990, fully half are expected to be exported," he said.

Administration Strategy

Aided by industry and labor groups and technical changes in the plane itself, the Administration was determined to save the SST.

Department of Transportation (DOT) scientists and officials, including William M. Magruder, SST development director, convinced the House Appropriations Committee that two SST prototypes should be funded, but the House overrode the Appropriations Committee.

Although Presidents Kennedy, Johnson and Nixon lined up in support of the SST project, the plane ran into trouble late in the 91st Congress when environmental groups, including the Sierra Club, applied enough pressure to make Congress take a second look at the aircraft.

After the Senate rejected all funds for the SST on Dec. 3, 1970, President Nixon stated, "The action of the U.S. Senate in disapproving the SST is a devastating mistake both because of its immediate impact and because it will have profound long-range consequences for this country. I urge both Houses of Congress to reverse this action."

The Nixon Administration failed in 1970 to generate enough support for full SST funding (fiscal 1971). It increased its pressure on Congress in 1971.

Directing arguments to two groups of legislators, new Members and those who voted against the SST in 1970, Secretary of Transportation John A. Volpe and Secretary of Treasury John Connally presented the case for the SST.

Testifying before the House Appropriations Subcommittee on Transportation March 1, Volpe pleaded for the SST: "The appeal I make to you...is as sincere an appeal as I have ever made in the 20 years since I entered public service. I want you to know what I say here comes from the heart and soul. It represents my deepest conviction. It is devoid of politics."

After 10 years and $1.1-billion invested in the SST program, Volpe said, "We have gone too far, invested too

much and are too near our goal to let this all go down the drain with no tangible results."

Opposition to the SST

The Coalition Against the SST, an alliance of 15 national and 14 state and local organizations, tried to persuade Congress the supersonic transport was an environmental threat and an economic disaster.

Joined by Common Cause—a new pressure group interested in re-ordering national priorities—and many prominent economists (Milton Friedman, John Kenneth Galbraith, Arthur M. Okun, Paul Samuelson), the coalition was composed of political, conservation and environmental organizations.

The national groups included: Citizens League Against the Sonic Boom, Environmental Action, Federation of American Scientists, National Taxpayers Union, Sierra Club, The Wilderness Society and Zero Population Growth.

At the state and local level, the Committee for Green Foothills (Calif.), Federation of Western Outdoor Clubs, Ecology Action for Rhode Island and the Texas Committee on Natural Resources are listed among the group's members.

Arthur Godfrey, the entertainer and the coalition's honorary chairman, spoke for the group March 10 before the Senate Appropriations Committee.

Expressing concern over a fleet of SSTs flying at stratospheric altitudes, Godfrey said that if the Air Force needed the plane he would enthusiastically support it because the "few and sporadic flights of military aircraft at higher altitudes apparently have little effect (on the environment)."

But, he said, "Since the proposed SST is strictly a civilian, commercial project, I am unalterably opposed to its development...."

Established in April 1970, the coalition's activities were directed by Friends of the Earth, an environmental group that is a registered lobbyist. The organization raised $20,600 which was spent for newspaper ads, staff salaries, research and organization expenses. In addition, the coalition's member organizations used their own funds to meet expenses of the anti-SST campaign.

George Alderson, legislative director of Friends of the Earth and coordinator of the SST coalition, said the group's attention was aimed at new Members of Congress, those who voted "inconsistently" on the SST last year, and others who were undecided about additional funding of the aircraft.

Alderson said that part of the coalition's money had been used to bring leaders of local environmental groups to Washington to persuade Congress that the SST should be voted down.

Environment. Tying SST environmental questions to economics, John Gardner, former Secretary of Health, Education and Welfare and now chairman of Common Cause, told the Senate Appropriations Committee March 14: "There remains much to be proven about possible atmospheric dangers." But, he said, "There is one environmental consequence that is virtually certain, and that is noise pollution. The problem is that development of quieter engines may cost from $60-million to $120-million and that efforts to recoup costs from users will cut into sales drastically."

(Continued on p. 112)

SST 1967-1970 Subcontract Awards, With Members' SST Votes

Includes: State, voting record of Senators on March 24, 1971 SST roll-call vote **(N, against funding; Y, for)**; City, Amount of Subcontract, voting record of Representatives on March 18 SST teller vote **(N, against funding; Y, for)**.

ARIZONA

Senators: Fannin (R) Y; Goldwater (R) Y
Phoenix—$14,298,774
Representatives: Rhodes (R), 1st Dist N; Steiger (R), 3rd Dist. N

CALIFORNIA

Senators: Cranston (D) N; Tunney (D) N
Chula Vista—$20,605,551
Representatives: Van Deerlin (D), 37th Dist. Y
El Cajon—$2,401,650
Representative: Bob Wilson (R), 36th Dist. Y
Hawthorne—$12,945,464
Representatives: Anderson (D), 17th Dist. Y; Charles H. Wilson (D), 31st Dist. Y
Irvine—$1,434,168
Representative: Schmitz (R), 35th Dist. Y
Los Angeles—$44,985,352
Representatives: Anderson (D), 17th Dist. Y; Bell (R), 28th Dist. Y; Corman (D), 22nd Dist. Y; Danielson (D), 29th Dist. N; Goldwater (R), 27th Dist. Y; Hawkins (D), 21st Dist. Y; Rees (D), 26th Dist. Y; Rousselot (R), 24th Dist. (Did not vote); Roybal (D), 30th Dist. N; Smith (R), 20th Dist. N; Teague (R), 13th Dist. Y; Charles H. Wilson (D), 31st Dist. Y.
North Hollywood—$1,822,525
Representative: Corman (D), 22nd Dist. Y
Oxnard—$1,460,241
Representative: Teague (R), 13th Dist. Y
San Diego—$6,446,832
Representatives: Schmitz (R), 35th Dist. Y; Bob Wilson (R), 36th Dist. Y; Van Deerlin (D), 37th Dist. Y
Santa Ana—$2,757,393
Representatives: Hanna (D), 34th Dist. Y; Schmitz (R), 35th Dist. Y
Torrance—$2,029,473
Representatives: Anderson (D), 17th Dist. Y; Bell (R), 28th Dist. Y

CONNECTICUT

Senators: Ribicoff (D) N; Weicker (R) N
East Granby—$1,039,216
Representative: Grasso (D), 6th Dist. N
Manchester—$2,034,416
Representative: Cotter (D), 1st Dist. Y
Warehouse Point—$1,455,985
Representative: Cotter (D), 1st Dist. Y
West Hartford—$2,034,534
Representative: Cotter (D), 1st Dist. Y
Windsor Locks—$5,197,481
Representative: Grasso (D), 6th Dist. N

ILLINOIS

Senators: Stevenson (D) N; Percy (R) N
Rockford—$6,496,809
Representative: Anderson (R) Y

INDIANA

Senators: Bayh (D) N; Hartke (D) N
Indianapolis—$4,232,889
Representatives: Bray (R), 6th Dist. Y; Jacobs (D), 11th Dist. N

KANSAS

Senators: Dole (R) Y; Pearson (R) Y
Wichita—$32,044,060
Representative: Shriver (R), 4th Dist. Y

MARYLAND

Senators: Beall (R) Y; Mathias (R) Y
Hagerstown—$10,000,000
Representative: Byron (D), 6th Dist., Y

MASSACHUSETTS

Senators: Kennedy (D) N; Brooke (R) N
Worcester—$5,358,531
Representative: Donahue (D), 4th Dist. N

MICHIGAN

Senators: Hart (D) N; Griffin (R) N
Detroit—$2,619,764
Representatives: Conyers (D), 1st Dist. N; Diggs (D), 13th Dist. N; Dingell (D), 16th Dist. N; O'Hara (D), 12th Dist. N; Griffiths (D), 17th Dist. N; Nedzi (D), 14th Dist. N
Kalamazoo—$2,969,191
Representative: Brown (R), 3rd Dist. N
Lansing—$1,526,326
Representative: Chamberlain (R), 6th Dist. N
Muskegon—$4,351,857
Representative: Vander Jagt (R) N

MINNESOTA

Senators: Humphrey (D) N; Mondale (D) N
Minneapolis—$2,610,703
Representative: Fraser (D), 5th Dist. N

NEW JERSEY

Senators: Williams (D) N; Case (R) N
Dover—$1,280,564
Representative: Frelinghuysen (R), 5th Dist. N

NEW YORK

Senators: Javits (R) N; Buckley (R-Cons) Y
Binghamton—$1,516,855
Representative: Robison (R), 33rd Dist. N
Buffalo—$3,092,957
Representative: Dulski (D), 41st Dist. N; Kemp (R), 39th Dist. Y; Smith (R), 40th Dist. N
East Aurora—$2,753,502
Representative: Kemp (R), 39th Dist. Y
Farmingdale—$24,973,000
Representative: Grover (R), 2nd Dist. Y
Utica—$1,597,894
Representative: Pirnie (R), 32nd Dist. Y

OHIO

Senators: Saxbe (R) Y; Taft (R) Y
Bedford—$1,420,137
Representative: Minshall (R), 23rd Dist., N

CINCINNATI

Cincinnati—$2,720,863
Representatives: Clancy (R), 2nd Dist. Y; Keating (R), 1st Dist. Y
Cleveland—$7,973,674
Representatives: Minshall (R), 23rd Dist. N; Stanton (D), 20th Dist., N, but voted Y on subsequent roll-call vote; Stokes (D), 21st Dist. N; Vanik (D), 22nd Dist. N
Dayton—$1,337,846
Representative: Whalen (R), 3rd Dist. Y
Middletown—$8,208,591
Representative: Powell (R) 24th Dist., Y
Minerva—$1,409,805
Representatives: Hays (D), 18th Dist. Y; Bow (R), 16th Dist. Y
Niles—$1,876,773
Representative: Carney (D), 19th Dist. Y
Toronto—$2,793,927
Representative: Hays (D), 18th Dist. Y
Xenia—$1,277,068
Representative: Brown (R), 7th Dist. N

OKLAHOMA

Senators: Harris (D) N; Bellmon (R) Y
Tulsa—$6,900,000
Representatives: Edmondson (D), 2nd Dist. Y; Belcher (R), 1st Dist. Y

OREGON

Senators: Hatfield (R) N; Packwood (R) N
Portland—$1,201,631
Representatives: Green (D), 3rd Dist. N; Wyatt (R), 1st Dist. Y

PENNSYLVANIA

Senators: Schweiker (R) N; Scott (R) Y
Erie—$1,165,847
Representative: Vigorito (D), 24th Dist. Y
Philadelphia—$1,372,336
Representatives: Barrett (D), 1st Dist. (Did not vote.); Byrne (D), 3rd Dist. Y; Eilberg (D), 4th Dist. Y; Green (D), 5th Dist. (Did not vote.); Nix (D), 2nd Dist. Y

TEXAS

Senators: Bentsen (D) N; Tower (R) Y
Dallas—$1,528,806
Representatives: Cabell (D), 5th Dist. Y; Collins (R), 3rd Dist. Y; Purcell (D), 13th Dist. Y; Teague (D), 6th Dist. Y

VIRGINIA

Senators: Byrd (I) N; Spong (D) N
Waynesboro—$1,165,847
Representative: Robinson (R), 7th Dist., Y

WASHINGTON

Senators: Jackson (D) Y; Magnuson (D) Y
Kent—$1,875,563
Representative: Adams (D), 7th Dist. Y

WISCONSIN

Senators: Nelson (D) N; Proxmire (D) N
Cudahy—$1,042,056
Representative: Zablocki (D), 4th Dist. Y

(Continued from p. 110)

The Coalition Against the SST has directed attention to the sonic boom created by the SST. When flying at supersonic speeds, the SST would create a continuous shock wave 50 miles wide. "Even if the boom were banned by law over U.S. territory, the noise would strike those working or traveling at sea—an estimated 4,000 persons for every flight across the North Atlantic," the coalition said in an "SST Fact Book."

Economics. Paradoxically, the Coalition Against the SST found itself a victim of its victories. Pleased that the Administration had ruled out SST flights over land at supersonic speeds and promised that the plane would not be built for commercial use if scientific research proved it hazardous to the environment, the coalition still wanted the SST project abandoned. The group shifted its attack to economic grounds where it found the support of a group of economists opposed to the SST.

In 1970, 16 economists submitted comments to the Senate on the financial disadvantages of building the SST. At that time, Arthur Okun, chairman of the Council of Economic Advisers during the Johnson Administration, said, "The very fact that proponents of the SST have turned to the Federal Government for funds is evidence itself that the SST does not pass the market test."

On March 11, Okun appeared before the Senate Appropriations Committee and charged Secretary Connally with engaging in "numerical science fiction" on the balance-of-trade issue.

Support for the SST

The National Committee for the SST and its adjunct, Industry and Labor for the SST, were organized in February to convince the public and Congress that production of the aircraft would create aerospace jobs and sales and to counter SST critics who, the committee said, had "grossly exaggerated" noise and polluting effects of the plane.

Messages in labor publications urged workers to write their Representatives and Senators in support of the SST; radio spots and newspaper ads in metropolitan areas (Boston, New York, Philadelphia, Minneapolis, Detroit, Hartford and Washington) warned that a decision not to build the SST would eliminate 50,000 jobs, reduce the nation's tax resources and add to its welfare rolls and adversely affect the U.S. balance of trade.

The leadership of the SST committee included George Meany, AFL-CIO president; Karl G. Harr, president, Aerospace Industries Association; I. W. Abel, president, United Steelworkers of America; and J. J. O'Donnell, president, Air Line Pilots Association.

In addition, Floyd E. Smith, president, International Association of Machinists (AFL-CIO), and Donald J. Strait, vice president of Fairchild Hiller Corporation's Republic Aviation Division, served as co-chairmen of American Industry and Labor for the SST, the SST committee's sister organization.

Fairchild Hiller has received $34-million in prototype subcontracts to develop the SST's tail and a midsection; the Association of Machinists represents aerospace workers.

John O'Shea, executive director of the SST committee, said that contributions to finance the SST media campaign had come from 41 companies, including Boeing and General Electric, the plane's two prime contractors.

However, he said, "Neither of the two companies contributed more than the machinists." Less than one-half of all donations came from the 41 companies and 268 individuals contributed from $1 to $25, O'Shea reported March 11.

The SST committee staged its campaign in the following manner: The legislative liaison staffs of organized labor and industry contacted Congressional staff members, Senators and Representatives. Then, vote "readings" were forwarded to the committee which sent out material and placed ads in newspapers and on radio.

According to O'Shea, the committee concentrated on new Members of Congress, including those who campaigned on environmental issues. The committee tried to let those Members know that "they can now face their constituents" with new positions on the SST "because the game has changed."

Environment. The committee for the SST maintained that the SST would have negligible effects on the earth's environment. In a letter to industry and labor groups, the committee answered charges from environmentalists that the SST would cause changes in climate: "The National Academy of Sciences and the Office of Meteorological Research both have (reported) that SSTs will have no appreciable effect on the earth's normal atmospheric balance."

Economics. Although the Administration and the committee devoted attention to countering environmental charges, the economic impact of the SST was of special concern to both.

Floyd Smith, who led labor forces in the SST struggle, told the House subcommittee that the economic plight of aerospace cities is due to unemployed workers. "Total employment at Boeing (Seattle) is expected to sink to 32,500 within the next nine months. If the SST prototype development is not funded it will drop even more drastically."

Final SST Effort

Opponents of the supersonic transport received a jolt May 12, 1971, when the House, which had voted to end the project March 18, turned an amendment to refund SST contractors inside out and approved $85.3-million to continue work on the controversial aircraft.

Led by Minority Leader Gerald R. Ford (R Mich.), SST forces, working quietly behind the scenes to revive the plane, lined up enough support to win a 201-187 roll-call vote on the SST amendment added to a fiscal 1971 supplemental appropriations bill (HR 8190).

Although leaders of the renewed SST fight insisted that it would cost the Government less to continue the project than to cancel it, the board chairman of the Boeing Company, William M. Allen, ruined the argument May 14 when he said from $500-million to $1-billion would be required to finish developing two SST prototypes.

On May 19 the White House conceded that termination costs would be less than development expenses, and the Senate, by a 58-37 vote, refused to appropriate funds for development of the commercial aircraft. A House-Senate conference on HR 8190 followed the Senate decision, thereby halting the surprise House effort to revive the SST.

1935 SPEECH BY HUGO L. BLACK ON UTILITIES PRESSURES

Following are excerpts from a nationally broadcast speech Aug. 8, 1935, by Sen. Hugo L. Black (D Ala.), who headed a Special Committee to Investigate Lobbying Activities. Congress that month enacted its first lobbyist registration law as Section 12i of the Public Utilities Holding Company Act. A bill (S 2512) sponsored by Black, the future Supreme Court Justice, was a source for Section 308 of the Federal Regulation of Lobbying Act of 1946.

"It is not only the right, but it is the duty of every patriotic citizen who loves his country, to give his honest and unselfish judgment on public questions to his representatives....

"There is no constitutional right to lobby. There is no right on the part of any greedy or predatory interest to use money taken from the pockets of the citizen to mislead him and thus enlist his aid in enabling the same greedy and predatory interest to take still more money out of the pocket of the same unsuspecting citizen. There is no constitutional right on the part of any sordid and powerful group to present its views behind a mask concealing the identity of the group. These money-maddened men behind the mask have no right to send their hired men out into the streets, into the places of business, into the homes and into the churches, to persuade or to frighten citizens into giving blanket authority to have their names signed to telegrams and letters, to be later manufactured by high-powered, high-priced publicity agents, and sent at company expense to the citizens' representatives in Washington, in such way and manner as to deliberately deceive those representatives. There is no constitutional right for the same group to seek out the intimate social friends of Senators and Representatives, their close political associates and campaign managers, and hire them from the four corners of the United States, to make intimate personal appeals and to frighten them as to the political consequences should they vote contrary to the wishes and the financial aggrandizement of the men behind the mask....

"On July 12th, Mr. Philip Gadsden, representing a large group of utility holding companies...testified before the committee. His group had spacious offices in the Mayflower Hotel in Washington for many months. It was headquarters for this group, and to these headquarters, there flocked power company agents from over the Nation. The expenses reported by this committee were a little more than $300,000 of which $150,000 went to two firms of the hundreds of lawyers whose services were used by companies in connection with this bill. This $300,000 was but a small part of the money expended against this bill. Most of the expenses have come from the individual companies themselves, and have been charged up to operating expenses of the various local power company units....

"One holding company system, serving electricity to the people in 26 States, has admitted spending $800,000 up to date. Some of you, of course, will pay for that.... Evidence now available to the committee...shows expenditures to defeat the bill of approximately $1,500,000....

"A flood of telegrams and a deluge of letters poured into the city of Washington since February of this year against the Wheeler-Rayburn bill. Immediately before the vote in each house they poured in relays, 50, 100, 200, 500, even 1,000 in a relay group. This movement was so planned, so timed and so arranged as to leave the impression on many that a perfect storm of public sentiment and indignation had spontaneously burst forth in vexed resentment against the Wheeler-Rayburn bill. If these letters and telegrams had not come in such flocks, droves and clouds, that it was impossible even to open them, Washington might have been left under the melancholy impression that a pestilence had spread abroad leaving millions of widows and orphans, all of whom were large stockholders in power holding companies. The fact that millions of our people were apparently honestly, genuinely and spontaneously so aroused, that they would spend hundreds of thousands of dollars to send such messages about a bill, naturally and rightfully gave concern to their representatives.

"Following these protests came long-distance telephone calls from friends back home, and finally there dropped into Washington the party chairman back home, a legislator's campaign manager or close personal friend —always the closest that could be found—willing to come to Washington....

"These letters and telegrams did not appear on their face to have been written, prepared, or paid for by any one but the persons whose names were signed. While they did not affirmatively assert in words that the persons whose names were signed, actually wrote and paid for them, certainly it was intended to leave that impression upon the Washington Senators and Congressmen and the President of the United States....

"Evidence before the Lobby Committee shows that one holding company system expended more than $134,000 for telegrams and telephone messages. At an average of 60 cents per message, this would mean more than 235,000 messages were sent by this one company on this one bill....

"Reports from 11 telegraph offices throughout the country...show that 14,782 telegrams were sent to Senators and Congressmen against the bill, and 14,779 of the messages were paid for by public utilities, while only three people had sufficient interest to pay for any such message. Probably more than 250,000 telegrams in all were sent in this way and paid for by the utilities. Sometimes the person presenting telegrams supposed to be signed by various citizens was a complete stranger in the community...perhaps 5,000,000 letters were sent under the same plan....

"The telegraph and letter factory usually worked in the office of the local power company. Regular or special stenographers turned them out...by the thousands, and later a signature was added either by some person who had never seen it before, or by the agent of the company, who claimed, and in most instances had, general authority to sign the name.

"No one single message contained any information to the Congressman or Senator that the message was conceived by a holding company beneficiary, actually written by a subordinate of this beneficiary, and actually paid for by a local power company.... Lately, publicity has been given by some companies to these payments by them, but in each instance, including one in my own State of Alabama, it was after our committee had asked the company for this particular information.

"These letter and telegram factories were supplied with prepared forms from the highly paid publicity men of the holding companies. Evidence in possession of the committee shows that holding company publicity men have been drawing as much as $100 per day, which, of course, goes back to the local company and into your electric light bill.

"I read from the case of *Marshall vs. Baltimore & Ohio Railroad Co.*, as follows:

'Any attempts to deceive persons in connection with the high functions of legislation, by secret compensations, or to create or bring into operation undue influence of any kind, have all the injurious effects of a fraud upon the public....

'Legislators should act with a single eye to the true interests of the whole people and courts of justice can give no countenance to the use of means which may subject them to be misled by the pertinacious importunity and indirect influence of interested and unscrupulous agents or solicitors.... Secrecy, as to the character under which the agent or solicitor acts, tends to deception and is immoral and fraudulent.'

"These words of the Supreme Court of the United States denounced a $50,000 lobby. Can we doubt what that court would say today of the high powered, deceptive, telegram fixing, letter framing, Washington visiting, $5,000,000 lobby?

"Listen to the words of Mr. Gadsden, spoken under oath, as chairman of the Committee of Holding Company Public Utility Executives. Here is the evidence:

Sen. Hugo L. Black (D Ala.), Committee Chairman: As the chairman of this board you insisted, did you not, that they bring everybody they could bring here who was close to a Congressman or Senator, from their State?

Gadsden: I certainly did.

Black: And you insisted—

Gadsden: I do not say I insisted, but I was in favor of it.

Black: And you did not bring these people here because they knew more about the bill than you did, did you?

Gadsden: No, they could not know more about it than I did.

Black: You brought them here and insisted that they be brought here because you thought they would personally have an influence in persuading the Congressmen or Senators how to vote?

Gadsden: I thought they would be able to impress the Congressman that the sentiment back home was against this bill and a great many of them did it, too.

Black: They did?

Gadsden: Yes. They were able to come here and say to a Congressman, 'John'—or 'Jim'—

Black: You consider that it is for the best interests of the Nation with reference to legislation, to try to find people back in the districts that may, by reason of personal relationship, a personal friendship, be able to influence Congressmen to vote your way?

Gadsden: Isn't that a constitutional right?

Black: Is that your conception of it?

Gadsden: My conception is that a Congressman wants to know what the sentiment of his constituents is, and if a prominent business man can come here and say, 'John or Jim, you had better watch out, the sentiment has changed in your district, and your constituents are opposed to this bill,' he is very apt to listen to him.

(In addition to testimony quoted by Black, Gadsden testified: "We feel that here was a great industry, about 12 billion dollars, which was threatened with destruction by the Government, and that we came down here and proposed to do whatever we could legally and properly to stop that destruction. That is our position.")

"In 1874 the Supreme Court of the United States in the case of *Trist vs. Child*, 88 U.S. 441, spoke again on the question of lobbying. In a case before the court a suit was brought on a contract for lobby services. The contract provided that a man named Child should endeavor to secure the passage of a bill. Child's method was outlined in a headnote to the opinion which is as follows:

A contract to take charge of a claim before Congress and prosecute it as an agent and attorney for the claimant (the same amounting to a contract to procure by 'lobby services'— that is to say, by personal solicitation in any way with members of Congress—the passage of a bill providing for the payment of a claim), is void.

"His letter explained the procedure as follows:

Please write to your friends to write to any member of Congress. Every vote tells, and a simple request may secure a vote, he not caring anything about it. Set every man you know at work, even if he knows a page, for a page often gets a vote.

"The Supreme Court, in declaring itself on this lobby practice, said, in part, as follows:

In our jurisprudence a contract may be illegal and fraudulent because it is contrary to a constitution or statute or inconsistent with sound policy and good morals....The question now before us has been decided in four American cases. They were all ably considered, and in all of them the contract was held to be against public policy and void.

"The court then distinguishes between purely professional services such as drafting petitions, taking testimony, etc., and personal solicitation with reference to such activities, and further said:

They rest on the same principles ethically as professional services rendered in a court of justice and are no more exceptional. But such services are separated by a broad line of demarcation from personal solicitation and other means and appliances which his correspondence shows were resorted to in this case....

The foundation of a republic is the virtue of its citizens. They are at once sovereigns and subjects. As the foundation is undermined, the structure is weakened. When it is destroyed, the fabric must fall. Such is the voice of universal history.... There is a correlative duty resting upon the citizen. In his intercourse with those in authority...he is bound to exhibit truth, frankness and integrity.... If any of the great corporations of the country were to hire adventurers who make market of themselves in this way, to procure the passage of a general law with a view to the promotion of their private interests, the moral sense of every rightminded man would instinctively denounce the employer and the employed as steeped in corruption and the employment as infamous.

If the instances were numerous, open and tolerated, they would be regarded as measuring the decay of public morals and the degeneracy of the time. No prophetic spirit would be needed to foretell the consequences near at hand.

We are aware of no case in English or American jurisprudence like the one here under consideration where the agreement has not been judged to be illegal and void.

"Contrary to tradition, against the public morals, and hostile to good government, the lobby has reached such a position of power that it threatens government itself. Its size, its power, its capacity for evil; its greed, trickery, deception and fraud condemn it to the death it deserves. You, the people of the United States, will not permit it to destroy you. You will destroy it."

PROBE OF 1935 LOBBYING ON UTILITIES LEGISLATION

Following are excerpts from a Feb. 27, 1936, report by the House Rules Committee on lobbying in connection with 1935 utility holding company legislation. The Committee endorsed a bill (HR 11223) on which the Federal Regulation of Lobbying Act of 1946 was partially based.

"B.B. Robinson, a broker dealing in Associated (the Associated Gas & Electric Co. and its affiliates) securities, testifies that he spent months here seeking to establish personal contacts which he might convert into votes. During this period he was in close touch with H.C. Hopson, head of the Associated group. Agents in this group in various parts of the country sent to Members of the House countless spurious messages purporting to come from investors and employees. These practices cannot be too vigorously condemned.

"Practically all the other holding companies maintained in Washington representatives, either officials or counsel, during the period the struggle over the death-sentence clause was raging. Such a group may come under the general definition of a lobby.

"They carried on a widespread, well-organized, and well-financed campaign intended to prevent the enactment of any legislation deemed inimical by the holding companies. The committee has found but little or no evidence of any improper contacts between this lobby and the membership of the House. In spite of all that was said and done, the membership generally understood the situation and conducted itself in a highly commendable manner. In fact, this extensive and expensive lobby accomplished at Washington little more than the lavish expenditure of money which really belonged to the stockholders of these companies.

"The companies acting in concert sought to bring home to utilities investors and employees, and to the public generally, the purport and consequences of this legislation as the companies saw them. The means used were telegrams, articles, letters, circulars, advertisements, and every form of communication practicable. Coupled with this country-wide dissemination of publicity were appeals that whoever agreed with the position of the companies communicate his attitude to his Representative in Congress. Field agents everywhere urged such actions. In many instances facilities were afforded and expenses paid for sending such communications.

"All this may be called, in a broad sense, propaganda. But the term 'propaganda' when used invidiously connotes insidious and indirect publicity, wherein the individual and public opinion sought to be created is hidden. In this instance, there is no evidence of propaganda of this kind.

"Ordinarily, the right of executives of corporations to keep their investors informed when in their judgment the value of their securities is imperiled, as well as the right of the investors to protest to their Representatives in Congress is without question.

"But this was no ordinary instance. The committee is of the opinion that to unloose upon Congress a highly charged avalanche of propaganda is unwholesome and inimical to the public interest. It seeks to impress upon the membership the sense of a popular uprising, when in fact it is an artificial product. The committee, therefore, condemns the activities of the companies acting in concert, as well as the nefarious practices of the Associated.

"A large amount of money was collected and expended in the course of this campaign. There is no evidence that resort was had to it in any efforts, directly undertaken to influence the membership of the House. It seems to have been expended mostly in the propaganda campaign and in keeping at Washington a highly expensive and ineffective aggregation. The scheme was to make a personal appeal to the membership of the House, and at the same time unloose upon them a highly charged avalanche of propaganda. The two worked hand in hand.

"The committee required to be filed with it as much detail as it could reasonably secure of the source, amount, and expenditure of money used in this connection. But it is very difficult to trace such matters to definite conclusions. These movements are always directed by people of ability and are so arranged and conducted from the beginning as to baffle and confuse the investigator. This investigation has disclosed a general condition that is unwholesome and should not be permitted to exist. Such has been the case with many other like investigations. They accomplish momentary good, but these sporadic investigations are not an adequate remedy for the evil. The truth is that coming as they frequently do, after the legislation in question has been disposed of, they are too much like closing the stable door after the horse has departed, usually leaving a very dim and uncertain trail. Under such circumstances, the procedure is necessarily slow, cumbersome, and expensive. Furthermore, they but infrequently produce concrete results and more infrequently result in punishment of offenders.

"Investigations of lobbying activities have been had from time to time. That they have no lasting benefit seems to be proven by the fact that the campaign to influence utility holding company legislation was probably as comprehensive, as well managed, as persistent and as well financed as any in the history of the country. This is doubtless due, in a large measure, to the fact that such committees encounter so much difficulty in getting concrete facts and that punishment of offenders so seldom results.... Time should be taken by the forelock, and something done in advance that will make it possible for such a committee to find concrete facts, detect unlawful practices and do so without any large expenditure.

"This committee believes that every American citizen and interest that may be affected by proposed legislation has the highest right and privilege to be heard—a right that should be neither denied nor abridged. But on the other hand, the membership of Congress, to whom appeal is made and upon whom it is sought to exert pressure, and the public likewise appealed to, and who is asked to exert that pressure, have a right to know by whom and in whose interest such appeals are made, by whom these movements are financed, and the manner in which money is expended. In other words, legislation should be enacted that would bring this whole condition into the open. If it cannot stand publicity, it should not be permitted to exist. The welfare of this Nation depends at last upon a sound public opinion. By it the representatives of the people must be guided and upon it they should ever be able to rely with confidence...."

FEDERAL REGULATION OF LOBBYING ACT OF 1946

(S 2177 -- PL 79-601)

Following is the text of the general lobbyist registration law enacted by Congress in 1946 as Title III of the Legislative Reorganization Act. Though never amended through 1970, the Act was narrowed in its coverage by the Supreme Court's 1954 decision in the Harriss-Moore-Linder case. (p. 118)

That decision restricted the scope of the Act to groups and individuals which collected or received money for the "principal" purpose of influencing legislation through direct contacts with Members of Congress. Grassroots lobbying, aimed at developing pressure on Congress indirectly by influencing public opinion, was exempted from coverage by the Court's 5-3 ruling. Critics contend the court rewrote the Act in holding it constitutional.

Title III -- Regulation of Lobbying Act

SHORT TITLE

SEC. 301. This title may be cited as the "Federal Regulation of Lobbying Act."

DEFINITIONS

SEC. 302. When used in this title --

(a) The term "contribution" includes a gift, subscription, loan, advance, or deposit of money or anything of value and includes a contract, promise, or agreement, whether or not legally enforceable, to make a contribution.

(b) The term "expenditure" includes a payment, distribution, loan, advance, deposit, or gift of money or anything of value, and includes a contract, promise, or agreement, whether or not legally enforceable, to make an expenditure.

(c) The term "person" includes an individual, partnership, committee, association, corporation, and any other organization or group of persons.

(d) The term "Clerk" means the Clerk of the House of Representatives of the United States.

(e) The term "legislation" means bills, resolutions, amendments, nominations, and other matters pending or proposed in either House of Congress and includes any other matter which may be the subject of action by either House.

DETAILED ACCOUNTS OF CONTRIBUTIONS

SEC. 303. (a) It shall be the duty of every person who shall in any manner solicit or receive a contribution to any organization or fund for the purposes hereinafter designated to keep a detailed and exact account of --

(1) all contributions of any amount or of any value whatsoever;

(2) the name and address of every person making any such contribution of $500 or more and the date thereof;

(3) all expenditures made by or on behalf of such organization or fund; and

(4) the name and address of every person to whom any such expenditure is made and the date thereof.

(b) It shall be the duty of such person to obtain and keep a receipted bill, stating the particulars, for every expenditure of such funds exceeding $10 in amount, and to preserve all receipted bills and accounts required to be kept by this section for a period of at least two years from the date of the filing of the statement containing such items.

RECEIPTS FOR CONTRIBUTIONS

SEC. 304. Every individual who receives a contribution of $500 or more for any of the purposes hereinafter designated shall within five days after receipt thereof render to the person or organization for which such contribution was received a detailed account thereof, including the name and address of the person making such contribution and the date on which received.

STATEMENTS TO BE FILED WITH CLERK OF HOUSE

SEC. 305. (a) Every person receiving any contributions or expending any money for the purposes designated in subparagraph (a) or (b) of section 307 shall file with the Clerk between the first and tenth day of each calendar quarter, a statement containing complete as of the day next preceding the date of filing --

(1) the name and address of each person who has made a contribution of $500 or more not mentioned in the preceding report; except that the first report filed pursuant to this title shall contain the name and address of each person who has made any contribution of $500 or more to such person since the effective date of this title;

(2) the total sum of the contributions made to or for such person during the calendar year and not stated under paragraph (1);

(3) the total sum of all contributions made to or for such person during the calendar year;

(4) the name and address of each person to whom an expenditure in one or more items of the aggregate amount or value, within the calendar year, of $10 or more has been made by or on behalf of such person, and the amount, date, purpose of such expenditure;

(5) the total of all expenditures made by or on behalf of such person during the calendar year and not stated under paragraph (4);

(6) the total sum of expenditures made by or on behalf of such person during the calendar year.

(b) The statements required to be filed by subsection (a) shall be cumulative during the calendar year to which they relate, but where there has been no change in an item reported in a previous statement only the amount need be carried forward.

STATEMENT PRESERVED FOR TWO YEARS

SEC. 306. A statement required by this title to be filed with the Clerk --

(a) shall be deemed properly filed when deposited in an established post office within the prescribed time, duly stamped, registered, and directed to the Clerk of the House of Representatives of the United States, Washington, District of Columbia, but in the event it is not received, a duplicate of such statement shall be promptly filed upon notice by the Clerk of its nonreceipt;

(b) shall be preserved by the Clerk for a period of two years from the date of filing, shall constitute part of the public records of his office, and shall be open to public inspection.

PERSONS TO WHOM APPLICABLE

SEC. 307. The provisions of this title shall apply to any person (except a political committee as defined in the Federal Corrupt Practices Act, and duly organized state or local committees of a political party), who by himself, or through any agent or employee or other persons in any manner whatsoever, directly or indirectly, solicits, collects, or receives money or any other thing of value to be used principally to aid, or the principal purpose of which person is to aid, in the accomplishment of any of the following purposes:

(a) The passage or defeat of any legislation by the Congress of the United States.

(b) To influence, directly or indirectly, the passage or defeat of any legislation by the Congress of the United States.

REGISTRATION WITH SECRETARY OF THE SENATE AND CLERK OF THE HOUSE

SEC. 308. (a) Any person who shall engage himself for pay or for any consideration for the purpose of attempting to influence the passage or defeat of any legislation by the Congress of the United States shall, before doing anything in furtherance of such object, register with the Clerk of the House of Representatives and the Secretary of the Senate and shall give to those officers in writing and under oath, his name and business address, the name and address of the person by whom he is employed, and in whose interest he appears or works, the duration of such employment, how much he is paid and is to receive, by whom he is paid or is to be paid, how much he is to be paid for expenses, and what expenses are to be included. Each such person so registering, shall, between the first and tenth day of each calendar quarter, so long as his activity continues, file with the Clerk and Secretary a detailed report under oath of all money received and expended by him during the preceding calendar quarter in carrying on his work; to whom paid; for what purposes; and the names of any papers, periodicals, magazines, or other publications in which he has caused to be published any articles or editorials; and the proposed legislation he is employed to support or oppose. The provisions of this section shall not apply to any person who merely appears before a committee of the Congress of the United States in support of or opposition to legislation; nor to any public official acting in his official capacity; nor in the case of any newspaper or other regularly published periodical (including any individual who owns, publishes, or is employed by any such newspaper or periodical) which in the ordinary course of business publishes news items, editorials, or other comments, or paid advertisements, which directly or indirectly urge the passage or defeat of legislation, if such newspaper, periodical, or individual, engages in no further or other activities in connection with the passage or defeat of such legislation, other than to appear before a committee of the Congress of the United States in support of or in opposition to such legislation.

(b) All information required to be filed under the provisions of this section with the Clerk of the House of Representatives and the Secretary of the Senate shall be compiled by said Clerk and Secretary, acting jointly, as soon as practicable after the close of the calendar quarter with respect to which such information is filed and shall be printed in the Congressional Record.

REPORTS AND STATEMENTS TO BE MADE UNDER OATH

SEC. 309. All reports and statements required under this title shall be made under oath, before an officer authorized by law to administer oaths.

PENALTIES

SEC. 310. (a) Any person who violates any of the provisions of this title, shall, upon conviction, be guilty of a misdemeanor, and shall be punished by a fine of not more than $5,000 or imprisonment for not more than twelve months, or by both such fine and imprisonment.

(b) In addition to the penalties provided for in subsection (a), any person convicted of the misdemeanor specified therein is prohibited, for a period of three years from the date of such conviction, from attempting to influence, directly or indirectly, the passage or defeat of any proposed legislation or from appearing before a committee of the Congress in support of or opposition to proposed legislation; and any person who violates any provision of this subsection shall, upon conviction thereof, be guilty of a felony, and shall be punished by a fine of not more than $10,000, or imprisonment for not more than five years, or by both such fine and imprisonment.

EXEMPTION

SEC. 311. The provisions of this title shall not apply to practices or activities regulated by the Federal Corrupt Practices Act nor be construed as repealing any portion of said Federal Corrupt Practices Act.

SUPREME COURT RULING ON 1946 LOBBY LAW

Majority Opinion

Following is the text of the majority opinion of the Supreme Court in the Harriss-Moore-Linder case, United States v. Harriss, handed down by Chief Justice Earl Warren, June 7, 1954:

I.

The constitutional requirement of definiteness is violated by a criminal statute that fails to give a person of ordinary intelligence fair notice that his contemplated conduct is forbidden by the statute. The underlying principle is that no man shall be held criminally responsible for conduct which he could not reasonably understand to be proscribed.

On the other hand, if the general class of offenses to which the statute is directed is plainly within its terms, the statute will be struck down as vague even though marginal cases could be put where doubts might arise. *United States v. Petrillo,* 332 U.S. 1,7. *Cf. Jordan v. De-George,* 341 U.S. 223, 231. And if this general class of offenses can be made constitutionally definite by a reasonable construction of the statute, this Court is under a duty to give the statute that construction. This was the course adopted in *Screws v. United States,* 325 U.S. 91, upholding the definiteness of the Civil Rights Act.

The same course is appropriate here. The key section of the Lobbying Act is Sec. 307, entitled "Persons to Whom Applicable." Section 307 provides:

"The provisions of this title shall apply to any person (except a political committee as defined in the Federal Corrupt Practices Act, and duly organized State or local committees of a political party), who by himself, or through any agent or employee or other persons in any manner whatsoever, directly or indirectly, solicits, collects, or receives money or any other thing of value to be used principally to aid, or the principal purpose of which person is to aid, in the accomplishment of any of the following purposes:

"(a) The passage or defeat of any legislation by the Congress of the United States.

"(b) To influence, directly or indirectly, the passage or defeat of any legislation by the Congress of the United States."

This section modifies the substantive provisions of the Act, including Sec. 305 and Sec. 308. In other words, unless a "person" falls within the category established by Sec. 307, the disclosure requirements of Sec. 305 and Sec. 308 are inapplicable. Thus coverage under the Act is limited to those persons (except for the specified political committees) who solicit, collect, or receive contributions of money or other thing of value, and then only if the principal purpose of either the persons or the contributions is to aid in the accomplishment of the aims set forth in Section 307 (a) and (b). In any event, the solicitation, collection, or receipt of money or other thing of value is a prerequisite to coverage under the Act.

The Government urges a much broader construction —namely, that under Sec. 305 a person must report his expenditures to influence legislation even though he does not solicit, collect, or receive contributions as provided in Sec. 307. Such a construction, we believe, would do violence to the title and language of Sec. 307 as well as its legislative history. If the construction urged by the Government is to become law, that is for Congress to accomplish by further legislation.

We now turn to the alleged vagueness of the purposes set forth in Sec. 307 (a) and (b). As in *United States v. Rumely,* 341 U.S. 41, 47, which involved the interpretation of similar language, we believe this language should be construed to refer only to "lobbying in its commonly accepted sense"—to direct communication with members of Congress on pending or proposed federal legislation.

The legislative history of the Act makes clear that, at the very least, Congress sought disclosure of such direct pressures, exerted by the lobbyists themselves or through their hirelings or through an artificially stimulated letter campaign. It is likewise clear that Congress would have intended the Act to operate on this narrower basis, even if a broader application to organizations seeking to propagandize the general public were not permissible.

There remains for our consideration the meaning of "the principal purpose" and "to be used principally to aid." The legislative history of the Act indicates that the term "principal" was adopted merely to exclude from the scope of Sec. 307 those contributions and persons having only an "incidental" purpose of influencing legislation. Conversely, the "principal purpose" requirement does not exclude a contribution which in substantial part is to be used to influence legislation through direct communication with Congress or a person whose activities in substantial part are directed to influencing legislation through direct communication with Congress. If it were otherwise—if an organization, for example, were exempted because lobbying was only one of its main activities—the Act would in large measure be reduced to a mere exhortation against abuse of the legislative process. In construing the Act narrowly to avoid constitutional doubts, we must also avoid a construction that would seriously impair the effectiveness of the Act in coping with the problem it was designed to alleviate.

To summarize, therefore, there are three prerequisites to coverage under Sec. 307: (1) the "person" must have solicited, collected, or received contributions; (2) one of the main purposes of such "person," or one of the main purposes of such contributions, must have been to influence the passage or defeat of legislation by Congress; (3) the intended method of accomplishing this purpose must have been through direct communication with members of Congress. And since Sec. 307 modifies the substantive provisions of the Act, our construction of Sec. 307 will of necessity also narrow the scope of Sec. 305 and Sec. 308, the substantive provisions underlying the information in this case. Thus Sec. 305 is limited to those persons who are covered by Sec. 307; and when so covered, they must report all contributions and expenditures having the purpose of attempting to influence legislation through direct communication with Congress. Similarly, Sec. 308 is limited to those persons (with the stated exceptions) who are covered by Sec. 307 and who, in addition, engage themselves for pay or for any other valuable consideration for the purpose of attempting to influence legislation through direct communication with Congress. Construed in this way, the Lobbying Act meets the constitutional requirement of definiteness.

II.

Thus construed, Sec. 305 and 308 also do not violate the freedoms guaranteed by the First Amendment—freedom to speak, publish, and petition the Government.

Present-day legislative complexities are such that individual members of Congress cannot be expected to explore the myriad pressures to which they are regularly subjected. Yet full realization of the American ideal of government by elected representatives depends to no small extent on their ability to properly evaluate such pressures. Otherwise the voice of the people may all too easily be drowned out by the voice of special interest groups seeking favored treatment while masquerading as proponents of the public weal. This is the evil which the Lobbying Act was designed to help prevent.

Toward that end, Congress has not sought to prohibit these pressures. It has merely provided for a modicum of information from those who for hire attempt to influence legislation or who collect or spend funds for that purpose. It wants only to know who is being hired, who is putting up the money, and how much. It acted in the same spirit and for a similar purpose in passing the Federal Corrupt Practices Act—to maintain the integrity of a basic governmental process. See *Burroughs and Cannon v. United States, 290 U.S. 534, 545.*

Under these circumstances, we believe that Congress at least within the bounds of the Act as we have construed it, is not constitutionally forbidden to require the disclosure of lobbying activities. To do so would be to deny Congress in large measure the power of self-protection. And here Congress has used that power in a manner restricted to its appropriate end. We conclude that Secs. 305 and 308, as applied to persons defined in Sec. 307, do not offend the First Amendment.

It is suggested, however, that the Lobbying Act, with respect to persons other than those defined in Sec. 307, may as a practical matter act as a deterrent to their exercise of First Amendment rights. Hypothetical borderline situations are conjured up in which such persons choose to remain silent because of fear of possible prosecution for failure to comply with the Act. Our narrow construction of the Act, precluding as it does reasonable fears, is calculated to avoid such restraint. But, even assuming some such deterrent effect, the restraint is at most an indirect one resulting from self-censorship, comparable in many ways to the restraint resulting from criminal libel laws. The hazard of such restraint is too remote to require striking down a statute which on its face is otherwise plainly within the area of congressional power and is designed to safeguard a vital national interest.

III.

The appellees further attack the statute on the ground that the penalty provided in Sec. 310 (b) is unconstitutional. That section provides:

"(b) In addition to the penalties provided for in subsection (a), any person convicted of the misdemeanor specified therein is prohibited, for a period of three years from the date of such conviction, from attempting to influence, directly or indirectly, the passage or defeat of any proposed legislation or from appearing before a committee of the Congress in support of or opposition to proposed legislation; and any person who violates any provision of this subsection shall, upon conviction thereof, be guilty of a felony, and shall be punished by a fine of not more than $10,000, or imprisonment for not more than five years, or by both such fine and imprisonment."

This section, the appellees argue, is a patent violation of the First Amendment guarantees of freedom of speech and the right to petition the Government.

We find it unnecessary to pass on this contention. Unlike Secs. 305, 307, and 308 which we have judged on their face, Sec. 310 (b) has not yet been applied to the appellees, and it will never be so applied if the appellees are found innocent of the charges against them. See *United States v. Wurzbach, 280 U.S. 396, 399; United States v. Petrillo, 322 U.S. 1, 9-12.*

Moreover, the Act provides for the separability of any provision found invalid. If Sec. 310 (b) should ultimately be declared unconstitutional, its elimination would still leave a statute defining specific duties and providing a specific penalty for violation of any such duty. The prohibition of Sec. 310 (b) is expressly stated to be "In addition to the penalties provided for in subsection (a)..."; subsection (a) makes a violation of Sec. 305 or Sec. 308 a misdemeanor, punishable by fine or imprisonment or both. Consequently there would seem to be no obstacle to giving effect to the separability clause as to Sec. 310 (b), if this should ever prove necessary. Compare *Electric Bond & Share Co. v. Securities & Exchange Commission, 303 U.S. 419, 433-437.*

The judgment below is reversed and the cause is remanded to the District Court for further proceedings not inconsistent with this opinion.

Reversed.

Mr. JUSTICE CLARK took no part in the consideration or decision of this case.

Dissent—Justice Jackson

Here is the dissenting opinion of Justice Robert H. Jackson in the Harriss-Moore-Linder case:

MR. JUSTICE JACKSON, dissenting.

Several reasons lead me to withhold my assent from this decision.

The clearest feature of this case is that it begins with an Act so mischievously vague that the Government charged with its enforcement does not understand it, for some of its important assumptions are rejected by the Court's interpretation. The clearest feature of the Court's decision is that it leaves the country under an Act which is not much like any Act passed by Congress. Of course, when such a question is before us, it is easy to differ as to whether it is more appropriate to strike out or to strike down. But I recall few cases in which the Court has gone so far in rewriting an Act.

The Act passed by Congress would appear to apply to all persons who (1) solicit or receive funds for the purpose of lobbying, (2) receive and expend funds for the purpose of lobbying, or (3) merely expend funds for the purpose of lobbying. The Court at least eliminates this last category from coverage of the Act, though I should suppose that more serious evils affecting the public interest are to be found in the way lobbyists spend their money than in the ways they obtain it. In the present indictments, six counts relate exclusively to failures to report expenditures while only one appears to rest exclusively on failure to report receipts.

Also, Congress enacted a statute to reach the raising and spending of funds for the purpose of influencing congressional action directly or indirectly. The Court entirely deletes "indirectly" and narrows "directly" to mean "direct communication with members of Congress." These two constructions leave the Act touching only a part of the practices Congress deemed sinister.

Finally, as if to compensate for its deletions from the Act, the Court expands the phrase "the principal purpose" so that it now refers to any contribution which "in substantial part" is used to influence legislation.

I agree, of course, that we should make liberal interpretations to save legislative Acts, including penal statutes which punish conduct traditionally recognized as morally "wrong." Whoever kidnaps, steals, kills, or commits similar acts of violence upon another is bound to know that he is inviting retribution by society, and many of the statutes which define these long-established crimes are traditionally and perhaps necessarily vague. But we are dealing with a novel offense that has no established bounds and no such moral basis. The criminality of the conduct dealt with here depends entirely upon a purpose to influence legislation. Though there may be many abuses in pursuit of this purpose, this Act does not deal with corruption. These defendants, for example, are indicted for failing to report their activities in raising and spending money to influence legislation in support of farm prices, with no charge of corruption, bribery, deception, or other improper action. This may be a selfish business and against the best interests of the nation as a whole, but it is in an area where legal penalties should be applied only by formulae as precise and clear as our language will permit.

The First Amendment forbids Congress to abridge the right of the people "to petition the Government for a redress of grievances." If this right is to have an interpretation consistent with that given to other First Amendment rights, it confers a large immunity upon activities of persons, organizations, groups and classes to obtain what they think is due them from government. Of course, their conflicting claims and propaganda are confusing, annoying and at times, no doubt, deceiving and corrupting. But we may not forget that our constitutional system is to allow the greatest freedom of access to Congress, so that the people may press for their selfish interests, with Congress acting as arbiter of their demands and conflicts.

In matters of this nature, it does not seem wise to leave the scope of a criminal Act, close to impinging on the right of petition, dependent upon judicial construction for its limitations. Judicial construction, constitutional or statutory, always is subject to hazards of judicial reconstruction. One may rely on today's narrow interpretation only at his peril, for some later Court may expand the Act to include, in accordance with its terms, what today the Court excludes. This recently happened with the anti-trust laws, which the Court cites as being similarly vague. This Court, in a criminal case, sustained an indict-

ment by admittedly changing repeated and long-established constitutional and statutory interpretations. *United States v. South-Eastern Underwriters Assn.,* 322 U.S. 533. The ex post facto provision of our Constitution has not been held to protect the citizen against a retroactive change in decisional law, but it does against such a prejudicial change in legislation. As long as this statute stands on the books, its vagueness will be a contingent threat to activities which the Court today rules out, the contingency being a change of views by the Court as hereafter constituted.

The Court's opinion presupposes, and I do not disagree, that Congress has power to regulate lobbying for hire as a business or profession and to require such agents to disclose their principals, their activities, and their receipts. However, to reach the real evils of lobbying without cutting into the constitutional right of petition is a difficult and delicate task for which the Court's action today gives little guidance. I am in doubt whether the Act as construed does not permit applications which would abridge the right of petition, for which clear, safe and workable channels must be maintained. I think we should point out the defects and limitations which condemn this Act so clearly that the Court cannot sustain it as written, and leave its rewriting to Congress. After all, it is Congress that should know from experience both the good in the right of petition and the evils of professional lobbying.

Dissent—Justices Douglas, Black

The dissenting opinion of Justice William O. Douglas and Hugo L. Black in the Harriss-Moore-Linder case follows:

Mr. JUSTICE DOUGLAS, with whom Mr. JUSTICE BLACK concurs, dissenting.

I am in sympathy with the effort of the Court to save this statute from the charge that it is so vague and indefinite as to be unconstitutional. My inclinations were that way at the end of the oral argument. But further study changed my mind. I am now convinced that the formula adopted to save this Act is too dangerous for use. It can easily ensnare people who have done no more than exercise their constitutional rights of speech, assembly, and press.

We deal here with the validity of a criminal statute. To use the test of *Connally v. General Construction Co.,* 269 U.S. 385, 391, the question is whether this statute "either forbids or requires the doing of an act in terms so vague that men of common intelligence must necessarily guess at its meaning and differ as to its application." If it is so vague, as I think this one is, then it fails to meet the standards required by due process of law. See *United States v. Petrillo,* 332 U.S. 1. In determining that question we consider the statute on its face. As stated in *Lanzetta v. New Jersey,* 306 U.S. 451, 453:

"If on its face the challenged provision is repugnant to the due process clause, specification of details of the offense intended to be charged would not serve to validate it....It is the statute, not the accusation under it, that prescribes the rule to govern conduct and warns against transgression....No one may be required at peril of life, liberty or property to speculate as to the meaning of penal statutes. All are entitled to be informed as to what the State commands or forbids."

And see, *Winters v. New York*, 333 U.S. 507, 515.

The question therefore is not what the information charges nor what the proof might be. It is whether the statute itself is sufficiently narrow and precise as to give fair warning.

It is contended that the Act plainly applies

—to persons who pay others to present views to Congress either in committee hearings or by letters or other communications to Congress or Congressmen and

—to persons who spend money to induce others to communicate with Congress.

The Court adopts that view, with one minor limitation which the Court places on the Act—that only persons who solicit, collect, or receive money are included.

The difficulty is that the Act has to be rewritten and words actually added and subtracted to produce that result.

Section 307 makes the Act applicable to anyone who "directly or indirectly" solicits, collects, or receives contributions "to be used principally to aid, or the principal purpose of which person is to aid" in either

—the "passage or defeat of any legislation" by Congress, or

—"To influence, directly or indirectly, the passage or defeat of any legislation" by Congress.

We start with an all-inclusive definition of "legislation" contained in Sec. 302 (e). It means "bills, resolutions, amendments, nominations, and other matters pending or proposed in either House of Congress, and includes any other matter which may be the subject of action by either House." What is the scope of "any other matter which may be the subject of action" by Congress? It would seem to include not only pending or proposed legislation but any matter within the legitimate domain of Congress.

What contributions might be used "principally to aid" in influencing "directly or indirectly, the passage or defeat" of any such measure by Congress? When is one retained for the purpose of influencing the "passage or defeat of any legislation"?

(1) One who addresses a trade union for repeal of a labor law certainly hopes to influence legislation.

(2) So does a manufacturers' association which runs ads in newspapers for a sales tax.

(3) So does a farm group which undertakes to raise money for an educational program to be conducted in newspapers, magazines and on radio and television, showing the need for revision of our attitude on world trade.

(4) So does a group of oil companies which puts agents in the Nation's capital to sound the alarm at hostile legislation, to exert influence on Congressmen to defeat it, to work on the Hill for the passage of laws favorable to the oil interests.

(5) So does a business, labor, farm, religious, social, racial, or other group which raises money to contact people with the request that they write their Congressman to get a law repealed or modified, to get a proposed law passed, or themselves to propose a law.

Are all of these activities covered by the Act? If one is included why are not the others? The Court apparently excludes the kind of activities listed in categories (1), (2), and (3) and includes part of the activities in (4) and (5)—those which entail contacts with the Congress.

There is, however, difficulty in that course, a difficulty which seems to me to be insuperable. I find no warrant in the Act for drawing the line, as the Court does, between "direct communication with Congress" and other pressures on Congress. The Act is as much concerned with one, as with the other.

The words "direct communication with Congress" are not in the Act. Congress was concerned with the raising of money to aid in the passage or defeat of legislation, whatever tactics were used. But the Court not only strikes out one whole group of activities—to influence "indirectly"—but substitutes a new concept for the remaining group—to influence "directly." To influence "directly" the passage or defeat of legislation includes any number of methods—for example, nationwide radio, television or advertising programs promoting a particular measure, as well as the "buttonholing" of Congressmen. To include the latter while excluding the former is to rewrite the Act.

...Judging from the words Congress used, one type of activity which I have enumerated is as much proscribed as another.

The importance of the problem is emphasized by reason of the fact that this legislation is in the domain of the First Amendment. That Amendment provides that "Congress shall make no law...abridging the freedom of speech, or of the press; or the right of the people... to petition the Government for a redress of grievances."

Can Congress require one to register before he writes an article, makes a speech, files an advertisement, appears on radio or television, or writes a letter seeking to influence existing, pending, or proposed legislation? That would pose a considerable question under the First Amendment, as *Thomas v. Collins,* 323 U.S. 516, indicates. I do not mean to intimate that Congress is without power to require disclosure of the real principals behind those who come to Congress (or get others to do so) and speak as though they represent the public interest, when in fact they are undisclosed agents of special groups. I mention the First Amendment to emphasize why statutes touching this field should be "narrowly drawn to prevent the supposed evil" (see *Cantwell v. Connecticut,* 310 U.S. 296, 307) and not be cast in such vague and indefinite terms as to cast a cloud on the exercise of constitutional rights....

If that rule were relaxed, if Congress could impose registration requirements on the exercise of First Amendment rights, saving to the courts the salvage of the good from the bad, and meanwhile causing all who might possibly be covered to act at their peril, the law would in practical effect be a deterrent to the exercise of First Amendment rights....

The language of the Act is so broad that one who writes a letter or makes a speech or publishes an article or distributes literature or does many of the other things with which appellees are charged has no fair notice when he is close to the prohibited line. No construction we give it today will make clear retroactively the vague standards that confronted appellees when they did the acts now charged against them as criminal. *Cf. Pierce v. United States,* 314 U.S. 306, 311. Since the Act touches on the exercise of First Amendment rights, and is not narrowly drawn to meet precise evils, its vagueness has some of the evils of a continuous and effective restraint.

1950 INVESTIGATION: MAJORITY AND MINORITY VIEWS

Majority Views

Following are excerpts from the General Interim Report, House Select Committee on Lobbying Activities, Oct. 20, 1950, signed by Reps. Frank Buchanan (D Pa.), chairman; Henderson Lanham (D Ga.); Carl Albert (D Okla.), and Clyde Doyle (D Calif.).

"Government must give cognizance to the great organized interests within society, but at the same time it has the equal responsibility of speaking on those issues which transcend group lines or which have no other effective voice. We recognize today that Government cannot be captive to the narrow force of private interest, that responsible public policy is not and cannot be the product of willy-nilly submission to the demands of whatever group has the largest material resources at its disposal. The true public interest in legislative policy is very often silent, but it is the responsibility of Government to ascertain this interest and to act in its behalf....

"...Even if pressure groups did compete instead of join forces, the advantage in lobbying would always lie with those interests which were best organized, best financed, and had the easiest access to mass media of communication. Organized business has always gained the most from lobbying because it has had the best organization, the most money, and the readiest access to publicity. It has had, in addition, the great advantage of seeking generally to prevent rather than encourage action by broadly based popular government. Given the strategic bottlenecks of our legislative procedure, it is far easier to obstruct than it is to create....

"The lobbying situation is basically a reflection of the state of our economy. As the management of this economy has drifted into fewer and fewer hands, so too has pressure on the legislative front been sharply intensified. The giant concentrations of corporate wealth which the Temporary National Economic Committee found to dominate the prewar economy have developed since at an accelerated pace. It is inevitable that such great concentrations of economic power should seek to extend their power to the political field as well, and we count this fact as one of the most serious problems which large-scale lobbying poses for our kind of easygoing institutional structure. Economic power provides one of the essential raw materials for successful pressure politics; the greater the power, the larger are the possibilities of success. And so to the extent that some groups are better endowed than others, there is a disparity in the pressure which these groups can exert on the policy-making process. As we said earlier, 'lobbying for all,' may be a sacred right but it is a right which some men can make more meaningful than others. It is said, for example, that the individual consumer and the billion-dollar corporation have equal rights before the law, but are they equal before the lawmakers?

"This, then is the problem: the great political imbalance between tightly organized economic power blocs, such as big labor, big business, and big agriculture, and more casually organized interests and a loosely patterned state. This imbalance is reflected in lobbying activities as it is in other aspects of our national life....It is ultimately the people who pay for the big front and the high pressure campaigns...."

Minority Views (Final Report)

Following are excerpts from minority views on the final report, House Select Committee on Lobbying Activities, Jan. 3, 1951. Signers were Reps. Charles A. Halleck (R Ind.), Clarence J. Brown (R Ohio) and Joseph P. O'Hara (R Minn.).

"The majority would extend the term 'lobbying' to cover all human endeavor in the United States. Various staff studies have sought to include under the heading of 'lobbying' any activity by anyone designed to influence another, or designed to inform another on any question which might be considered by the Congress at any indefinite time in the future.

"The majority also sought to establish that all sums spent on institutional advertising, or in the form of contributions to business organizations of any sort, were legislative expenditures....

"The majority of the committee...began the investigation with several preconceived ideas, and thereafter proceeded to gather such evidence as they hoped would substantiate these ideas;

"(1) The majority of the committee was determined to prove that lobbying by Government agencies is in the public interest and not subject to criticism.

"(2) The majority of the committee was determined to prove that lobbying by organizations openly opposed to Fair Deal legislation was selfish and reprehensible while lobbying in support of Fair Deal objectives was perfectly all right.

"(3) The majority of the committee was determined to use the material it gathered and the outpourings of its large staff to influence the recent election....

"The so-called interim report issued by the chairman...is an attempt to smear American enterprise and to discredit our American system....

"The report prepared by the committee staff and issued by the chairman and his Democratic colleagues clearly is designed to help the leftists who are running for office on administration tickets. It is a 'Socialist white paper' for the 1950 campaign.

"The majority members of the committee say all lobbying by business and conservative elements is bad; all lobbying by left-wingers, labor organizations, and Fair Deal officeholders is good....

"We would like to emphasize once again the difficulties of attempting to legislate in this field. We doubt whether the so-called indirect lobbying, which, on the surface at least, is no more or less than constitutionally protected freedom of speech, can, or should be, regulated by the Congress. We do feel that those individuals whose principal purpose is to attempt to persuade individual members of Congress to follow a certain course of action might well be required to identify themselves and their source of support. Whether any lobbying statute should go further than this is seriously open to question....

"It is salutary to suggest that any action taken by a Congress must remain responsive and responsible to the will of the people. By taking steps to discourage, limit, or prohibit the right...to petition...not only does the Congress do a disservice, but it initiates the steps which strike at the foundation of our Republic."

COURT VIEWS ON TEXAS LAW REQUIRING REGISTRATIONS

A 1945 opinion by the U.S. Supreme Court on a Texas registration law could have an impact on any future legislation by Congress requiring lobbyists to register and report.

In *Thomas v. Collins,* 323 U.S. 516 (1945), the Court discussed constitutional questions raised by a Texas statute requiring labor organizers to register with and obtain a card from a state official before soliciting memberships in unions.

The Court held that as applied in that case, the law imposed a previous restraint on the rights of free speech and free assembly of the president of the United Auto Workers in violation of the First and Fourteenth Amendments to the U.S. Constitution.

Associate Justices William O. Douglas and Hugo L. Black cited the case in their 1954 dissent from the landmark Harriss-Moore-Linder decision. Douglas wrote that a requirement that one register before engaging in specified communication aimed at influencing legislation would present "a considerable question under the First Amendment," as indicated in *Thomas v. Collins.*

Lambert H. Miller, senior vice president and general counsel of the National Association of Manufacturers, cited the case at a 1971 House hearing on a proposed new Federal lobby law. He said the bill (HR 5259) would encompass "a much larger area for possible recordkeeping and reporting than seems necessary or desirable."

Under the bill, Miller said, "four phone calls, four letters or four visits with legislative representatives in any half-year period, communicating a point of view and urging action, would bring such communication within the reporting requirements. The final question is whether this limitation would stand up constitutionally or whether it would be an infringement of the First Amendment rights of freedom of speech, the press, and the right to petition. Why is the fourth or fifth communication any less protected than the first three and does not such a limitation raise the question as to whether or not this is a 'prior restraint' in the exercise of these First Amendment rights?"

The case of *Thomas v. Collins,* the NAM counsel said, "should be examined very carefully, for it would seem to have an important bearing on this particular aspect" of the bill. The proposal was patterned after one recommended by the McClellan committee in 1957.

Thomas Case

The Court's 1945 opinion was written by Associate Justice Wiley Rutledge. It said the case "confronts us again with the duty our system places on this Court to say where the individual's freedom ends and the State's power begins."

The Court said any attempt to restrict the liberties secured by the First Amendment "must be justified by clear public interest, threatened not doubtfully or remotely, but by clear and present danger. The rational connection between the remedy provided and the evil to be curbed, which in other contexts might support legislation against attack on due process grounds, will not suffice. These rights rest on firmer foundation. Accordingly, whatever occasion would restrain orderly discussion and persuasion, at appropriate time and place, must have clear support in public danger, actual or impending. Only the gravest abuses, endangering paramount interests, give occasion for permissible limitation. It is therefore in our tradition to allow the widest room for discussion, the narrowest range for its restriction, particularly when this right is exercised in conjunction with peaceable assembly. It was not by accident or coincidence that the rights to freedom in speech and press were coupled in a single guaranty with the rights of the people peaceably to assemble and to petition for redress of grievances. All these, though not identical, are inseparable....

"The idea is not sound...that the First Amendment's safeguards are wholly inapplicable to business or economic activity. And it does not resolve where the line shall be drawn in a particular case merely to urge, as Texas does, that an organization for which the rights of free speech and free assembly are claimed is one 'engaged in business activities' or that the individual who leads it in exercising these rights receives compensation for doing so...."

After saying it believed the union leader was within his rights in going ahead and speaking freely at a meeting despite a court order against it, the Court said:

"We do not mean to say there is not, in many circumstances, a difference between urging a course of action and merely giving and acquiring information. On the other hand, history has not been without periods when the search for knowledge alone was banned. Of this we may assume the men who wrote the Bill of Rights were aware. But the protection they sought was not solely for persons in intellectual pursuits.... 'Free trade in ideas' means free trade in the opportunity to persuade to action, not merely to describe facts.... Indeed, the whole history of the problem shows it is to the end of preventing action that repression is primarily directed and to preserving the right to urge it that the protections are given....

"If one who solicits support for the cause of labor may be required to register as a condition to the exercise of his right to make a public speech, so may he who seeks to rally support for any social, business, religious or political cause. We think a requirement that one must register before he undertakes to make a public speech to enlist support for a lawful movement is quite incompatible with the requirements of the First Amendment.

"Once the speaker goes further, however, and engages in conduct which amounts to more than the right of free discussion comprehends, as when he undertakes the collection of funds or securing subscriptions, he enters a realm where a reasonable registration or identification requirement may be imposed....

"The restraint is not small when it is considered what was restrained. The right is a national right, federally guaranteed. There is some modicum of freedom of thought, speech and assembly which all citizens of the Republic may exercise throughout its length and breadth, which no State, nor all together, nor the Nation itself, can prohibit, restrain or impede. If the restraint were smaller than it is, it is from petty tyrannies that large ones take root and grow. This fact can be no more plain than when they are imposed on the most basic rights of all. Seedlings planted in that soil grow great and, growing, break down the foundations of liberty."

NGRESS AND THE NATION
1945-1968

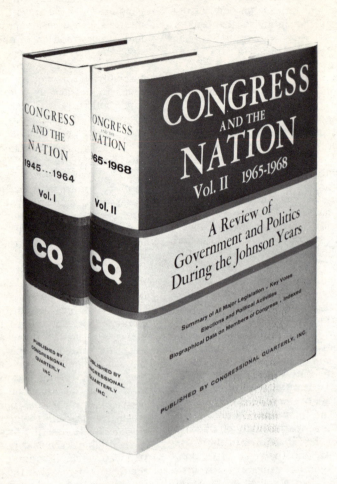

This 3,100 page, two-volume resource brings detail and perspective to the important legislative issues and political events of 24 years, spanning five Presidencies. Organization and indexing make the contents readily accessible for reference.

Volume I (1945-1964) 1965, 2,000 pages	$27.50
Volume II (1965-1968) 1969, 1,100 pages	$35.00
The Set: Volumes I & II	$55.00

CONGRESSIONAL QUARTERLY, INC.

1735 K Street, N.W.   Washington, D.C. 20006